P

DIRECTIONS

WRITTEN AND RESEARCHED BY

Ruth Blackmore and
James McConnachie

ROUGH GUIDES

NEW YORK • LONDON • DELHI

www.roughguides.com

Contents

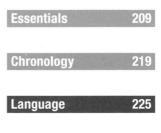

Introduction to

Paris

A trip to Paris, famous as the most romantic of destinations, is one of those lifetime musts. The very fabric of the city is elegant, its grand avenues and atmospheric little backstreets lined with harmonious apartment blocks and interspersed by exquisitely designed gardens and squares. The Parisians are no less stylish than their city: a sophisticated, cosmopolitan people renowned for their chic and their hauteur.

Through the heart of the city flows the Seine, skirting the pair of islands where Paris was founded. The historic pillars of the city, the church of Notre-Dame and the royal palace of the Louvre, stand on the riverbank, along with one of the world's most distinctive landmarks – the Eiffel Tower. There are legions of art galleries and museums too: between the Musée du Louvre, the Musée d'Orsay and the Pompidou Centre, you can see an

unhealthy proportion of the world's finest works of art. For those willing to venture beyond the city limits, the glorious Gothic cathedral of St-Denis, the sumptuous royal palace of Versailles and the all-singing, all-dancing Disneyland Paris, are easily accessible.

When to visit

Spring is the classic time to visit Paris, when the weather is mild (average daily 6–20°C), with bright days balanced by rain showers. **Autumn**, similarly mild, and **winter** (1–7°C) can be very rewarding, but on overcast days the city can feel melancholy; winter sun on the other hand is the city's most flattering light, and hotels and restaurants are relatively uncrowded in this season. By contrast, Paris in high **summer** (15–25°C) is not the best time to go: large numbers of Parisians desert the capital between July 15 and the end of August for the beach or mountains, and many restaurants and shops close down for much of this period.

▲ Sacré-Coeur, Montmartre

▼ The Seine from Pont des Arts

Alongside the great civic museums and monuments lie well-defined *quartiers* that make Paris feel more a collection of sophisticated villages than a true metropolis. Traditional communities still revolve around the local cafés, while wealthier enclaves preserve their exclusive boutiques and restaurants. Quarters such as the elegant Marais, chichi St-Germain and romantic Montmartre are ideal for shopping, sitting in cafés and just aimlessly wandering, while throughout the city you can find peaceful green spaces, ranging from formal gardens and avant-garde municipal parks to ancient cemeteries.

▼ Ile St-Louis and the Seine

Few cities can compete with the thousand-and-one cafés, brasseries and restaurants that dot Paris's boulevards and back-alleys, from ultra-modern fashion temples to traditional mirrored palaces, and from tiny gourmet *bistrots* to crowded Vietnamese diners. After dark, the theatres and concert halls host world-leading productions, and tiny venues put on jazz gigs and Parisian *chanson* nights, while the café-bars and clubs of the Champs-Elysées, Bastille and the Left Bank fill with the young and style-conscious from all over Europe, and beyond.

◀ View from Tour Montparnasse

Paris
AT A GLANCE

THE ISLANDS

The Ile de la Cité's soaring Notre-Dame and glittering Sainte-Chapelle have been inspiring visitors for centuries, while picturesque Ile Saint-Louis is ideal for leisurely *quai*-side strolling.

▲ Notre-Dame

THE MARAIS

One of Paris's most captivating districts, the Marais brims with trendy bars and cafés, not to mention gorgeous Renaissance mansions, some of which house outstanding museums.

CHAMPS-ELYSÉES

Synonymous with glitz and glamour, the Champs-Elysées sweeps through one of the city's most exclusive districts, studded with luxury hotels and top fashion boutiques.

BEAUBOURG

At the heart of the ancient Beaubourg *quartier* stands the resolutely modern Pompidou Centre, its riot of coloured tubing concealing a matchless collection of modern art.

▼ Beaubourg metro

▲ Le Petit Fer à Cheval, The Marais

LEFT BANK

Paris's Left Bank, south of the Seine, is a real haven from the urban bustle of the city's Right-Bank core. The studenty Quartier Latin, fashionable St-Germain, arty Montparnasse and the elegant quarter around the Eiffel Tower all share a relaxed, village-like feel.

MONTMARTRE

Hilltop views of the city, traffic-free streets, rich artistic associations and great cafés make Montmartre the most charming of Paris's neighbourhoods.

▲ Yves Saint Laurent, Left Bank

▶ Place du Tertre, Montmartre

EASTERN PARIS

Traditionally the working-class area, eastern Paris's diverse student, arty and ethnic mix ensures a vibrant café and nightlife scene.

Ideas

The big six

The appeal of Paris very much lies in its ability to feel like two cities. One is a place of grand monuments and world-class museums; the other a surprisingly small-town kind of place of low-rise apartments, local shops and neighbourhood cafés. You should save a little time to explore the more intimate side of the city, but the landmark sights certainly shouldn't be missed, especially if it's your first time in Paris – even if you've visited many times before, it would be hard to tire of the Notre-Dame or Eiffel Tower, and you could spend days strolling around the Louvre alone.

▲ Champs-Elysées

The "Elysian Fields" is now a giant, tree-lined avenue plunging down from the Arc de Triomphe towards the Louvre, right through the heart of upper-class Paris.

P.79 ▸THE CHAMPS-ELYSÉES AND TUILERIES

▼ Notre-Dame

The great Gothic cathedral of Notre-Dame, with its delicate tracery, exquisite rose windows and soaring nave, is an awe-inspiring sight.

P.70 ▸ THE ISLANDS

▼ Pompidou Centre

Famous for its radical "inside-out" architecture, the Pompidou Centre is one of the city's most recognizable and popular landmarks.

P.101 ▶ BEAUBOURG AND LES HALLES

▼ The Louvre

The Louvre is simply one of the greatest art galleries in the world, with a palatial setting worthy of the collection inside.

P.74 ▶ THE LOUVRE

▲ The Eiffel Tower

The closer you get, the more impressive the Eiffel Tower becomes. From the top, it's just magnificent.

P.142 ▶ THE EIFFEL TOWER AREA

▲ Musée d'Orsay

A nineteenth-century railway station makes a cathedral-like setting for France's greatest collection of Impressionist and post-Impressionist paintings.

P.136 ▶ ST-GERMAIN

Paris calendar

Famously described by Hemingway as "a moveable feast", Paris won't disappoint whatever time of year you visit. You'll see another side to the city, however, if you time your trip to coincide with one of its key festivals or events, such as Bastille Day, when Parisians celebrate the 1789 storming of the Bastille with fireworks and parties, or the Tour de France, when crowds line the Champs-Elysées to cheer home the triumphant cyclists.

▲ Bastille Day

July 14 is the country's most important national holiday, celebrated with dancing, fireworks and a military parade down the Champs-Elysées.

P.216 ▸ ESSENTIALS

▶ Paris Plage

For four weeks in summer, tonnes of sand are laid out as a beach along a stretch of the Seine, creating a kind of Paris-sur-Mer.

P.216 ▶ ESSENTIALS

◀ The Tour de France

The world's most famous cycle race sprints home down the Champs-Elysées at the end of July.

P.216 ▶ ESSENTIALS

▶ Nuit Blanche

During Nuit Blanche (Sleepless Night) hundreds of galleries, cafés and public buildings remain open all night, with music and cultural events held city-wide.

P.216 ▶ ESSENTIALS

◀ Paris in spring

The flirtatious parks and Seine-side beach of summer, the brazier-heated café terraces of winter and the celebrated autumn leaves all have their appeal, but spring remains the loveliest time to visit Paris.

P.4 ▶ INTRODUCTION

14

The Seine

Sometimes referred to as Paris's main avenue, the Seine sweeps through the city centre in a broad arc, dividing the Left Bank from the Right Bank and taking in the capital's grandest monuments on its way. Its leafy *quais* provide welcome havens from the city's bustle, and its numerous bridges afford fine and unexpected vistas, while river trips are a relaxing way to see some of the capital's best-known sights.

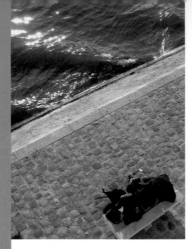

▲ The quais

The tree-lined *quais* are perfect for relaxing walks or a restful pause, especially on Sundays when sections of road on both sides of the river are closed to traffic.

P.121 ▸ QUARTIER LATIN

▼ Pont des Arts

The Pont des Arts is a graceful link between the Louvre and St-Germain, its benches perfect for sitting out in the sunshine and gazing at the river flowing by.

P.132 ▸ ST-GERMAIN

◀ Bateaux Mouches

An hour's trip in a Bateau Mouche is a great way to get a close-up view of the classic buildings along the Seine.

P.217 ▶ ESSENTIALS

▶ Pont Neuf

Built in 1607, this twelve-arched bridge of warm yellow stone is Paris's oldest and surely its most handsome.

P.67 ▶ THE ISLANDS

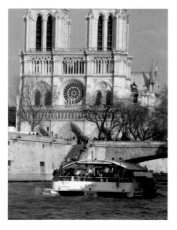

▼ Pont Alexandre III

This is the most extravagant bridge in the city – witness its single iron arch spanning 109m, topped off with exuberant Art Deco lamps and statues of river nymphs.

P.142 ▶ THE EIFFEL TOWER AREA

▲ Batobus

This handy river bus calls at many of the city's biggest sights, but the river journey is more than half the point – certainly more picturesque than the métro…

P.214 ▶ ESSENTIALS

Contemporary architecture

Over the past few decades Paris has commissioned dozens of ambitious, boldly designed projects by leading architects such as Gehry, Koolhaas and I.M. Pei. A large number are the legacy of François Mitterrand, who, like many a leader of France before him, was keen to leave his stamp on the capital. Some of his "*grands projets*", such as the glass pyramid erected in the very heart of the Louvre, were hugely controversial at first, but are now widely accepted – testament to a new go-ahead spirit in the city.

▲ Grande Arche de la Défense

The sheer scale of this contemporary riposte to the Arc de Triomphe is staggering.

P.187 ▸ WESTERN PARIS

▲ Institut du Monde Arabe

The Arab institute is best loved for its exquisite *moucharabiyah* facade, which blends traditional Arabic art with the latest technology.

P.121 ▸ QUARTIER LATIN

▼ Musée du Quai Branly

With its walls of vegetation and glass, sumptuous terrace and blocks of colour, Jean Nouvel's new museum of non-European art is playful and inspiring.

P.144 ▶ THE EIFFEL TOWER AREA

▼ Cité des Sciences

Four times the size of the Pompidou Centre, this science museum complex is nothing less than a giant playground for contemporary architecture.

P.177 ▶ EASTERN PARIS

▲ The Pyramid

As beautiful by night as by day, I.M. Pei's shocking glass pyramid rises up in the very centre of the Louvre's historic courtyard.

P.74 ▶ THE LOUVRE

▲ Bibliothèque Nationale

Dominique Perrault's four book-shaped glass towers are an astounding sight, but it's the garden sunk between them that makes this one of Paris's boldest buildings.

P.155 ▶ SOUTHERN PARIS

Art galleries

Paris has some big-league art galleries, not least the mighty Louvre and the Musée d'Orsay, with its shimmering collection of Impressionist masterpieces. As well as exceptional paintings by native artists such as Matisse, Monet and Renoir, the city's galleries contain a rich legacy of works by foreign painters – Kandinsky, Picasso and Dalí among them – drawn to the city in the early twentieth century, a time when, for any aspiring artist, Paris was the only place to be.

▲ Musée Marmottan

Monet's paintings of Giverny, including several of his *Waterlilies*, steal the show at this gallery of Impressionists.

P.184 ▶ WESTERN PARIS

▲ Musée de l'Art Moderne de la Ville de Paris

The city's own art collection is a fitting tribute to Paris and the many celebrated artists who made it their home in the course of the twentieth century.

P.89 ▶ TROCADÉRO

▼ Musée d'Orsay

This converted railway station provides a cathedral-like setting for the greatest works of French Impressionism.

P.136 ▶ ST-GERMAIN

▲ Musée Picasso

This is the largest collection of Picassos anywhere, displayed in a beautiful Renaissance mansion.

P.111 ▶ THE MARAIS

▶ Musée National d'Art Moderne, Pompidou Centre

The "Beaubourg" houses one of the finest collections of modern art in the world, with major holdings of works by Kandinsky, Picasso and Matisse.

P.102 ▶ BEAUBOURG AND LES HALLES

◀ The Louvre

The Louvre's collections represent not just the best of all French painting and sculpture, but also the finest art from right across Europe – and beyond into Egypt, the Arab world and ancient Greece and Rome.

P.74 ▶ THE LOUVRE

Museums

You could spend days on end in the Louvre, but it's also worth seeking out some of the city's smaller, specialist museums, dedicated to exploring subjects as diverse as the French Revolution, medieval Paris and ancient Khmer art. Many of these museums, moreover, enjoy beautiful settings, such as handsome Renaissance mansions, and in some cases the original studio of an artist has been carefully preserved and converted into a museum of their work.

▲ Musée National du Moyen Age

Set in a fine Renaissance mansion, Paris's Museum of the Middle Ages houses all manner of exquisite *objets d'art*, including the city's single most enthralling sight: the tapestry series of *The Lady and the Unicorn*.

P.121 ▸ QUARTIER LATIN

▲ Musée Rodin

Rodin's elegant mansion now houses the definitive collection of the sculptor's powerful, mould-breaking works.

P.146 ▸ THE EIFFEL TOWER AREA

▶ Musée Carnavalet

This fascinating museum brings the history of Paris alive through a wealth of paintings and artefacts, and some wonderful old interiors, rescued from houses pulled down to make way for Haussmann's redevelopments in the nineteenth century.

P.112 ▶ THE MARAIS

◀ Musée Moreau

Gustave Moreau's eccentric canvases cover every inch of his spacious studio's walls; immediately below, you can visit the tiny apartment where the artist lived with his parents.

P.165 ▶ MONTMARTRE AND NORTHERN PARIS

▶ Musée Guimet

Visiting the beautifully designed Musée Guimet, with its refined statues and sculptures from all over the Buddhist world, is a distinctly spiritual experience.

P.88 ▶ Trocadéro

◀ Musée Jacquemart-André

This sumptuous Second Empire residence, built for the art-loving Jacquemart-André couple, displays their choice collection of Italian, Dutch and French masters.

P.82 ▶ THE CHAMPS-ELYSÉES AND TUILERIES

Churches

Many of Paris's churches have long, stormy histories. The most turbulent period was the Revolution, when, as symbols of wealth and privilege, some churches were destroyed, others looted or turned into temples of Agriculture, Reason and the like. Fortunately, splendid examples of Gothic, Renaissance and Classical architecture have survived more or less intact, with some providing fine settings for classical music concerts.

▲ Soldiers' church in Les Invalides

Built as a church for wounded former soldiers, this masterpiece of French classicism has an unusual restraint and dignity – especially in comparison to the bombastic King's Church, with which it shares an altar.

P.146 ▸ THE EIFFEL TOWER AREA

▶ The Madeleine

This imposing Neoclassical church, with its ranks of massive columns, is often used for society weddings.

P.94 ▶ THE GRANDS BOULEVARDS AND PASSAGES

◀ Sainte-Chapelle

The Sainte-Chapelle, with its stunning stained-glass windows, is one of the jewels of the Middle Ages.

P.68 ▶ THE ISLANDS

▼ St Eustache

This beautiful Gothic-Renaissance church cuts a flamboyant figure, flanked by giant flying buttresses.

P.104 ▶ BEAUBOURG AND LES HALLES

▲ St Sulpice

Now that the fuss of its notorious appearance in *The Da Vinci Code* has died down, St-Sulpice can recover the reputation it once had – as one of the city's most fascinating churches.

P.136 ▶ ST-GERMAIN

Secret gardens

Of all the ways to get under the skin of Paris, perhaps the most satisfying is just to appreciate the peace in one of the city's harder-to-find little gardens, or take a short walk along the elegant promenades that can be found here and there, with a bit of looking. Quite apart from their charm, and the pleasure to be found in discovering them, these hidden nooks and quiet breathing spaces are wonderful for people-watching: this is where you'll find Parisians walking their dogs, playing with their kids, reading, hand-holding, and just taking time out from the city.

▲ Jardin Atlantique

Although a public park, the Jardin Atlantique is actually hidden away on top of the Montparnasse railway tracks – a triumph of engineering and contemporary garden design.

P.149 ▸ MONTPARNASSE

▲ Promenade Plantée

Get a different angle on the city from this old railway viaduct, now an elevated walkway planted with a glorious abundance of trees and flowers.

P.170 ▸ BASTILLE AND BERCY

▼ Place Dauphine

Relax and watch a spot of leisurely boules being played under the chestnuts of this peaceful and secluded square.

P.68 ▸ THE ISLANDS

▲ Jardin du Palais Royal

Enclosed by a stately ensemble of arcaded buildings and little frequented, the Jardin du Palais Royal feels like a secret garden in the middle of the city.

P.95 ▸ THE GRANDS BOULEVARDS AND PASSAGES

▶ Parc de Bagatelle

A heady perfume fills the air when the Parc de Bagetelle's roses, of which there are more than 1500 varieties, burst into bloom in June.

P.186 ▸ WESTERN PARIS

◀ Allée des Cygnes

One of the most unusual Paris walks, this takes you along a tree-lined embankment adrift in the Seine and proffers dramatic views of the post-industrial western riverbanks.

P.153 ▸ SOUTHERN PARIS

Dead Paris

From the royal tombs at St-Denis to the memorials at the Panthéon and Napoleon's tomb at Les Invalides, the dead of Paris certainly make their presence felt. It's the cemeteries, however, that make the biggest impact on the city's landscape. From vantage points like the Eiffel Tower they seem to fill a surprising amount of the city's area, looking like green islands speckled with miniature stone apartment blocks. Père-Lachaise is a major draw, but don't miss the smaller graveyards at Montmartre and Montparnasse. Finally, there's the most morbid sight of all – the bone-lined catacombs.

▲ Père-Lachaise cemetery

Pay homage to Chopin, Oscar Wilde or Jim Morrison – just some of the countless notables buried in what is arguably the world's most famous cemetery.

P.180 ▸ EASTERN PARIS

▼ Panthéon

Moving their remains to the crypt of the Panthéon is the greatest honour the French Republic can bestow on its artists, poets, thinkers and politicians.

P.124 ▸ QUARTIER LATIN

▶ The Catacombs

The tunnel-like quarries underneath Montparnasse are lined with literally millions of human bones, evacuated from the overcrowded Paris cemeteries in the nineteenth century.

P.152 ▶ MONTPARNASSE

◀ Napoleon's tomb

The emperor's magnificently pompous tomb is the highlight of the great military complex of Les Invalides.

P.146 ▶ THE EIFFEL TOWER AREA

▶ Montmartre cemetery

Zola's grave, its effigy often graced by a rose, is found at Montmartre, along with other artistic greats Stendhal, Degas and François Truffaut.

P.163 ▶ MONTMARTRE AND NORTHERN PARIS

◀ St-Denis Necropolis

In the glorious setting of the world's first Gothic cathedral lie the monumental tombs of French kings and queens – from the Merovingians right through to Marie Antoinette.

P.191 ▶ EXCURSIONS

Gastronomic restaurants

Paris boasts an unparalleled concentration of haute-cuisine restaurants and is the perfect place to blow out on the meal of a lifetime. Gastronomic cuisine doesn't have to mean astronomic prices: some restaurants offer a special set lunch menu for around €75. In the evening prices average at €150 for three courses, and there's no limit on the amount you can pay for fine wines. Be sure to book well in advance – many places are shut at weekends or on Sundays – and dress smartly.

▲ L'Arpège

For once, you won't find much meat or fish on Alain Passard's unique menu, just exquisitely inventive morsels of rare vegetables in elegant sauces – with the odd pigeon breast or lobster for traditionalists.

P.147 ▸ THE EIFFEL TOWER AREA

▲ Taillevent

Michelin three-star rated since 1973 – no mean achievement – *Taillevent,* with its ever-inventive dishes and outstanding wine cellar, is a rare treat.

P.86 ▸ THE CHAMPS-ELYSÉES AND TUILERIES

▶ Alain Ducasse at the Plaza Athénée

One of the most innovative chefs around, Alain Ducasse sends diners into raptures over his exquisite food and ultra-stylish decor – Louis XV chandeliers draped with shimmering, metallic organza.

P.85 ▶ THE CHAMPS-ELYSÉES AND TUILERIES

◀ Jules Verne

It's hard to decide which is better at *Jules Verne*, the view from the second floor of the Eiffel Tower or the contemporary French cuisine. You'll need to book a few months in advance to guarantee this unforgettable experience.

P.147 ▶ THE EIFFEL TOWER AREA

▶ Lasserre

This classic haute-cuisine establishment has a lovely belle époque dining room and a roof that is rolled back to reveal the Paris sky on balmy summer evenings.

P.85 ▶ THE CHAMPS-ELYSÉES AND TUILERIES

◀ L'Ambroisie

Beautiful tapestries provide a fitting backdrop to this intimate and refined restaurant, which serves exquisite and creative cuisine.

P.118 ▶ THE MARAIS

Bistrots

Every Paris *quartier* has its own local *bistrot*, relaxed and informal places where you'll often be sitting elbow to elbow with your neighbours. *Bistrots* are usually the least expensive places to eat out and most have good-value set menus. The cuisine is warming and homely, the sort your grandmother might cook, though increasingly *bistrots* are garnering reputations for the most exciting creative cuisine in the capital – pioneered by young chefs who are not afraid to experiment with more exotic ingredients.

▲ Au 35

Number 35 is exactly the sort of perfect Left Bank *bistrot* you wish you could somehow roll up, put in your pocket and set up on your own street at home. In fact, it's so adorably tiny, you could almost try.

P.140 ▸ ST-GERMAIN

▲ Astier

A convivial and bustling place, serving well-cooked traditional dishes at very reasonable prices.

P.182 ▸ EASTERN PARIS

▼ Le Villaret

Diners come from the other end of Paris to sample the good-value inventive cuisine at this little neighbourhood *bistrot*, hidden away on a backstreet in the Oberkampf district.

P.183 ▸ EASTERN PARIS

▼ L'Os a Moëlle

If even Right-Bankers are making the trip out here to the very edge of the city, it's a strong clue that this chef-run *bistrot* is the real thing. The communal tables, groaning with produce, in the "Cave" across the road are almost even more tempting.

P.157 ▸ SOUTHERN PARIS

▲ Aux Lyonnais

This revamped old *bistrot*, with beautiful tiled decor, serves up refined Lyonnais cuisine and is currently one of the capital's hottest dining spots.

P.99 ▸ THE GRANDS BOULEVARDS AND PASSAGES

Classic brasseries

First brought to Paris by immigrant Alsatians in the late nineteenth century, brasseries were originally beer taverns ("brasserie" means "brewery") that soon started serving full dinner menus little changed over the years; you can count on classic dishes such as steak, oysters and tarte tatin cooked to perfection. Little of the decor has changed either, with many places preserving their fine belle époque interiors – globe lamps, glass cupolas, brass fittings and dark-leather banquettes.

▲ Bofinger

Bastille opera-goers pack the tables beneath this classic brasserie's splendid glass cupola.

P.174 ▶ BASTILLE AND BERCY

▲ Le Vaudeville

This lively establishment, attractively decorated with marble and mosaics, serves gigantic seafood platters and is especially popular with the post-theatre crowd.

P.99 ▶ THE GRANDS BOULEVARDS AND PASSAGES

▶ Flo

This deeply old-fashioned brasserie is hidden away in an atmospheric courtyard near the Porte St-Denis in northern Paris, but it's well worth the journey.

P.166 ▶
MONTMARTRE AND
NORTHERN PARIS

◀ La Coupole

You can recapture something of the spirit of Montparnasse's fashionable heyday at this giant, high-ceilinged brasserie, packed with drinkers and diners into the small hours.

P.152 ▶ MONTPARNASSE

▶ Lipp

Lipp is a St-Germain classic: the haunt of powerful editors and media faces, it serves wonderful sauerkraut, among other traditional brasserie *plats*.

P.140 ▶
ST-GERMAIN

◀ Le Square Trousseau

Set on an attractive square, with outside tables on sunny days, this handsome brasserie attracts a chic but relaxed clientele.

P.174 ▶ BASTILLE
AND BERCY

Cafés

Chilling out in a café is one of the chief pleasures of a trip to Paris and the best way to get your finger on the city's pulse. A mainstay of Parisian society, cafés are places where people come to pose and people-watch, debate and discuss or simply read a book. Some places have a chameleon-like existence, changing from quiet places for coffee in the daytime to buzzing venues – more like bars – in the evening.

▲ Le Petit Fer à Cheval

This appealingly small café has a marble-topped bar in the shape of a horseshoe (*fer à cheval*), and is ideal for an apéritif or pick-me-up espresso.

P.119 ▸ THE MARAIS

▲ L'Apparement Café

A chic café, with a warren of cosy back rooms that makes it perfect for unwinding and forgetting all about those museums and galleries…. The Sunday brunch is an institution.

P.117 ▸ THE MARAIS

▼ Bar du Marché

The thrumming and fashionable "market bar" pulls in the punters from all around St-Germain's busy old market street, rue de Buci.

P.139 ▶ ST-GERMAIN

▲ Pause Café

What starts as a laidback café in the daytime becomes a busy, trendy nightspot after midnight, with packed-out pavement tables, relaxed music and lots of chatter.

P.174 ▶ BASTILLE AND BERCY

▶ Café Flore

The most authentic of the Left Bank's literary cafés, though these days you're more likely to be rubbing shoulders with fashionistas than philosophers.

P.139 ▶ ST-GERMAIN

◀ Café de l'Industrie

One of Bastille's best cafés – young and busy yet comfortable and unpretentious – this is the kind of place that's hard to leave once you're ensconced.

P.174 ▶ BASTILLE AND BERCY

Paris nightlife

Many of Paris's best café-bars stay open very late, so after midnight you're not necessarily committed to a full-on club. If you do go clubbing, you'll find most Parisian DJs playing house or techno, but the musical style and general vibe really depends on who's running the individual soirée. Check out gay and lesbian venues too (see p.50), many of which attract trendy, mixed crowds. Taxis are hard to find after hours, so Parisian clubbers often keep going until after 5.30am, when the métro restarts, or stay up even later at a fashionable "after" event.

▲ Bastille bars

The Bastille area is the liveliest place in Paris for nightlife, with excellent venues ranging from trendy, late-opening little cafés to club-bars with DJs.

P.174–175 ▶ BASTILLE AND BERCY

▲ Rex Club

For music, the *Rex* is one of the best, with an excellent sound system, lots of space and enough clout to pull in the top promoters.

P.100 ▶ THE GRAND BOULEVARDS AND PASSAGES

▶ Le Pulp

There's something very different
about this lesbian-run, mostly mixed
club. It's friendlier, more laidback and
yet trendier than many others in Paris
– and it plays the best music.

**P.100 ▶ THE GRANDS
BOULEVARDS AND PASSAGES**

◀ Batofar

The boats moored beside
the Bibliothèque Nation-
ale host some of Paris's
liveliest and least preten-
tious nightlife venues.
This former lighthouse
ship is one of the best,
with live music and DJs
later on.

**P.158 ▶ SOUTH-
ERN PARIS**

▶ Le Triptyque

A live-music and club
venue in one, with a cool,
eclectic music policy, the
Triptyque has become the
new mecca for "alterna-
tive" Paris.

**P.100 ▶ THE GRAND
BOULEVARDS AND
PASSAGES**

◀ La Folie en Tête

The Butte-aux-Cailles,
down in southern Paris, is
renowned for its alterna-
tive, left-wing spirit, and *La
Folie en Tête* is the most
characterful of its friendly,
laidback bars.

**P.158 ▶ SOUTHERN
PARIS**

Musical Paris

Paris's musical scene is stimulating and diverse. Classical music flourishes, while opera-lovers can choose between the glittering Opéra Garnier and the modern Opéra Bastille (see p.175). Every night there are high-end jazz and world music gigs, while in the city's clubs, techno and "electro" rule. Meanwhile, that most French of musical traditions, *chanson*, has recently made a comeback and can be heard in select, intimate venues around the city.

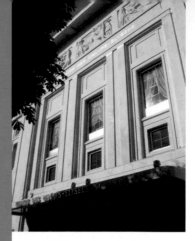

▲ Théâtre des Champs-Elysées

The premiere of Stravinsky's *Rite of Spring* caused a riot here in 1913; these days its varied programme of classical music, opera and dance is more likely to meet with hearty applause.

P.86 ▸ THE CHAMPS-ELYSÉES AND TUILERIES

▼ Café de la Danse

An intimate and attractive club hosting rock, pop, world and folk music.

P.175 ▸ BASTILLE AND BERCY

▲ Opéra Garnier

A more opulent setting for grand opera and ballet would be hard to imagine.

P.100 ▸ THE GRAND BOULEVARDS AND PASSAGES

◀ New Morning

A cavernous space with spartan decor and often standing room only, but the jazz and world music aficionados who flock here to hear the big names on the circuit don't seem to mind.

P.168 ▸ MONTMARTRE AND NORTHERN PARIS

▶ Au Limonaire

This tiny dinner and *chanson* venue could hardly be more Parisian, showcasing up-and-coming talent in the best jazzy, comic-romantic-philosophical French tradition.

P.100 ▸ THE GRANDS BOULEVARDS AND PASSAGES

Gourmet Paris

You don't have to dine out to experience the best of French food in Paris. Supermarkets may have driven out some of the everyday grocers' and butchers' shops, but at the top end of the market you'll find plenty of deluxe pâtisseries, chocolatiers, charcuteries, fromageries, traîteurs and épiceries. Some are grand-scale, luxury food emporia, others bijou specialists where you can buy what the owner swears is the very best chocolate truffle, pâté or goat's cheese in the world. You'll also get the best advice on how to buy, keep, serve and ultimately eat your chosen treat, and it'll be meticulously well wrapped.

▲ Rue des Martyrs

Cutting through the heart of the urbane 9ᵉ arrondissement, rue des Martyrs is lined with high-quality food shops and cafés as it climbs towards Montmartre. Neighbourhood shopping at its most refined.

P.168 ▸ MONTMARTRE AND NORTHERN PARIS

▲ Legrand

One of the oldest wine merchants in Paris, opened in 1900, this is a must for any oenophile.

P.98 ▸ THE GRANDS BOULEVARDS AND PASSAGES

▶ Barthélémy

The old shop front dates back to the days when Bartélémy was a dairy. Now it sells the very best French cheeses.

P.137 ▶
ST-GERMAIN

◀ Au Bon Marché

The food hall at the Bon Marché department store has a huge range of fine French foods, as well as luxury deli goods from around the world.

P.138 ▶
ST-GERMAIN

▶ Debauve & Gallais

A temple to chocolate in the heart of St-Germain. Endless inventive varieties are made, displayed and finally wrapped up with serious devotion to the art.

P.138 ▶
ST-GERMAIN

◀ Fauchon

If there's a luxury French delicacy this food emporium doesn't stock, then it isn't worth knowing about.

P.97 ▶
THE GRANDS
BOULEVARDS
AND PASSAGES

Markets

Paris proudly maintains its tradition of food markets, of which the most traditional is the rue Montorgueil market, a last remnant of the great working-class produce market that once occupied Les Halles. A more thriving example is the place d'Aligre market, with a great wine bar adjacent. The organic market, on boulevard Raspail, couldn't be more different: a middle-class mecca – for foodies and the ecologically minded alike. The rue Dejean African market, past the Gare du Nord, delivers a powerfully contrasting flavour of the vibrant, ethnically mixed city that lies beyond the centre. Further still, at the northern and southern fringes of the city, squat two huge flea markets, where you can pick up wonderful curiosities among the bric-a-brac and antiques.

▲ Marché Dejean

Perhaps the best way to visit Paris's African quarter, the Goutte d'Or, is to make a shopping trip to the colourful African and exotic street-market on rue Dejean.

P.165 ▸ MONTMARTRE AND NORTHERN PARIS

▲ Place d'Aligre and Le Baron Rouge

The market at place d'Aligre is one of Paris's liveliest and most authentic – a perfect prelude to a glass of Muscadet and some oysters at the down-to-earth wine-bar, *Le Baron Rouge*.

PP.170 & 173 ▸ BASTILLE AND BERCY

▼ Boulevard Raspail Marché "Bio"

Every Sunday, the reservation in the middle of the broad boulevard Raspail blooms with the mouthwatering products of organic farmers and specialist food producers.

P.136 ▶ ST-GERMAIN

▲ Rue Montorgueil

A permanent street market full of traditional grocers and fishmongers and even a horse butchers, all vying for space with some of the city's trendiest cafés and bars.

P.104 ▶ BEAUBOURG AND LES HALLES

▶ Puces de St-Ouen

A giant antiques emporium with an equally massive cheap clothing, jumble and grey-import market hanging onto its coat-tails, St-Ouen is the king of Paris's flea markets.

P.163 ▶ MONTMARTRE AND NORTHERN PARIS

◀ Puces de Vanves

The Puces de Vanves is the most faithful to Paris's flea-market traditions, with stall after stall of curiosities, bric-a-brac and antique junk.

P.153 ▶ SOUTHERN PARIS

Romantic hideaways

Paris's hotels, with their all-too-often tiny rooms and rather old-fashioned decor, don't always match up to the romantic promise of the rest of the city. However, special places to stay do exist, especially among the raft of boutique hotels that have opened recently, and then there are time-worn classics that have always held a certain romantic appeal.

▲ Hôtel du Petit Moulin

At this new and stylish boutique hotel, all the decor – down to the numbers on the doors – was designed by Christian Lacroix.

P.202 ▸ ACCOMMODATION

▼ Hôtel Bonséjour Montmartre

Romance isn't just for the wealthy: at this friendly budget hotel you may not find velvet curtains and a four-poster, but you can have your own balcony in the heart of Montmartre.

P.204 ▸ ACCOMMODATION

▼ Hôtel Pavillon de la Reine

This handsome, ivy-covered, luxury hotel is just off the place des Vosges, and has a more personal feel than many hotels of its class.

P.202 ▸ ACCOMMODATION

▲ Hôtel du Bourg Tibourg

The rooms are tiny, but exquisitely furnished in neo-Gothic style, with a dash of Orientalism thrown in.

P.201 ▸ ACCOMMODATION

▶ Relais Christine

Hidden behind high walls and a little courtyard on a quiet Left-Bank back street, the *Christine* feels like a well-kept secret. One of the city's most intimate luxury hotels.

P.203 ▸ ACCOMMODATION

◀ L'Hôtel

Famously, Oscar Wilde died in this hotel, and it has been restored with more than a touch of camp decadence, as well as serious luxury.

P.203 ▸ ACCOMMODATION

Paris fashion

Paris remains the capital of world fashion – even if you agree with Yves Saint Laurent that Paris Fashion Week is "a ridiculous spectacle better suited to a concert stage". If you're in the market for haute couture, or are enough of a fashion devotee to visit the exquisite, historic clothes on display at the Musée de la Mode, you'll find the shopping superb. Glitzy couture names and international ready-to-wear brands are thick on the ground in the Champs-Elysées and St-Germain quarters, while for independent little boutiques, scour the Marais and Bastille, or the area around Abbesses métro, near Montmartre.

▲ Galeries Lafayette

The queen of Paris's department stores, with floor upon floor of clothes and cosmetics – and even its own dome.

P.97 ▶ THE GRANDS BOULEVARDS AND PASSAGES

▲ Isabel Marant

Isabel Marant may be young but she's a fully fledged designer with a fast-growing reputation. Yet the prices of her exciting, sometimes showy ready-to-wear collections aren't stratospheric.

P.173 ▶ BASTILLE AND BERCY

▶ Abbesses boutiques

Shoppers with an original frame of mind should make for the little streets around place des Abbesses, where there's a cluster of independent designers and boutiques for smaller women.

P.159 ▶ MONTMARTRE AND NORTHERN PARIS

▼ Musée de la Mode

If you can't wear the best, you can at least stare at it at the Fashion Museum, which holds fascinating exhibitions on exquisite and historic designer wear.

P.89 ▶ TROCADÉRO

◀ Zadig & Voltaire

If the budget doesn't stretch to couture you can find well-cut, original and flattering designs at this Paris-based chain, which has branches all over the city.

P.139 ▶ ST-GERMAIN

Glamorous Paris

To the rest of the world Paris epitomizes glamour and style, so much so that any other city seeking to project a glamorous image calls itself "Paris of the Orient", "Paris of the Americas" and so on. The very make-up of the city, with its wide boulevards and harmonious squares, is elegant; its inhabitants are famously chic and impeccably turned out, and there's no shortage of beautiful places in which to see and be seen.

▲ Kong

This ultra-stylish, Philippe Starck-fashioned bar-restaurant on top of the flagship Kenzo building is a favourite haunt of fashionistas.

P.106 ▸ BEAUBOURG AND LES HALLES

▲ Costes

Slip a copy of *Vogue* under your arm and you'll fit right in with the fashion and media crowd that frequents the luxuriously decorated bar-restaurant of the *Hôtel Costes*.

P.86 ▸ CHAMPS-ELYSÉES AND TUILERIES

▼ Bar Hemingway

Named after Ernest Hemingway, who famously "liberated" the *Ritz* in 1944, the hotel's discreetly elegant bar serves up exquisite cocktails to the rich and famous.

P.99 ▸ THE GRANDS BOULEVARDS AND PASSAGES

▼ Le Cab

Currently one of the city's hottest nightspots, *Le Cab* draws in international celebs and top fashion models.

P.100 ▸ THE GRANDS BOULE-VARDS AND PASSAGES

▲ Renoma Café Gallery

The beautiful people and their financiers come day and night to lounge about in this trendy café-restaurant just off the Champs-Elysées, done out in minimalist tones of white and steel-grey.

P.86 ▸ CHAMPS-ELYSÉES AND TUILERIES

▼ Le Train Bleu

All the glamour of the belle époque lives on in the Gare de Lyon's sumptuous restaurant, sporting dazzling gilt decor, spectacular ceiling frescoes and crystal chandeliers.

P.174 ▸ BASTILLE AND BERCY

Gay Paris

Paris isn't just gay- and lesbian-friendly, it positively revels in an atmosphere of openness, especially in the "pink triangle" around rue Ste-Croix de la Bretonnerie, in the heart of the fashionable Marais district. Even the city's mayor, Bertrand Delanoë, is openly gay. An excellent monthly magazine, *Têtu* ("Headstrong"), lists the best bars and clubs, and there's an ever-growing number of gay-oriented hotels and restaurants too. The best gay clubs and bars have long attracted a cool, straight clientele – so don't rule out these venues even if you're not gay.

▼ Le Carré

The best of the new breed of designer gay bars in the Marais, this café-bar attracts a sophisticated Parisian gay and mixed crowd.

P.119 ▶ THE MARAIS

▼ Bliss Kfé

This slightly grungy lesbian bar welcomes a cool, often mixed crowd.

P.118 ▶ THE MARAIS

▼ Le Mixer

Just a tiny little bar but a very lively one, with a DJ mixing it up from a pulpit-like platform, lots of stylish lighting and a friendly, gay/lesbian/bi/straight crowd.

P.119 ▶ THE MARAIS

▲ Gay Pride

The big event of the calendar is the half-million-strong pride march on the last Saturday of June, with lots of spin-off concerts, parties and events.

P.216 ▶ ESSENTIALS

◀ Amnésia Café

One of the most relaxed and upmarket gay venues in the city, affecting a cosy, sofa-filled "Friends" vibe by day and lots of cocktail-fuelled bonhomie at night.

P.118 ▶ THE MARAIS

Kids' Paris

The obvious lure of Disneyland aside, Paris has plenty of attractions and activities to keep most children happy: puppet shows, funfairs, zoos and adventure parks, not to mention more off-beat attractions such as the creepy catacombs (see p.152) and dingy sewers (see p.144). In addition, nearly every park, big or small, has its play area with swings and slides. Just as much of a delight for many children is Paris's vibrant atmosphere, with its street performers and buskers, lively pavement cafés and brightly lit carousels.

▼ Jardin d'Acclimatation

No child could fail to be enchanted by this wonderland of mini-canal and train rides, adventure parks, trampolines, bumper cars, puppet theatres and farm animals.

P.187 ▶ WESTERN PARIS

▼ Sandpits

Paris seems to have sandpits in spades – at least one in every park and recreation area, as in the Palais Royal garden here.

P.95 ▶ THE GRANDS BOULEVARDS AND PASSAGES

▲ Disneyland

Disney's vast theme park may not be very French but the children will love it. Even cynical adults may find it hard to resist the more exciting rides.

P.192 ▸ EXCURSIONS

▶ Parc de la Villette

The Géode Omnimax cinema is just one of the many attractions for kids in this futuristic park.

P.177 ▸ EASTERN PARIS

◀ Jardin du Luxembourg boats

One of the timeless pleasures of the Luxembourg gardens is hiring a toy boat and sailing it to and fro across the circular pond.

P.132 ▸ ST-GERMAIN

Ethnic food

Parisians are not renowned for their adventurous tastes, and the vast majority of restaurants remain resolutely, traditionally French. Unless you have the budget for cutting-edge contemporary cuisine, the best way to dine creatively in Paris is to investigate the many ethnic foods on offer, starting with falafel takeaways in the Jewish quarter. Given France's colonial past, North African food is particularly well represented in the city, with some excellent restaurants offering groaning plates of couscous or Moroccan tagines, and cafés serving mint tea and achingly sweet pastries. Pungent Vietnamese dishes can be found here and there in Paris, and you can also taste fiery West African dishes that would be hard to track down in Anglophone countries.

▲ **Café de la Mosquée**

Mint tea, Arab-style sweetmeats and a perfectly North African ambiance are all found in the tearoom of the Paris Mosque.

P.129 ▸ THE QUARTIER LATIN

▲ **Waly Fay**

This cosy but elegant West African restaurant is distinctly upmarket. The stews are richly spiced and the ambience warm and welcoming.

P.174 ▸ BASTILLE AND BERCY

▼ L'As du Fallafel

On Sundays, the queues for the utterly more-ish falafel pitta pockets stretch way down rue des Rosiers, in the core of the miniature Jewish quarter.

`P.117` ▸ THE MARAIS

▼ Chez Omar

Couscous is North Africa's gift to Paris. You can find it everywhere, from fast-food cafés with just a couple of seats to more elaborate settings, such as the fine belle époque *Chez Omar* in the Marais.

`P.118` ▸ THE MARAIS

▲ Le Bambou

The best restaurants in so-called Chinatown, in the south of Paris, are the Vietnamese ones – and *Le Bambou* is one of the best of those.

`P.157` ▸ SOUTHERN PARIS

Green Paris

Paris's green spaces are places where people come to meet each other, relax and have fun: families stroll or sit out in the open-air cafés, elderly men play chess under the chestnut trees and children mess around in sandpits or get treated to pony rides. Paris is justly renowned for its formal gardens, from the majestic expanses of the Tuileries and Jardin du Luxembourg to the hyper-contemporary space of the Parc André-Citroën and the elegant square at the centre of the place des Vosges. Out on the city's periphery you can roam more freely in the wilder expanses of the Bois de Boulogne, while in the north of the city you can explore the thread of green that traces the line of the Canal St-Martin.

▲ Jardin des Tuileries

The French formal garden *par excellence*: sweeping vistas, symmetrical flowerbeds and straight avenues.

P.83 ▸ THE CHAMPS-ELYSÉES AND TUILERIES

▲ Jardin du Luxembourg

For all its splendid Classical design, the Luxembourg is still the most relaxed and friendly of Paris's parks.

P.132 ▸ ST-GERMAIN

◄ Bois de Boulogne

This huge swathe of parkland, with its many attractions, such as the Parc de Bagatelle rose garden, is a favourite Parisian retreat.

P.186 ▶ WESTERN PARIS

▶ Place des Vosges

The place des Vosges's harmonious ensemble of pink-brick buildings form an elegant backdrop to the attractive and popular garden at its centre.

P.113 ▶ THE MARAIS

▲ Parc André-Citroën

On the edge of the city, sloping down to the river, this public park is famous for its imaginative design, balloon ride and its capricious, computer-controlled fountains.

P.153 ▶ SOUTHERN PARIS

▶ Canal St-Martin

With its elegant arched bridges and leafy *quais*, the Canal St-Martin is a charming spot for a stroll.

P.176 ▶ EASTERN PARIS

Images of Paris

Paris is one of those rare cities that it's almost impossible to visit for the first time, so familiar is it from paintings, photographs and cinema. As Europe's cultural capital for much of the past two centuries, the city has harboured many of the greatest artists of the modern era. Painters such as Renoir, Manet and Toulouse-Lautrec, and photographers like Henri Cartier-Bresson, Robert Doisneau and Brassaï have defined their city and made its image famous throughout the world. Since the 1960s, film has taken the lead – so much so that certain streets and areas of Paris are now indelibly marked by the classic movie sequences that were shot there.

▼ Les Amants du Pont Neuf

Homeless lovers Juliette Binoche and Dennis Lavant transform the Pont Neuf into the most painfully romantic of locations. It's almost unbelievable that the entire set was actually rebuilt in the south of France – at staggering expense.

P.67 ▶ THE ISLANDS

▼ Henri Cartier-Bresson

The father of photo-journalism never forgot his home, and his shots of Paris – today often on show at his own Fondation Henri Cartier-Bresson – are among the most iconic images of the city ever created.

P.151 ▶ MONTPARNASSE

◀ A bout de souffle

In 1960, Paris staked its claim to being the world's sexiest film location, thanks to director Jean-Luc Godard, who had Jean Seberg and Jean-Paul Belmondo flirting so dangerously as they walked along the Champs-Elysées.

P.79 ▶ THE CHAMPS-ELYSÉES AND TUILERIES

▶ Le Fabuleux Destin d'Amélie Poulain

Whether you think it's deliciously kookie or grotesquely chocolate-box, *Amélie* defined the new, contemporary Montmartre: young, stylish and quirky.

P.159 ▶ MONTMARTRE AND NORTHERN PARIS

◀ Zazie dans le métro

Louis Malle's farcical 1960 feature follows a twelve-year-old girl's zany, knockabout weekend in Paris, as she and her cross-dressing uncle fail to ride the métro. Shown here, the place de la Concorde. No métro trains in sight.

P.83 ▶ THE CHAMPS-ELYSÉES AND TUILERIES

▶ Bal du Moulin de la Galette

Renoir captured the spirit of turn-of-the-twentieth-century Montmartre, the festive haunt of prostitutes and painters, drunks and dilettantes, bohemians and bon-viveurs.

P.159 ▶ MONTMARTRE AND NORTHERN PARIS

Paris views

From on high, Paris looks like a sea of nineteenth-century mansion buildings, their pale stone facades turning creamy-golden in the sun. The long boulevards look like leafy canyons and the parks like great green pools, but it's the cemeteries that stand out most of all, studded with pale stone graves that could almost be miniature apartment blocks. There are no skyscrapers to hide the old city centre, so it's easy to pick out the great landmarks, from the towers of Notre-Dame and the giant sculpted swathe of the Louvre to the multicoloured pipes and tubes of the Pompidou Centre.

▲ **Sacré-Cœur**

The steps of the Sacré-Cœur are famously romantic, with Paris spread out below you to the south, and the sun full on your face.

P.162 ▶ MONTMARTRE AND NORTHERN PARIS

▲ **Parc de Belleville**

A little out of the way, but worth a trek for the splendid views of the city afforded by the park's heights.

P.181 ▶ EASTERN PARIS

▶ Arc de Triomphe

Views from the top are best towards dusk on a sunny day when the marble of the Grande Arche de la Défense sparkles in the setting sun and the Louvre is bathed in warm light.

P.80 ▶ THE CHAMPS-ELYSÉES AND TUILERIES

▲ Tour Montparnasse

The vista from the tower-top helipad is stunning, and you can have a drink in the panoramic 56th-floor restaurant afterwards.

P.148 ▶ MONTPARNASSE

▼ Georges, Pompidou Centre

Eating and drinking is very much a secondary affair here – it's the stunning view of the Paris rooftops that's the real draw.

P.105 ▶ BEAUBOURG AND LES HALLES

▲ Eiffel Tower

The view from the Eiffel Tower is especially spectacular at night when the whole tower is lit up from within, and the searchlight sweeps the skies above.

P.142 ▶ THE EIFFEL TOWER AREA

Parisians' Paris

Some of the greatest pleasures Paris has to offer somehow fall off the list of many visitors. For many Parisians, their city isn't defined by the Louvre or the Eiffel Tower so much as by a relaxed Sunday brunch with friends in the Marais, a *hammam* steam bath, or an afternoon escape to one of the Quartier Latin's many art-house cinemas. More recently, ice-skating has become a real Parisian passion – understandable given the venues outside the historic Hôtel de Ville and halfway up the Eiffel Tower. Most quintessentially Parisian of all, and not to be missed even if you're a devoted taxi-taker or pavement-pounder, is a ride on the métro – the secret heart of Paris.

▲ **Ice-skating at the Hôtel de Ville**

Skating within a stone's throw of the Seine must be one of the most romantic dates in the world. Some years you can even skate up on the first level of the Eiffel Tower.

P.115 ▸ THE MARAIS

▼ The métro

More than just a way to get around, you'll rub up closer to the "real" Paris in the métro than anywhere else in the city, and the station designs are often fascinating, too.

P.213 ▶ ESSENTIALS

▲ Les Bains du Marais

Parisians have a fetish for *hammams*, or Turkish-style steam rooms, and the most elegant and upmarket of them all is in the Marais.

P.116 ▶ THE MARAIS

▶ Cinema

Every good Parisian is a passionate cinemaphile, and there are scores of specialist *salles* to indulge them, especially in the Quartier Latin, and at the kitsch 1930s *Grand Rex*.

P.217 ▶ ESSENTIALS

◀ Brunch in the Marais

The breakfast-style menus may pay homage to New York, but Parisians brunch with their own sense of sociable style – and a glass of wine as often as OJ.

P.117 ▶ THE MARAIS

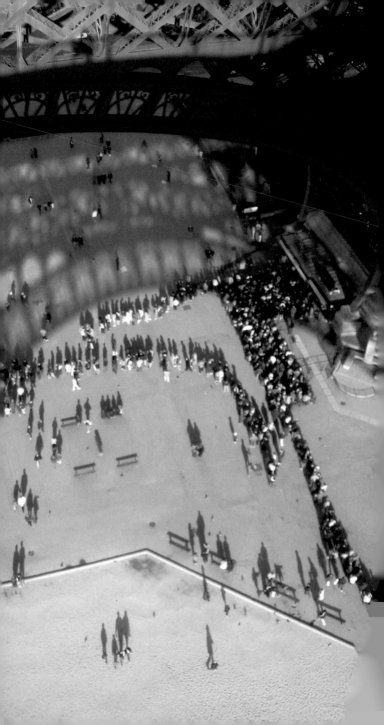

Places

The Islands

There's no better place to start a tour of Paris than with its two river islands, Ile de la Cité, the city's ancient core, and charming, village-like Ile St-Louis. The Ile de la Cité is where Paris began. It was settled in around 300 BC by a Celtic tribe, the Parisii, and in 52 BC was overrun by Julius Caesar's troops. The Romans called the settlement Lutetia Parisiorum and turned it into an administrative centre, building a palace-fortress at the western end of the Ile de la Cité. In the tenth century the Frankish kings transformed this fortress into a splendid palace, of which the Sainte-Chapelle and the Conciergerie prison survive today.

At the other end of the island they erected the great cathedral of Notre-Dame. It takes some stretch of the imagination today to picture what this medieval settlement must have looked like, for most of it was erased in the nineteenth century by Baron Haussmann, Napoleon III's Préfet de la Seine (a post equivalent to mayor of Paris). Some ninety streets were destroyed and in their place were raised four vast Neoclassical edifices, including the Préfecture de Police. The few corners of the island that escaped Haussmann's attentions include the leafy square du Vert-Galant and charming place Dauphine.

Pont Neuf

Ⓜ Pont Neuf. Despite its name, the Pont Neuf is Paris's oldest surviving bridge, built in 1607 by Henri IV, one of the city's first great town planners. A handsome stone construction with twelve arches, the bridge

▲ PONT NEUF

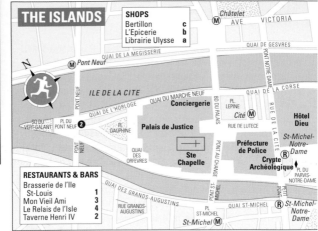

THE ISLANDS

SHOPS
Bertillon   c
L'Epicerie   b
Librairie Ulysse   a

RESTAURANTS & BARS
Brasserie de l'Ile
St-Louis   1
Mon Vieil Ami   3
Le Relais de l'Isle   4
Taverne Henri IV   2

links the western tip of the Ile de la Cité with both banks of the river. It was the first in Paris to be made of stone rather than wood, hence the name. Henri is commemorated with a stately equestrian statue halfway across.

Square du Vert-Galant

Ⓜ Pont Neuf. Enclosed within the triangular "stern" of the island, the square du Vert-Galant is a tranquil, tree-lined garden and a popular haunt of lovers. The square takes its name (a "Vert-Galant" is a "green" or "lusty" gentleman) from the nickname given to Henri IV, whose amorous exploits were legendary.

Place Dauphine

Ⓜ Cité. Red-brick seventeenth-century houses flank the entrance to place Dauphine, one of the city's most secluded and attractive squares, lined with venerable town houses. The noise of traffic recedes here, likely to be replaced by nothing more intrusive than the gentle tap of boules being played in the shade of the chestnuts.

The Sainte-Chapelle

4 bd du Palais. Ⓜ Cité. Daily: March–Oct 9.30am–6pm; Nov–Feb 9am–5pm. €6.50, combined ticket with the Conciergerie €11. The slender spire of the Sainte-Chapelle soars high above the Palais de Justice buildings. Though damaged in the Revolution, it was sensitively restored in the mid-nineteenth century and remains one of the finest achievements of French High Gothic, renowned for its exquisite stained-glass windows.

The building was constructed by Louis IX between 1242 and 1248 to house a collection of holy relics, including Christ's crown of thorns and a fragment of the True Cross, bought from the bankrupt empire of Byzantium. First you enter the lower chapel, where servants would have worshipped; very simply decorated, it gives no clue as to the splendour that lies ahead in the upper chapel (accessed via a spiral staircase). Here you're greeted by a truly dazzling sight – a vast, almost uninterrupted expanse of magnificent stained glass, supported by deceptively fragile-looking stone columns.

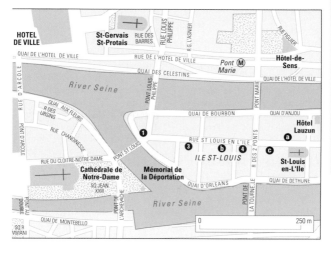

When the sun streams through, the glowing blues and reds of the stained glass dapple the interior and it feels as if you're surrounded by myriad brilliant butterflies. The windows, two-thirds of which are original (the others are from the nineteenth-century restoration), tell virtually the entire story of the Bible, beginning on the north side with Genesis and various other books of the Old Testament, continuing with the Passion of Christ (east end) and ending with the Apocalypse in the rose window.

The Conciergerie

2 bd du Palais. Ⓜ Cité. Daily: March–Oct 9.30am–6pm; Nov–Feb 9am–5pm. €8, combined ticket with Sainte-Chapelle €11.

Located within the Palais de Justice complex, the Conciergerie is Paris's oldest prison, where Marie-Antoinette and, in their turn, the leading figures of the Revolution were incarcerated before execution. It was turned into a prison – and put in the charge of a "concierge", or steward – after

Etienne Marcel's uprising in 1358 led Charles V to decamp to the greater security of the Louvre.

One of its towers, on the corner of the quai de l'Horloge, bears Paris's first public clock, built in 1370 and now fully restored.

▼ SAINTE-CHAPELLE

Inside the Conciergerie are several splendidly vaulted Gothic halls, among the few surviving vestiges of the original Capetian palace. Elsewhere a number of rooms and prisoners' cells, including Marie-Antoinette's cell, have been reconstructed to show what they might have been like at the time of the French Revolution.

Cathédrale de Notre-Dame

Ⓜ Cité & Ⓜ/RER St-Michel. Cathedral daily 7.45am–6.45pm; free. Towers daily: April–Sept 9.30am–7.30pm; Oct–March 10am–5.30pm; €7.50, under-18s free. Guided tours in English Wed & Thurs 2pm, Sat 2.30pm; 1hr–1hr 30min; free; gather at the welcome desk near the entrance.

One of the masterpieces of the Gothic age, the Cathédrale de Notre-Dame rears up from the Ile de la Cité like a ship moored by huge flying buttresses. It was among the first of the great Gothic cathedrals built in northern France and one of the most ambitious, its nave reaching an unprecedented 33m. Built on the site of the Merovingian cathedral of Saint-Etienne, Notre-Dame was begun in 1160 and completed around 1345. In the seventeenth and eighteenth centuries it fell into decline, suffering its worst depredations during the Revolution when the frieze of Old Testament kings on the facade was damaged by enthusiasts who mistook them for the kings of France.

It was only in the 1820s that the cathedral was at last given a much-needed restoration, a task entrusted to the great architect-restorer Viollet-le-Duc, who carried out a thorough – some would say too thorough – renovation, remaking much of the statuary on the facade (the originals can be seen in the Musée National du Moyen Age; see p.121) and adding the steeple and baleful-looking gargoyles, which you can see close up if you brave the ascent of the towers.

The cathedral's facade is one of its most impressive exterior features; the Romanesque influence is still visible, not least in its solid H-shape, but the overriding impression is one of lightness and grace, created in part by the delicate filigree work of the central rose window and the gallery above. There are some wonderful carvings over the portals; the oldest

▲ CONCIERGERIE

▲ NOTRE-DAME

are those over the right portal depicting the Virgin enthroned, and below, episodes from the life of Saint Anne (Mary's mother) and the life of Christ.

Inside, you're struck by the dramatic contrast between the darkness of the nave and the light falling on the first great clustered pillars of the choir. It's the end walls of the transepts that admit all this light, being nearly two-thirds glass, including two magnificent rose windows coloured in imperial purple. These, the vaulting and the soaring shafts reaching to the springs of the vaults, are all definite Gothic elements, while there remains a strong sense of Romanesque in the stout round pillars of the nave and the general sense of four-squareness.

The kilomètre zéro

On the pavement by the west door of Notre-Dame is a spot, marked by a bronze star, known as kilomètre zéro, from which all main-road distances in France are calculated.

The Crypte Archéologique

place du Parvis-Notre-Dame. Ⓜ Cité & Ⓜ/RER St-Michel. Tues–Sun 10am–6pm. €3.30. The atmospherically lit Crypte Archéologique is a large excavated area under the place du Parvis revealing the remains of the original cathedral, as well as vestiges of the streets and houses that once clustered around Notre-Dame: most are medieval, but some date as far back as Gallo-Roman times.

Le Mémorial de la Déportation

Ⓜ Cité. Daily 10am–noon & 2–7pm, closes 5pm in winter. Free. Scarcely visible above ground, the stark and moving Mémorial de la Déportation is the symbolic tomb of the 200,000 French who died in Nazi concentration camps during World War II – among them Jews, Resistance fighters and forced labourers. Stairs barely shoulder-wide descend into a space like a prison yard and then into a crypt, off which is a long, narrow, stifling corridor, its walls covered in thousands of points of light representing

▲ L'EPICERIE

the dead. Above the exit are the words "Pardonne, n'oublie pas" ("Forgive; do not forget").

Ile St-Louis

Ⓜ Pont-Marie. The smaller of the two islands, Ile St-Louis, is prime strolling territory. Unlike its larger neighbour, it has no heavyweight sights; rather the island's allure lies in its handsome ensemble of austerely beautiful seventeenth-century houses, tree-lined quais and narrow streets, harbouring restaurants, art galleries and gift shops. For centuries the Ile St-Louis was nothing but swampy pastureland, a haunt of lovers, duellists and miscreants on the run, until in the seventeenth-century the real-estate developer, Christophe Marie, had the bright idea of filling it with elegant mansions. Two of the finest, the Hôtel Lambert at 2 rue St-Louis-en-l'Ile, now owned by Baron Rothschild, and the Hôtel Lauzun at 17 quai d'Anjou, were built by Versailles architect Le Vau and decorated by Le Brun.

Shops

Berthillon

31 rue St-Louis-en-l'Ile. Ⓜ Pont-Marie. Wed–Sun 10am–8pm. Long queues form for these exquisite ice creams and sorbets that come in all sorts of unusual flavours, such as rhubarb and Earl Grey tea.

L'Epicerie

51 rue St-Louis-en-l'Ile. Ⓜ Pont-Marie. Daily 10.30am–7pm. Attractively packaged vinegars, oils, jams and mustards, with some unusual flavourings such as orange- and rosemary-flavoured white-wine vinegar from Champagne.

Librairie Ulysse

26 rue St-Louis-en-l'Ile. Ⓜ Pont-Marie. Tues–Fri 2–8pm. A tiny bookshop, piled from floor to ceiling with new and secondhand travel books.

Restaurants

Brasserie de l'Ile St-Louis

55 quai de Bourbon. Ⓜ Pont-Marie.

☎01.43.54.02.59 Daily except Wed noon–midnight; closed Aug. A friendly brasserie with a rustic, dark-wood interior and a sunny terrace, serving moderately priced (around €25 a head) Alsatian cuisine such as sauerkraut with ham and sausage.

Mon Vieil Ami

69 rue St-Louis-en-l'Ile. Ⓜ Pont-Marie. ☎01.40.46.01.35. Wed–Sun 11.30– 2.30pm & 7–10.30pm. Recently opened by renowned Alsatian chef Antoine Westermann, this charming little bistro already ranks as a firm favourite with locals and is arguably the best place to eat on the island. The cuisine is bold and zesty, using seasonal ingredients, and the wine list includes a fine selection of Alsatian vintages. The minimalist decor of chocolate browns and frosted-glass panels makes a stylish backdrop. Three courses around €40. Booking recommended.

Le Relais de l'Isle

37 rue St-Louis-en-l'Ile. Ⓜ Pont-Marie. ☎01.46.34.72.34. Wed–Sun noon–2pm & 7.30–11pm. A cosy, candlelit jazz-restaurant serving

tasty dishes such as rabbit in prune sauce and lemon chicken with honey. It's the convivial ambience that makes this place special, though: friendly service, the pianist tinkling away and the chef occasionally popping out from the kitchen to join in. Set menu €30, plus €3 extra added for the jazz.

Bars

Taverne Henri IV

13 place du Pont-Neuf. Ⓜ Pont-Neuf. Mon–Fri 11.30am–3.30pm & 6–9pm, Sat noon–4pm; closed Aug. An old-style wine bar, serving reasonably priced wine and snacks, buzziest at lunchtime when lawyers from the nearby Palais de Justice drop in.

Live music

Sainte-Chapelle

☎01.42.77.65.65; bookings also at any FNAC store (see p.172) or Virgin Megastore. Classical music concerts are held in the splendid surroundings of the chapel more or less daily. Tickets €16–27.50.

▲ LIVE JAZZ ON THE ILE ST-LOUIS

The Louvre

The Louvre is one of the world's truly great museums. Opened in 1793, during the Revolution, it soon acquired the largest art collection on earth, thanks to Napoleon's conquests. Today, it houses paintings, sculpture and precious art objects, covering everything from Ancient Egyptian jewellery to the beginnings of Impressionism. Even if you're not venturing inside, the palace itself is breathtaking, cutting a grand classical swathe right through the centre of the city.

Quite separate from the Louvre proper, but still within the palace, are three museums under the aegis of the Union Centrale des Arts Décoratifs, dedicated to fashion and textiles, decorative arts and advertising.

The palace

For centuries the site of the French court, the palace was originally little more than a feudal fortress, begun by Philippe-Auguste in 1200. In fact, it wasn't until the reign of François I, in the first flowering of the Renaissance, that the foundations of the present-day building were laid, and from then on almost every sovereign added to the Louvre, leaving the palace a surprisingly harmonious building. Even with the addition in 1989 of the initially controversial glass **Pyramide** in the cour Napoléon – an extraordinary leap of imagination conceived by the Chinese-born architect I. M. Pei – the overall effect of the Louvre is of a quintessentially French grandeur and symmetry.

Painting

By far the largest of the museum's collections is its paintings. The early **Italians** are perhaps the most interesting,

Visiting the Louvre

☎08.92.68.36.22 ⓦwww.louvre.fr. Mon, Thurs, Sat & Sun 9am–6pm, Wed & Fri 9am–9.45pm. €8.50; €6 after 6pm; free to under-18s; free first Sun of the month except public hols & to under-26s Fri after 6pm. Same-day readmission allowed.

Tickets can be bought in advance by phone, online or from branches of FNAC and Virgin Megastore, as found everywhere in Paris. The main entrance is via the Pyramide; if the queues look too long, then try the entrance directly under the Arc du Carrousel, which you can also access from 99 rue de Rivoli and from the line #1 Palais Royal-Musée du Louvre métro stop. The Porte des Lions, on the riverfront quai des Tuileries, near the western end of the museum, provides another quick way in. Pre-booked ticket holders can enter from the Passage Richelieu, which has views of the dramatically glazed-over sculpture courtyards.

Due to the sheer volume of exhibits (not to mention visitors), even if you spent the entire day here you'd see only a fraction of the collection. The Denon wing is a very popular place to start: as well as the Mona Lisa, it houses all of the Italian paintings, some magnificent French nineteenth-century canvases, and the great Italian and Classical sculptures. Rewarding and relatively peaceful alternatives are the grand chronologies of French painting and sculpture, or a stroll through the sensual collection of Objets d'Art. *Da Vinci Code* enthusiasts should make for the Grande Galerie, in the Denon wing, and the inverted pyramid, under the Arc du Carrousel. Don't miss the dramatic Medieval Louvre section, on the lower ground floor of Sully, where the foundations of Philippe-Auguste's keep stand alongside vestiges of Charles V's medieval palace walls. Wherever you're headed, pick up a free floor plan – essential for navigation.

among them Leonardo da Vinci's *Mona Lisa*. If you want to get near her, go during one of the evening openings, or first thing in the day. Other highlights of the Italian collection include two complete Botticelli frescoes, Giotto's *Stigmatization of St Francis of Assisi*, and Fra Angelico's *Coronation of the Virgin*. Fifteenth- to seventeenth century Italian paintings line the magnificent length of the Grande Galerie – the setting for the notorious opening scene of *The Da Vinci Code*. Outstanding works here are Leonardo's *Virgin and Child with St Anne* and *Virgin of the Rocks,* several Raphael masterpieces and Mantegna's *Crucifixion*. Epic-scale nineteenth-century French works are displayed in the parallel suite of rooms, among them the glorious *Coronation of Napoleon I*, by David, Ingres' languorous nude, *La Grande Odalisque*, and Géricault's harrowing *Raft of the Medusa*, which depicts a notorious incident in which shipwrecked sailors on a raft turned to cannibalism.

▲ VIEW FROM INSIDE THE PYRAMID

A good place to start a circuit of **French paintings** is with the master of French Classicism, Poussin; his profound themes, taken from antiquity, the Bible and mythology, together with his harmonious style, were to influence generations of artists. You'll need a healthy appetite for Classicism in the next suite of rooms, but there are some arresting portraits, and the paintings of Georges de la Tour are superbly idiosyncratic. When you move into the rather less severe eighteenth century, the more intimate paintings of Watteau come as a relief, as do Chardin's intense still lifes. In the later part of the collection, the chilly wind of Neoclassicism blows through the paintings of Gros, Gérard, Prud'hon, David and Ingres, contrasting with the more sentimental style that begins with Greuze and continues into the Romanticism of Géricault and Delacroix. The final rooms take in Corot and the Barbizon school, the precursors of Impressionism. The Louvre's collection of French painting stops at 1848, a date picked up by the Musée d'Orsay (see p.136).

In the **Dutch** and **Spanish** collections, works worth lingering over are Rembrandt's superb *Supper at Emmaus*, with its dramatic use of chiaroscuro, Murillo's tender *Beggar Boy*, and the Goya portraits. Interspersed throughout the painting section are rooms dedicated to the Louvre's impressive collection of prints and drawings, exhibited by rotation.

Antiquities

The **Oriental Antiquities** and **Arts of Islam** categories cover the Mesopotamian, Sumerian, Babylonian, Assyrian and Phoenician civilizations, and the art of ancient Persia, India and Spain. One of the collection's most important exhibits is the Code of Hammurabi, a basalt stele dating from around 1800 BC covered in Akkadian script setting down King Hammurabi's rules of conduct for his subjects.

The **Egyptian Antiquities** collection starts with the atmospheric crypt of the Sphinx. Everyday life is illustrated through cooking accessories, jewellery, the principles of hieroglyphics, musical instruments, sarcophagi and a host of mummified cats. The collection continues with the development of Egyptian art; highlights include the expressive *Seated Scribe* (c.2500 BC) and the huge bust of Amenophis IV (1365–1349 BC).

The biggest crowd-pullers in the museum after the *Mona Lisa* are found in the **Greek and**

▲ THE LOUVRE PALACE

Roman Antiquities section: the dramatic *Winged Victory of Samothrace,* and the late-second-century BC *Venus de Milo,* striking a classic model's pose. Her antecedents are all on display, too, from the graceful marble head of the *Cycladic Idol* and the delightful *Dame d'Auxerre* to the Classical perfection of the *Athlete of Benevento.* The Roman section includes some wonderful frescoes from Pompeii and Herculaneum.

Objets d'Art

The vast Objets d'Art section presents the finest tapestries, ceramics, jewellery and furniture commissioned by France's most wealthy and influential patrons, beginning with the rather pious Middle Ages section and continuing through 81 relentlessly superb rooms to a salon decorated in the style of Louis-Philippe, the last king of France. Numerous rooms have been partially re-created in the style of a particular epoch, and walking through the complete chronology, where suites are often devoid of other visitors, gives a powerful sense of the evolution of aesthetic taste at its most refined and opulent.

Towards the end, the circuit passes through the breathtaking apartments of Napoleon III's minister of state.

Sculpture

The sculpture section covers the entire development of the art in France from the Romanesque to Rodin in the Richelieu wing, and Italian and northern European sculpture in the Denon wing, including Michelangelo's *Slaves,* designed for the tomb of Pope Julius II. The huge glass-covered courtyards of the Richelieu

▲ GRANDE GALERIE

wing – the cour Marly with the Marly Horses, which once graced place de la Concorde, and the cour Puget with Puget's *Milon de Crotone* as the centrepiece – are very impressive, if a bit overwhelming.

Union Centrale des Arts Décoratifs

107 rue de Rivoli. ⓦwww.ucad.fr. Tues–Fri 11am–6pm, Sat & Sun 10am–6pm. €8. The other museums housed in the Louvre under the umbrella organization Union Centrale des Arts Décoratifs are among the city's most innovative.

The **Musée de la Mode et du Textile** holds high-quality temporary exhibitions demonstrating the most brilliant and cutting-edge of Paris fashions from all eras, such as Jackie Kennedy's famous 1960s dresses.

On the top floor, the **Musée de la Publicité** shows off its collection of advertising posters through cleverly themed, temporary exhibitions. The space is appropriately trendy – half exposed brickwork and steel panelling and half crumbling Louvre finery.

The newly revamped **Musée des**

▲ COUR NAPOLEON

and furnished entirely as a late-medieval bedroom. Changing contemporary collections display works by French, Italian and Japanese designers, including some great examples of the work of Philippe Starck.

Cafés

Café Denon

Lower ground floor, Denon wing. It's worth seeking out this cosy little tearoom and restaurant, hidden away among the Louvre's vaults. Like all the Louvre cafés, it's fairly expensive for what it is.

Café Mollien

First floor, Denon wing. The busiest of the Louvre's cafés has a prime position near the Grande Galerie, with huge windows giving onto a terrace (in summer) overlooking the Pyramide.

Café Richelieu

First floor, Richelieu wing. The most prim and elegant of the Louvre's cafés, with full meals available as well as drinks and snacks. The spectacular outdoor terrace is open on warm days.

Arts Décoratifs seems something of the odd man out, though its eclectic collection of art and superbly crafted furniture fits the Union Centrale's "design" theme. The medieval and Renaissance rooms show off curiously shaped and beautifully carved chairs, dressers and tables, religious paintings, and Venetian glass. There are also some wonderful tapestries – including the delightful late-fifteenth-century *Le Berger*, depicting a shepherd surrounded by a very woolly flock – and a room decorated

▼ SCULPTURAL DETAIL, LOUVRE PALACE

The Champs-Elysées and Tuileries

The breathtakingly ambitious Champs-Elysées is part of a grand, nine-kilometre axis, often referred to as the "Voie Triomphale", or Triumphal Way, that extends from the Louvre at the heart of the city to the Défense business district in the west. Combining imperial pomp and supreme elegance, it offers impressive vistas along its entire length and incorporates some of the city's most famous landmarks – the place de la Concorde, Tuileries gardens and the Arc de Triomphe. The whole ensemble is so regular and geometrical it looks as though it might have been laid out by a single town planner rather than successive kings, emperors and presidents, all keen to add their stamp and promote French power and prestige.

The Champs-Elysées

Scene of the annual Bastille Day procession, the Champs-Elysées is the nation's best-known avenue. Its heyday was during the Second Empire when members of the *haute bourgeoisie* built themselves splendid mansions along its length and fashionable society frequented the avenue's cafés and theatres. Nowadays, tree-lined and broad, it looks at its most impressive from a distance, thanks to its constant traffic, fast-food outlets and chain stores. It has, however, experienced something of a renaissance in the last few years, as chic designer outlets such as Louis Vuitton (see p.84) have moved in and once-dowdy shops such as the Renault show room at no. 53 and the Publicis drugstore, near the Arc de Triomphe, have undergone stylish makeovers. New, fashionable restaurants and bars have opened in the streets that spar off the avenue.

▲ CHAMPS-ELYSEES AT NIGHT

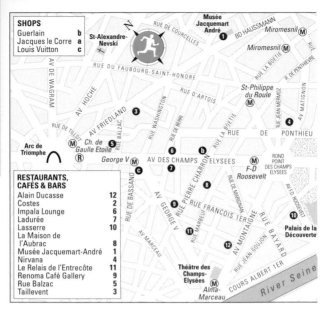

The Arc de Triomphe

Ⓜ Charles-de-Gaulle. Daily:
April–Sept 10am–11pm; Oct–March
10am–10.30pm. €8. Crowning
the Champs-Elysées, the Arc
de Triomphe sits imposingly in
the middle of place Charles de
Gaulle, also known as l'Etoile
("star") on account of the
twelve avenues radiating from
it. Modelled on the ancient
Roman triumphal arches, this
imperial behemoth was built by
Napoleon as a homage to the
armies of France and is engraved
with the names of 660 generals
and numerous French battles.
The best of the exterior reliefs
is François Rude's *Marseillaise*, in
which an Amazon-type figure
personifying the Revolution
charges forward with a sword,
her face contorted in a fierce
rallying cry. A quiet reminder
of the less glorious side of war is
the tomb of the unknown soldier
placed beneath the arch and
marked by an eternal flame that is
stoked up every evening by war
veterans. The climb up to the top
is well worth it for the panoramic
views.

The Grand Palais

Ⓜ Champs-Elysées-Clemenceau.
Ⓦ www.rmn.fr/galeriesnationales
dugrandpalais. Galeries nationales
du Grand Palais: daily except Tues
10am–8pm, Wed until 10pm. €10. At
the lower end of the Champs-
Elysées is the Grand Palais, a
grandiose Neoclassical building
with a fine glass and ironwork
cupola, created for the 1900
Exposition Universelle. The
glass of the dome – some 15,000
square metres – has recently
been restored and the ironwork
spruced up with a new coat of
sea-green paint. Renovation
work on the exterior will be fully
complete in 2007; meanwhile
the palais is gradually resuming
its role as a cultural centre,
hosting music festivals and art
exhibitions, as well as trade fairs

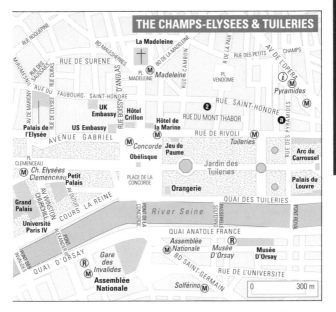

PLACES

and fashion shows.
In the north wing of
the building is the
Galeries nationales,
Paris's prime venue
for major art
retrospectives.

Palais de la Découverte

Av Franklin D. Roosevelt.
Ⓜ Champs-Elysées-
Clemenceau. ⓦwww.
palais-decouverte.fr.
Tues–Sat 9.30am–6pm,
Sun & hols 10am–7pm.
Museum €6.50,
including planetarium
€10. Occupying
the west wing of
the Grand Palais is
the city's original
science museum,
dating from the late
1930s. It does a fairly
good job of bringing
science alive,
using audiovisual

▲ THE ARC DE TRIOMPHE

▲ PLACE DE LA CONCORDE

material, models and interactive exhibits. Temporary exhibitions explore themes such as climate change and biotechnology, and there's also a planetarium, with occasional English-language sessions in summer.

The Petit Palais

av Winston Churchill. Ⓜ Champs-Elysées-Clemenceau. Tues–Sun 10am–6pm. Free. The Petit Palais houses the Musée des Beaux Arts. Built at the same time as its larger neighbour the Grand Palais, the building is hardly "petit" but certainly palatial, with beautiful spiral wrought-iron staircases and a grand gallery on the lines of Versailles' Hall of Mirrors. What's more, a major renovation completed in 2005 has returned the building to its original splendour, allowing more natural light to flood in and illuminate the restored stained-glass windows and ceiling frescoes. It has also freed up more space for the museum's extensive collection of paintings, sculpture and decorative artworks, ranging from the ancient Greek and Roman period up to the early twentieth century. At first sight it looks like it's mopped up the leftovers after the city's other galleries have taken their pick, but there are some real gems here, such as Monet's *Sunset at Lavacourt* and Courbet's *Young Ladies on the Bank of the Seine*. There's also fantasy jewellery of the Art Nouveau period, a fine collection of seventeenth-century Dutch landscape painting, Russian icons and effete eighteenth-century furniture and porcelain. A newly installed café overlooks the restored interior garden.

Musée Jacquemart-André

158 bd Haussmann. Ⓜ Miromesnil/St-Philippe-du-Roule. Ⓦwww.musee-jacquemart-andre.com. Daily 10am–6pm. €9.50. The Musée Jacquemart-André is set in a magnificent nineteenth-century *hôtel particulier* (mansion), hung with the superb artworks accumulated on the travels of banker Edouard André and his wife, former society portraitist Nélie Jacquemart. A stunning distillation of fifteenth- and

sixteenth-century Italian genius, including works by Tiepolo, Botticelli, Donatello, Mantegna and Uccello, forms the core of the collection. Almost as compelling as the splendid interior and paintings is the insight gleaned into a grand nineteenth-century lifestyle.

Place de la Concorde

Ⓜ Concorde. The vast place de la Concorde has a much less peaceful history than its name suggests. Between 1793 and 1795, some 1300 people died here beneath the Revolutionary guillotine, Louis XVI, Marie-Antoinette, Danton and Robespierre among them. Today, constantly circumnavigated by traffic, the centrepiece of the *place* is a gold-tipped obelisk from the temple of Ramses at Luxor, offered as a favour-currying gesture by the viceroy of Egypt in 1829. From the centre of the square there are sweeping vistas in all directions: the Champs-Elysées looks particularly impressive and you can also admire the alignment of the Assemblée Nationale, in the south, with the church of the Madeleine – both sporting identical Neoclassical facades – at the end of rue Royale, to the north.

Jardin des Tuileries

Ⓜ Concorde/Tuileries. Daily: April–June & Sept 7.30am–9pm; July & Aug 7.30am–11.45pm; Oct–March 7.30am–7.30pm. The Jardin des Tuileries, the formal French garden *par excellence*, dates back to the 1570s, when Catherine de Médicis had the site cleared of the medieval warren of tilemakers (*tuileries*) to make way for a palace and grounds. One hundred years later, Louis XIV commissioned André Le Nôtre to redesign them, and the results are largely what you see today: straight avenues, formal flowerbeds and splendid vistas. The grand central alley is lined with shady, clipped chestnuts and manicured lawns, and framed at each end by ornamental pools, surrounded

▲ PLACE DE LA CONCORDE FROM TUILERIES

▲ JARDIN DES TUILERIES

by an impressive gallery of copies of statues by the likes of Rodin and Coysevox; you can see the originals in the Louvre.

Orangerie

Jardin des Tuileries. Ⓜ Concorde. ⓦwww.musee-orangerie.fr. Daily except Tues 12.30–7pm, Fri until 10pm. Group bookings only 9am–12.30pm. €6.50. The Jardin des Tuileries' Orangerie houses a private art collection of late nineteenth-century art, and has recently reopened after a major renovation project from 2000 to 2006. It involved replacing the concrete ceiling with glass, allowing the centrepiece of the collection – eight of Monet's giant waterlily paintings – to be displayed in line with the artist's original request that as much natural light as possible be allowed to reach them. The rest of the collection includes works by Renoir, Matisse, Cézanne, Utrillo and Modigliani.

Jeu de Paume

Jardin des Tuileries. Ⓜ Concorde. ⓦwww.jeudepaume.org. Tues noon–

9pm, Wed–Fri noon–7pm, Sat & Sun 10am–7pm. €6. The Jeu de Paume was once a royal tennis court and later the place where French Impressionist paintings were displayed before being transferred to the Musée d'Orsay. The Centre National de la Photographie now resides here and mounts major photographic exhibitions.

Shops

Guerlain

68 av des Champs-Elysées. Ⓜ Franklin-D.-Roosevelt. Mon–Sat 10.30am–8pm, Sun 3–7pm. A beautiful belle époque boutique selling heady perfumes from the Guerlain range.

Jacques Le Corre

193 rue Saint-Honoré. Ⓜ Tuileries. Mon–Sat 11am–7pm. Creative, original hats, footwear and handbags. The stylish, unisex hats come in interesting colours and shapes; Jacques is famed for his classic cotton cloche, perfecting the vagrant-chic look.

Louis Vuitton

101 av des Champs-Elysées. Ⓜ George V. Mon–Sat 10am–8pm. Louis Vuitton's stylishly revamped store doesn't just sell luxury luggage and handbags, it also has a contemporary art exhibition space on its seventh floor, accessed from within the store or round the corner at 60 rue de Bassano. Artworks, such as a video wall by Olafur Eliasson (who did the sun-like installation *The Weather Project* at the Tate Modern in London), have also been incorporated into the shop.

Cafés

Ladurée

75 av des Champs-Elysées. Ⓜ George V. Daily 7.30am–11.30pm. This Champs-Elysées branch of the Ladurée tea rooms, with its luxurious gold and green decor, is perfect for a shopping break. Try their melt-in-your-mouth macaroons or the thick hot chocolate (€6.10 for a jug enough for two cups).

Musée Jacquemart-André

158 bd Haussmann. Ⓜ Miromesnil/ St-Philippe-du-Roule. Daily 11.30am– 5.30pm. Admire ceiling frescoes by Tiepolo while savouring fine pastries in this sumptuously appointed *salon de thé* in the Musée Jacquemart-André.

Restaurants

Alain Ducasse at the Plaza-Athénée

Hotel Plaza-Athénée, 25 av Montaigne. Ⓜ Alma Marceau. ☎01.53.67.65.00. Mon–Fri 7.45–10.15pm and Thurs & Fri 12.45–2.15pm; closed mid-July to mid-Aug. One of the world's top haute-cuisine temples, run by star chef Alain Ducasse; his sublime dishes are likely to revive even the most jaded palate. The decor is Louis XV with a modern gloss, and the service – as you'd expect – is impeccable. Reckon on around €200 upwards and book well in advance.

Lasserre

17 av Franklin D. Roosevelt. Ⓜ Franklin-D.-Roosevelt. ☎01.43.59.02.13, ☷www.restaurant -lasserre.com. Mon–Sat 7–10pm and Thurs & Fri noon–2pm; closed Aug. A classic haute-cuisine restaurant with a lovely belle époque dining room and a roof that's rolled back on balmy summer evenings. From €120.

La Maison de l'Aubrac

37 rue Marbeuf. Ⓜ Franklin-D.-Roosevelt. ☎01.43.59.18.40. Daily 24hr. An all-night restaurant with rustic decor serving meaty Auvergnat cuisine, such as sausage with *aligot* (creamy mashed potato with cheese) for €17.50. There's also a twenty-page wine list to choose from, with bottles from €30.

▲ MUSÉE JACQUEMART-ANDRE: SALON DE THE

Le Relais de l'Entrecôte

15 rue Marbeuf. Ⓜ Franklin-D.-Roosevelt. Daily noon–2.30pm & 7–11.30pm; closed Aug. *Le Relais de l'Entrecôte* has only one main dish on the menu: steak and frites. This is no ordinary steak though – the secret is in the delicious sauce. €21.80 including a salad starter. No reservations taken.

Rue Balzac

3 rue Balzac. Ⓜ George-V. ☎01.53.89.90.91. Mon–Fri noon–2pm & 7–9.30pm, Sat & Sun 7–9.30pm; closed Aug. A stylish, buzzing restaurant owned by Johnny Hallyday. The low lighting and subdued reds and yellows of the decor provide an atmospheric backdrop to modern French cuisine, available in small or large servings (*petit modèle* or *grand modèle*). Around €50 a head.

Taillevent

15 rue Lamennais. Ⓜ George-V. ☎01.44.95.15.01. Mon–Fri 12.30–2.30pm & 7.30–11.30pm; closed Aug. One of Paris's finest gourmet restaurants. The Provençal-influenced cuisine and wine list are exceptional, the decor classy and refined. There's a set menu for €70 at lunch only, otherwise reckon on an average of €150 a head, excluding wine, and book well in advance.

Bars

Costes

Hôtel Costes, 239 rue St-Honoré. Ⓜ Concorde/Tuileries. Daily until 2am. A favourite haunt of fashionistas and celebs, this is a romantic place for an aperitif or late-night drinks amid decadent nineteenth-century decor of red velvet, swags and columns, set around an Italianate courtyard. Cocktails around €15.

Impala Lounge

2 rue de Berri. Ⓜ George V. Daily until 4am. A trendy, *Out of Africa*-themed bar with great atmosphere and music – mostly reggae, funk and Afro-jazz.

Nirvana

3 av Matignon. Ⓜ St-Philippe-du-Roule. Daily until 4am. A hip bar-restaurant-club with Indian-inspired decor where you can sip drinks next to tired models flanked by their Hermès bags, and dance till dawn in the club downstairs. Cocktails €13.

Renoma Café Gallery

32 av George V. Ⓜ George-V. ☎01.47.20.46.19. Daily 9am–2am. A trendy bar-café-restaurant hung with photos by avant-garde fashion designer Maurice Renoma. By day you can sit in the comfy lounge area and browse design and architecture magazines, and by night chill out with a vodka cocktail (€9). It also does a popular, decent-portioned Sunday brunch (noon–5pm; €28).

Live music

Théâtre des Champs-Elysées

15 av Montaigne. Ⓜ Alma Marceau. ☎01.49.52.50.50, ⓦwww.theatredes champselysees.fr. Built in 1913, this historic theatre, where Stravinsky premiered his *Rite of Spring*, is home to the Orchestre National de France and also hosts many international concerts and ballets. Tickets are as cheap as €5 for a seat with no view, otherwise they range from around €12 to €115.

Trocadéro

The swish little strip of the 16ᵉ arrondissement that runs alongside the Seine is unusually thick with good museums, even for Paris. Between place de l'Alma, notorious as the scene of Princess Diana's fatal car crash, and place du Trocadéro stretch broad, leafy and largely residential boulevards, lined with the homes of wealthy Parisians and their expensive little dogs. The atmosphere of the quarter isn't exactly lively, but the views across the river to the Eiffel Tower and the 7ᵉ arrondissement are wonderful, especially from the terrace of the Palais de Chaillot.

Palais de Chaillot

From behind its elaborate park and fountains, the sweeping arcs of the Palais de Chaillot seem designed to embrace the view of the Eiffel Tower, which stands on the far side of the river. The distinctly totalitarian Modernist-Classical architecture dates the palace to 1937, when it was built as the showpiece of the Exposition Universelle, one of Paris's regular trade and culture jamborees. The central terrace between the palace's two wings forms a perfect platform for photo opportunities, curio-sellers and skateboarders.

Cité de l'Architecture et du Patrimoine

Palais de Chaillot, 17 place du Trocadéro. Ⓜ Trocadéro. ⓦwww.citechaillot.org. Opens spring 2007. The all-new Cité de l'Architecture et du Patrimoine, which fills the east wing of the Palais de Chaillot, is a combined institute, library and museum of architecture. The

▲ PALAIS DE CHAILLOT

CAFÉS
Aux Marchés du Palais 3
Salon de Porcelain 1
Tokyo Eat & Tokyo Idem 2

top floor showcases modern and contemporary architecture with models, designs and a reconstruction of an entire apartment from Le Corbusier's Cité Radieuse, in Marseille. The most impressive gallery is on the vaulted level below, where the **Galerie des Moulages** displays giant-sized plastercasts that were taken from great French buildings at the end of the nineteenth century. The idea is to tell the story of French architecture from the Middle Ages through to the nineteenth century, but it's an exercise in national pride as much as education. **The Galerie des Peintures Murales**, on the top floor of the central Pavillon de Tête, features full-scale copies of great French frescoes and wall-paintings.

Temporary exhibitions include studies of contemporary architecture, while two rooftop terraces give superb views across the river to the Eiffel Tower.

Musée de la Marine

Palais de Chaillot, 17 place du Trocadéro. Ⓜ Trocadéro. ⓦ www. musee-marine.fr. Mon & Wed–Sun 10am–6pm. €8. The Musée de la Marine is worth visiting for its beautiful, super-scale models of French ships. These range from ancient galleys to Napoleonic three-deckers, and from giant trawlers to the latest nuclear submarines.

Musée Guimet

place d'Iéna. Ⓜ Iéna. ⓦwww. museeguimet.fr. Mon & Wed–Sun 10am–6pm. €6. The airy, light-filled atrium of the Musée National des Arts Asiatiques-Guimet is peopled with exquisite Buddha statues and figurines from Cambodia's ancient Khmer dynasty. It's a breathtaking introduction to the museum's world-renowned collection of Buddhist and Asian art. Above, the museum winds round four floors groaning with dramatically lit statues of Buddhas and gods.

The third-floor rotunda was used by the collection's philanthropist founder, Emile Guimet, for the first Buddhist ceremony ever held in France. Guimet's original collection, brought back from his travels in Asia in 1876, is exhibited in the temple-like **Galeries du Panthéon Bouddhique**, around the corner (entrance at 19 avenue d'Iéna; same hours and ticket as museum).

Musée de la Mode et du Costume

Palais Galliera, 10 av Pierre 1er de Serbie. Ⓜ Iéna/Alma-Marceau. ☎01.56.52.86.00, ⓦwww.galliera. paris.fr. Tues–Sun 10am–6pm. €7. The exquisite Palais Galliera is home to the Musée de la Mode et du Costume, which runs two or three major exhibitions of clothes and fashion each year, often drawing from the museum's exceptional collection. Themes range from the work of individual *couturiers* to historical shows looking at the style of a particular era. During changeovers the museum is closed, so check in advance.

Musée d'Art Moderne de la Ville de Paris

Palais de Tokyo, 13 av du Président Wilson. Ⓜ Iéna/Alma-Marceau. ⓦwww.mam.paris.fr. Tues–Sun 10am–6pm, Wed till 10pm during exhibitions; closed public hols. Free. The Musée d'Art Moderne de la Ville de Paris displays the city's own collection of modern art. It may not rival the Pompidou Centre for super-celebrity works, but many of the paintings have

a rewarding Parisian theme, and the setting in the elegant, Modernist Palais de Tokyo is perfect, as there's a strong collection of early twentieth-century artists – notably Braque, Chagall, Delaunay, Derain, Léger, Modigliani and Picasso. Highlights are the chapel-like salle Matisse, devoted to Matisse's *La Danse de Paris*, and Dufy's enormous mural *La Fée Electricité* (*The Electricity Fairy*), which fills an entire, curved room with 250 lyrical, colourful panels recounting the story of electricity from Aristotle to the 1930s. Since the 1960s, the collection has been kept up to the minute by an active buying policy, and the visit usually ends with the latest video or installation acquisition.

In the courtyard garden you can have a drink and admire the smooth columns framing a view of the Eiffel Tower.

Site de Création Contemporaine

Palais de Tokyo, 13 av du Président Wilson. Ⓜ Iéna/Alma-Marceau. ⓦwww.palaisdetokyo.com. Tues–Sun noon–midnight. €6. The semi-derelict interior of the Palais de Tokyo's western wing looks

▲ MUSEE D'ART MODERNE DE LA VILLE DE PARIS

as if it has been hit by a bomb, with its wires, concrete beams and pipes haphazardly exposed. The effect is in fact deliberate, an avant-garde "anti-museum" statement made by the building's occupants: the Site de Création Contemporaine. This is the French state's chief space for cutting-edge contemporary art events, with a constant flow of French conceptual art shows. Paris-born Louise Bourgeois has exhibited here, and the site has been occupied – with official sanction – by groups as diverse as a squat-living art collective and a posse of skateboard artistes. Artists and art students pay just €1 for entry.

Place de l'Alma

From most angles, place de l'Alma looks like just another busy Parisian junction, with cars rattling over the cobbles and a métro entrance on the pavement. Over in one corner, however, stands a replica of the flame from the Statue of Liberty, which was given to France in 1987 as a symbol of Franco-American relations.

This golden torch has now been adopted by mourners from all over the world as a memorial to Princess Diana, who was killed in the underpass beneath in 1997. A low wall is covered with loving graffiti messages, though they're periodically cleaned off by the disapproving authorities.

Cafés

Aux Marchés du Palais

5 rue de la Manutention. Ⓜ Iéna/Alma-Marceau. ☎ 01.47.23.52.80. Mon–Fri noon–2pm & 7.30–10.30pm. This friendly, traditional bistro makes a good lunch stop, with sunny tables on the pavement opposite the Palais de Tokyo, and a menu of respectable, quintessentially French dishes. You can eat well for around €25.

Salon de Porcelain

Musée Guimet, place d'Iéna. Ⓜ Iéna. Mon & Wed–Sun 10am–5.30pm. The museum café offers an intriguing menu of speciality dishes and teas from all over Asia – dim sum, Thai, Japanese – though the basement ambience lacks equivalent style. *Menus* under €20.

Tokyo Eat & Tokyo Idem

Site de Création Contemporaine, Palais de Tokyo. Ⓜ Iéna/Alma-Marceau. Tues–Sun noon–1am. The café and restaurant inside the gallery are self-consciously hip places to hang out – the Benetton-bright decor of both venues is actually the gallery's permanent art collection. The restaurant, *Tokyo Eat*, serves cool, modern Mediterranean and fusion flavours, with a good weekday-lunchtime deal of a main course for €12. The downstairs cáfe, *Tokyo Idem*, is a good bet for a drink and a snack.

▲ PLACE DE L'ALMA FLAME

The Grands Boulevards and passages

Built on the old city ramparts, the Grands Boulevards are the eight broad streets that extend in a long arc from the Eglise de la Madeleine eastwards. In the nineteenth century, the boulevards were where *Paris vivant* was to be found, from the fashionable cafés in the west to the more colourful eastern end, with its street theatre and puppet shows. There's nothing that remarkable about the boulevards these days, but vestiges of their past live on in the brasseries, cafés, theatres and cinemas (notably the splendid Art Deco cinemas Grand Rex and Max Linder; see p.217).

To the south of the Grands Boulevards lies the city's main commercial and financial district, while just to the north, beyond the glittering Opéra Garnier, are the large department stores Galeries Lafayette and Printemps. Rather more well-heeled shopping is concentrated on the rue St-Honoré in the west and the streets around aristocratic place Vendôme, lined with top couturiers, jewellers and art dealers. Scattered around the whole area are the delightful *passages* – nineteenth-century arcades that hark back to shopping from a different era.

Musée Grévin

bd Montmartre. Ⓜ Grands-Boulevards. Mon–Fri 10am–5.30pm, Sat & Sun 10am–7pm. €17, children €10. A remnant from the fun-loving times on the Grands Boulevards are the waxworks in the Musée Grévin, comprising mainly French personalities and the usual bunch of Hollywood actors. The best thing about the museum is the original rooms: the magical Palais des Mirages (Hall of Mirrors), built for the Exposition Universelle in 1900; the theatre with its sculptures by Bourdelle; and the 1882 Baroque-style

▲ GALERIES LAFAYETTE

PLACES

The Grands Boulevards and passages

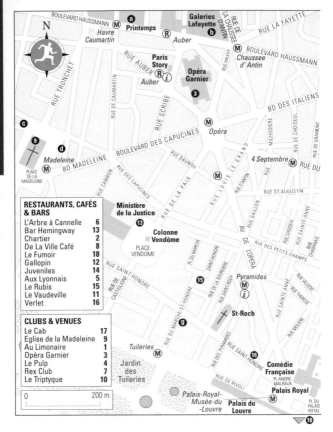

RESTAURANTS, CAFÉS & BARS

L'Arbre à Cannelle	6
Bar Hemingway	13
Chartier	2
De La Ville Café	8
Le Fumoir	18
Gallopin	12
Juveniles	14
Aux Lyonnais	5
Le Rubis	15
Le Vaudeville	11
Verlet	16

CLUBS & VENUES

Le Cab	17
Eglise de la Madeleine	9
Au Limonaire	1
Opéra Garnier	3
Le Pulp	4
Rex Club	7
Le Triptyque	10

Hall of Columns, where among other unlikely juxtapositions, Lara Croft prepares for action a few feet away from a dignified Charles de Gaulle, while Voltaire smiles across at the billowing skirts of Marilyn Monroe.

Opéra Garnier

Ⓜ Opéra. Daily 10am–4.30pm. €7; see p.100 for booking information.
The fantastically ornate Opéra Garnier, built by Charles Garnier for Napoleon III, exemplifies the Second Empire in its show of wealth and hint of vulgarity. The theatre's facade is a fairytale concoction of white, pink and green marble, colonnades, rearing horses, winged angels and gleaming gold busts. No less opulent is the interior with its spacious, gilded-marble and mirrored lobbies. The auditorium itself is all red velvet and gold leaf, hung with a six-tonne chandelier; the colourful ceiling was painted by Chagall in 1964 and depicts scenes from well-known operas and ballets jumbled up with famous Parisian landmarks. You can visit the interior, including the auditorium, as long as there are

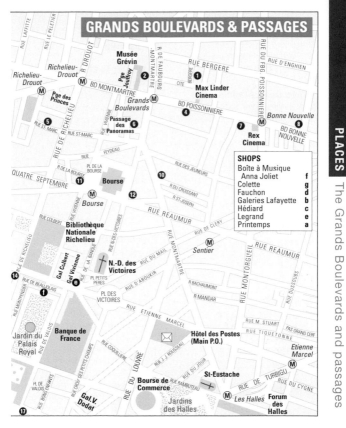

GRANDS BOULEVARDS & PASSAGES

SHOPS

Boîte à Musique Anna Joliet	**f**
Colette	**g**
Fauchon	**d**
Galeries Lafayette	**b**
Hédiard	**c**
Legrand	**e**
Printemps	**a**

no rehearsals (your best chance is 1–2pm).

Paris-Story

11 bis rue Scribe. Ⓜ Opéra. Shows daily on the hour 9am–7pm. €10. Paris-Story is a multimedia show tracing the history of Paris – it's a brief and highly romanticized overview, but quite enjoyable all the same. The 45-minute film, "narrated" by Victor Hugo, with simultane-

▲ OPERA GARNIER

ous translation in English, uses a kaleidoscope of computer-generated images and archive footage, set against a luscious classical-music soundtrack.

Eglise de la Madeleine

Ⓜ Madeleine. Mon–Sat 7.30am–7pm, Sun 8am–1pm & 4–7pm. See p.100 for concert information. The imperious-looking Eglise de la Madeleine is the parish church of Parisian high society. Originally intended as a monument to Napoleon's army, it's modelled on the Parthenon and is surrounded by Corinthian columns and fronted by a huge pediment depicting *The Last Judgement*. Inside, the wide single nave is decorated with Ionic columns and surmounted by three huge domes – the only source of natural light. A theatrical stone sculpture of the Magdalene being swept up to heaven by two angels draws your eye to the high altar, and above is a half-dome painted with a fresco commemorating the concordat signed between the Church and Napoleon, healing the rift after the Revolution.

Place de la Madeleine

Ⓜ Madeleine. Flower market Tues–Sat 8am–7.30pm. Place de la Madeleine is home to some of Paris's top gourmet food stores, best known of which are Fauchon and Hédiard (see pp.97 & 98). On the east side is one of the city's oldest flower markets dating back to 1832, while nearby, some rather fine Art Nouveau public toilets are definitely worth inspecting.

Place Vendôme

Ⓜ Opéra. Built by Versailles architect Hardouin-Mansart, place Vendôme is one of the city's most impressive set pieces. It's a pleasingly symmetrical, eight-sided *place*, enclosed by a harmonious ensemble of elegant mansions, graced with Corinthian pilasters and steeply pitched roofs. Once the grand residences of tax collectors and financiers, they now house such luxury establishments as the *Ritz* hotel, Cartier, Bulgari and other top-flight jewellers, lending the square a decidedly exclusive air. No. 12, now occupied by Chaumet jewellers, is where Chopin died, in 1849.

Somewhat out of proportion with the rest of the square, the centrepiece is a towering triumphal column, surmounted by a statue of Napoleon dressed as Caesar. It was raised in 1806 to celebrate

▲ PLACE VENDOME

the Battle of Austerlitz and features bronze reliefs of scenes of the battle, cast from 1200 recycled Austro-Russian cannons, spiralling their way up.

Rue St-Honoré

Rue St-Honoré – especially its western end and its extension the Faubourg St-Honoré – is a preserve of top fashion designers and art galleries. In recent years newer, cutting-edge designers have begun colonizing the stretch between rue Cambon and rue des Pyramides – a trend that started with the ultra-cool *Hôtel Costes* in the late 1990s, followed by the concept store, Colette (see p.97).

Palais Royal

Ⓜ Palais-Royal-Musée-du-Louvre. Gardens daily dawn–dusk. Free.

The Palais Royal was built for Cardinal Richelieu in 1624, though little now remains of the original palace. The current building, mostly dating from the eighteenth century, houses various governmental bodies and the Comédie Française, longstanding venue for the classics of French theatre. To the rear lie sedate gardens with fountains and avenues of clipped limes, bounded by stately eighteenth-century mansions built over arcades housing mainly antique and designer shops. You'd hardly guess that for a time these peaceful arcades and gardens were a site of gambling dens, brothels and funfair attractions until the prohibition on public gambling in 1838 put

an end to the fun. Folly, some might say, has returned – in the form of contemporary artist Daniel Buren's black-and-white striped pillars, rather like sticks of Brighton rock, all of varying heights, dotted about the main courtyard in front of the palace.

Galerie Véro-Dodat

Between rue Croix-des-Petits-Champs and rue Jean-Jacques Rousseau. Ⓜ Palais-Royal-Musée-du-Louvre. With its tiled floors, ceiling decorations and mahogany shop fronts divided by faux marble columns, Galerie Véro-Dodat is one of the most attractive and homogeneous *passages*. Fashionable new shops rub shoulders with older businesses.

PLACES

▲ PALAIS ROYAL

The passages

Conceived by town planners in the early nineteenth century to protect pedestrians from mud and horse-drawn vehicles, the *passages*, elegant glass-roofed shopping arcades, were for decades left to crumble and decay, but many have recently been renovated and restored to something approaching their former glory, and chic boutiques have moved in alongside the old-fashioned traders and secondhand dealers. Most are closed at night and on Sundays.

Galerie Vivienne

Links rue Vivienne with rue des Petits-Champs. Ⓜ Bourse. The flamboyant decor of Grecian and marine motifs of charming Galerie Vivienne establishes the perfect ambience in which to buy Jean-Paul Gaultier gear, or you can browse in the antiquarian bookshop, Librairie Jousseaume, which dates back to the *passage*'s earliest days.

Passage des Panoramas

Off rue Vivienne. Ⓜ Grands-Boulevards. The grid of arcades collectively known as the passage des Panoramas is scruffier but has an appealing old-fashioned chic. Standing out among the

▲ GALERIE VIVIENNE

bric-a-brac shops, stamp and secondhand postcard dealers are a *salon de thé*, *L'Arbre à Cannelle*, with fantastic carved wood panelling, and a fine old printshop with its original 1867 fittings.

Passages Jouffroy and Verdeau

Off bd Montmartre. Ⓜ Grands-Boulevards. Across boulevard Montmartre, passage Jouffroy is full of the kind of stores that make shopping an adventure rather than a chore. M. Segas sells eccentric walking canes and theatrical antiques opposite a shop stocking every conceivable fitting and furnishing for a doll's house, while near the romantic *Hôtel Chopin* (see p.201), Paul Vulin spreads his secondhand books along the passageway, and Ciné-Doc appeals to cinephiles with its collection of old film posters. Crossing rue de la Grange-Batelière, you enter passage Verdeau, where old postcard and camera dealers trade alongside smart new art galleries.

Passage du Grand-Cerf

Between rue St-Denis and rue Dessoubs. Ⓜ Etienne-Marcel. The three-storey Grand-Cerf is stylistically the best of all the *passages*. The wrought-iron work, glass roof and plain-wood shop fronts have all been cleaned, attracting stylish arts, crafts and contemporary design shops.

Bibliothèque Nationale Richelieu

Ⓜ Bourse. 🌐www.bnf.fr. Exhibitions Tues–Sun 10am–7pm; €4.50–7. Cabinet des Monnaies, Médailles et Antiques Mon–Fri 1–5.45pm, Sat 1–4.45pm, Sun noon–6pm; free. The Bibliothèque Nationale Richelieu, the French National Library, is a huge, forbidding-looking building, dating back to the 1660s. Visiting its temporary exhibitions will give you access to some of the more beautiful parts of the building – the Galerie Mazarine in particular, with its panelled ceilings painted by Romanelli. You can also see a rich and absorbing display of coins and ancient treasures in the Cabinet des Monnaies, Médailles et Antiques. There's no restriction on entering the library, nor on peering into the atmospheric reading rooms, though many of the books have now been transferred to the new François Mitterrand site in the 13ᵉ (see p.155).

Shops

As well as the shops below be sure to check out the *passages*, fertile hunting ground for curios and one-off buys.

Boîte à Musique Anna Joliet

9 rue de Beaujolais, Jardin du Palais Royal. Ⓜ Palais Royal-Musée du Louvre. Mon 1–7pm, Tues–Sat 10am–7pm. A delightful, minuscule shop selling every style of music box, from inexpensive self-winding toy models to grand cabinets costing thousands of euros.

Colette

213 rue St-Honoré. Ⓜ Tuileries. Mon–Sat 11am–7pm. Style-conscious young Parisians peruse the latest Anya Hindmarch handbags and Prada offerings at this cutting-edge concept store, combining high fashion and design. Coolest of all is the downstairs *Water Bar*, offering eighty different kinds of bottled H_2O.

Fauchon

24–30 place de la Madeleine. Ⓜ Madeleine. Mon–Sat 9.30am–7pm. A cornucopia of extravagant and beautiful groceries, charcuterie and wines. Just the place for presents of tea, jam, truffles, chocolates, exotic vinegars and mustards.

Galeries Lafayette

40 bd Haussmann. Ⓜ Chaussée d'Antin. Mon–Sat 9.30am–7pm, Thurs until 9pm. This venerable department store's forte is high fashion, with two floors given

▲ MUSIC BOXES AT ANNA JOLIET

▲ DOME OF THE GALERIES LAFAYETTE

over to the latest creations by leading designers and nearly a whole floor devoted to lingerie. Then there's a host of big names in men's and women's accessories and a huge *parfumerie* – all under a superb 1900 dome. Just down the road at no. 35 is a new addition to the emporium, Lafayette Maison, five floors of quality kitchenware, linen and furniture.

Hédiard

21 place de la Madeleine. Ⓜ Madeleine. Mon–Sat 8am–10pm. Since the 1850s, Hédiard has been the aristocrat's grocer, selling superlative-quality food.

Legrand

1 rue de la Banque. Ⓜ Bourse. Mon 11am–7pm, Tues–Fri 10am–7.30pm, Sat 10am–7pm. This wine shop with beautiful old decor is the place to stock up on your favourite vintages and discover some little-known ones, too. There's also a bar (noon–7pm) where you can do some sampling and snack on saucisson and pâté.

Printemps

64 bd Haussmann. Ⓜ Havre-Caumartin. Mon–Sat 9.30am–7pm, Thurs until 10pm. Books, records, a *parfumerie* and an excellent fashion department for men and women. The sixth-floor restaurant is right underneath the beautiful Art Nouveau glass dome.

Cafés

L'Arbre à Cannelle

57 passage des Panoramas. Ⓜ Grands-Boulevards. Mon–Sat 11.30am–6pm. This café/*salon de thé*, formerly a brasserie, dating back to the early twentieth century, has exquisite wood panelling and ceiling frescoes and makes an excellent spot for lunch or tea.

Verlet

256 rue St-Honoré. Ⓜ Palais-Royal-Musée-du-Louvre. Mon–Sat 9am–7pm. A heady aroma of freshly ground coffee greets you as you enter this old-world coffee merchants and café. Choose from 25 varieties, such as Mokka Harar d'Ethiopie. There's also a selection of teas and cakes.

Restaurants

Chartier

7 rue du Faubourg-Montmartre. Ⓜ Grands-Boulevards. Daily 11.30am–3pm & 6–10pm. Brown linoleum floor, dark-stained woodwork, brass hat-racks, waiters in long aprons – the original decor of an early twentieth-century soup kitchen. Worth seeing, though crowded and rushed, the food here is cheap (mains €7–9) and good value.

Gallopin

40 rue Notre-Dame-des-Victoires. Ⓜ Bourse. ☎01.42.36.45.38. Daily noon–midnight. A lovely old brasserie, with original brass and mahogany fittings and a

beautiful painted glass roof in the back room. Classic French dishes and excellent *foie gras maison*. Set menu from €23.

Aux Lyonnais

32 rue St-Marc. Ⓜ Bourse/Richelieu-Drouot. ☎01.42.96.65.04. Tues–Fri noon–2pm & 7.30–11pm, Sat 7.30–11pm. This attractive *bistrot*, with belle époque tiles and mirrored walls, has been taken over by top chefs Alain Ducasse and Thierry de la Brosse. As the name implies, the accent is on Lyonnaise specialities, such as *quenelles* (delicate fish dumplings). Service is friendly and there's a buzzy atmosphere. Set menu for €28; be sure to book.

Le Vaudeville

29 rue Vivienne. Ⓜ Bourse. ☎01.40.20.04.62. Daily noon–3pm & 7pm–1am. There's often a queue to get a table at this lively, late-night brasserie, attractively decorated with marble and mosaics and serving fine cuisine at around €30 a head.

Bars

Bar Hemingway

Ritz Hotel, place Vendome. Ⓜ Tuileries/Opéra. Mon–Sat 6.30pm–2am. Hidden away at the back of the *Ritz*, this discreetly elegant bar with leather armchairs and deferential white-suited bar staff was once Hemingway's regular haunt, and the walls are covered with photos of him. His favourite drink, dry martini, is on the menu, but if you're feeling adventurous go for one of the more unusual cocktails (€24) concocted by award-winning barman Colin Field.

De La Ville Café

34 bd de la Bonne Nouvelle. Ⓜ Bonne-Nouvelle. Daily 11am–2am, Fri & Sat until 4am. This ex-bordello, with grand staircase, gilded mosaics and marble columns, draws in crowds of pre-clubbers who sling back a mojito or two before going on to one of the area's clubs. At weekends, DJs spin the discs till the early hours. Cocktails €8.

Le Fumoir

6 rue de l'Amiral-Coligny. Ⓜ Louvre-Rivoli. Daily 11am–2am. Animated chatter rises above a mellow jazz soundtrack and the sound of cocktail shakers in this coolly designed and relaxing bar-restaurant, situated just by the Louvre. Cocktails €8.

Juveniles

47 rue de Richelieu. Ⓜ Palais-Royal-Musée-du-Louvre. Mon–Sat noon–11pm. A very popular, tiny wine bar run by a Scot, *Juveniles* has a great selection of wines from €13 a bottle. *Plats du jour* for €11, cheese platters and other snacks €7.

Le Rubis

10 rue du Marché-St-Honoré. Ⓜ Pyramides. Mon–Fri 7.30am–10pm, Sat 9am–3pm; closed mid-Aug. This very small and crowded wine

▲ VIEW OF THE LOUVRE FROM LE FUMOIR

PLACES The Grands Boulevards and passages

bar is one of the oldest in Paris, known for its excellent wines and home-made *rillettes* (a kind of pork pâté).

Clubs

Le Cab

2 pl du Palais Royal. Ⓜ Palais-Royal. ⓦwww.cabaret.fr. Mon–Sat 11.30pm–5am. Entry €20. Currently one of the city's more celebrated venues, it's somehow dragging the designer-clad away from the Champs-Elysées – on weekend nights you'll need to look good to get in. There are a network of underground rooms below the associated café-restaurant, with a small dancefloor and lots of low tables in nooks and corners. The decor is designer retro-meets-futuristic lounge, with a music policy to match.

Le Pulp

25 bd Poissonnière. Ⓜ Bonne-Nouvelle. ☎01.40.26.01.93. Wed–Sat midnight–6am. Fri & Sat €9. Paris's lesbian club *par excellence*, playing music from techno to Madonna. So cool that it pulls in a huge straight crowd on the free Wednesday (rock) and Thursday (electro) nights.

Rex Club

5 bd Poissonnière. Ⓜ Bonne-Nouvelle. ☎01.42.36.28.83. Wed–Sat 11.30pm–5am. €10–13. The clubbers' club: serious about its music, which is strictly electronic, notably techno. Attracts big-name DJs.

Le Triptyque

142 rue Montmartre. Ⓜ Bourse. ⓦwww.letriptyche.com. Hours vary, usually 8pm–6am. Sometimes free, more often around €6–10. *Les physios* (the bouncers) won't turn you away at this unpretentious, innovative grunge-cool club, packed with anyone from local students to lounge lizards. For once, it's all about the music. It features an eclectic mix of concerts and DJ-led lounge sessions earlier on, then club soirées from around midnight, on themes which change nightly – everything from electro to post-rock to UK drum 'n' bass; check the website for what's on.

Live music

Au Limonaire

18 Cité Bergère. Ⓜ Grands-Boulevards. ☎01.45.23.33.33, ⓦhttp://limonaire. free.fr. Tues–Sat. This tiny backstreet place is the perfect intimate and informal venue for Parisian *chanson*, often showcasing committed young singers or zany music/poetry/performance acts trying to catch a break. Dinner beforehand (traditional, fairly inexpensive and usually quite good) guarantees a seat for the show at 10pm, otherwise you'll be crammed up against the bar – if you can get in at all.

Eglise de la Madeleine

Ⓜ Madeleine. ☎ 01.42.50.96.18, ⓦwww.eglise-lamadeleine.com. A regular venue for organ recitals and choral concerts. Tickets €15–23.

Opéra Garnier

Ⓜ Opéra. ☎08.36.69.78.68, ⓦwww. opera-de-paris.fr. The Opéra Garnier is generally used for ballets and smaller-scale opera productions than those put on at the Opéra Bastille. For programme and booking details consult their website or phone the box office. Tickets can cost as little as €7 if you don't mind being up in the gods, though most are in the €40–60 range.

Beaubourg and Les Halles

One of the city's most recognizable and popular landmarks, the Pompidou Centre, or Beaubourg as the building is known locally, draws large numbers of visitors to its excellent modern art museum and high-profile exhibitions. Its ground-breaking architecture provoked a storm of controversy on its opening in 1977, but since then it has won over critics and public alike. By contrast, nearby Les Halles, a shopping complex built at around the same time as the Pompidou Centre to replace the old food market that once stood here, has never really endeared itself to the city's inhabitants, though it's worth seeking out some of Les Halles' surviving old bistros and food stalls, which preserve traces of the old market atmosphere.

The Pompidou Centre

Ⓜ Rambuteau/Hotel-de-Ville. Ⓦwww. cnac-gp.fr. Built at the heart of one of Paris's oldest districts, the

BEAUBOURG & LES HALLES

0   300 m

RESTAURANTS, CAFÉS & BARS		L'Imprévu	9	VENUES		SHOPS	
Café Beaubourg	7	Kong	11	Le Duc des Lombards	10	Agnès b.	b
Au Chien qui Fume	5	Le Petit Marcel	4	Le Sunset &		Comptoir des Ecritures	c
A la Cloche des Halles	1	La Tour de Montlhéry	3	Le Sunside	8	Pâtisserie Stohrer	a
Georges	6	Au Vieux Molière	2				

resolutely modern Pompidou Centre is among the twentieth century's most radical buildings. Wanting to move away from the traditional idea of galleries as closed treasure chests to create something more open and accessible, the architects Renzo Piano and Richard Rogers stripped the "skin" off the building and made all the "bones" visible. The infrastructure was put on the outside: escalator tubes and utility pipes, brightly colour-coded according to their function, climb around the exterior in a crazy snakes-and-ladders fashion. The centre's main draw is its modern art museum and exhibitions, but there are also two cinemas and performance spaces. One of the added treats of visiting the museum is that you get to ascend the transparent escalator on the outside of the building, affording superb views over the city.

Musée National d'Art Moderne

Pompidou Centre. Ⓜ Rambuteau/ Hotel-de-Ville. Daily except Tues 11am–9pm. €10, under-18s free (pick up a free pass at the ticket office), free for everyone on first Sun of the month. The Musée National d'Art Moderne collection, spread over floors four and five of the Pompidou Centre, is one of the finest of its kind in the world, and is so large that only a fraction of the 50,000-plus works are on show at any one time (they're frequently rotated).

The section covering the years 1905 to 1960 is a near-complete visual essay on the history of modern art: Fauvism, Cubism, Dada, abstract art, Surrealism and Abstract Expressionism are all well represented. There's a particularly rich collection of Matisses, ranging from early Fauvist works to his late masterpieces – a standout is his *Tristesse du Roi*, a moving meditation on old age and memory. Other highlights include a number of Picasso's and Braque's early Cubist paintings and a substantial collection of Kandinskys, including his pioneering abstract works *Avec l'arc noir* and *Composition à la tache rouge*. A whole room is devoted to the characteristically colourful paintings of Robert and Sonia Delaunay, while the

▲ POMPIDOU CENTRE

▲ PASSAGE MOLIERE

state on condition that the rooms be arranged exactly as he left them, and they provide a fascinating insight into how the artist lived and worked. Studios one and two are crowded with Brancusi's trademark abstract bird and column shapes in highly polished brass and marble, while studios three and four comprise the artist's private quarters.

mood darkens in later rooms with unsettling works by Surrealists Magritte, Dalí and Ernst.

In the Pop Art section is Andy Warhol's easily recognizable *Ten Lizes,* in which the actress Elizabeth Taylor sports a Mona Lisa-like smile. Elsewhere Yves Klein prefigures performance art with his *Grande anthropophagie bleue; Hommage à Tennessee Williams,* one in a series of "body prints" in which the artist turned female models into human paintbrushes, covering them in paint to create his artworks.

Established contemporary artists you're likely to come across include Claes Oldenburg, Christian Boltanski – known for his large *mise-en-scène* installations, often containing veiled allusions to the Holocaust – and Daniel Buren, whose works are easy to spot: they all bear his trademark stripes, exactly 8.7cm in width.

Atelier Brancusi

Pompidou Centre. Ⓜ Rambuteau/Hotel-de-Ville. Daily except Tues 2–6pm. Free. The Atelier Brancusi is the reconstructed home and studio of Constantin Brancusi, one of the greatest sculptors of the twentieth century. He bequeathed the contents of his *atelier* to the

Quartier Beaubourg

Ⓜ Rambuteau/Hotel-de-Ville. The lively quartier Beaubourg around the Pompidou Centre also offers much in the way of visual art. The colourful, swirling sculptures and fountains in the pool in front of Eglise St-Merri on **place Igor Stravinsky**, on the south side of the Pompidou Centre, were created by Jean Tinguely and Niki de St-Phalle; this squirting waterworks pays homage to Stravinsky – each fountain was inspired by one of his compositions (*The Firebird, The Rite of Spring* and so on) – but shows scant respect for passers-by.

North of the Pompidou Centre, numerous commercial galleries take up the contemporary art theme on **rue Quincampoix**, the most attractive street in the area: narrow, pedestrianized and lined with fine old *hôtels particuliers.* Also worth exploring is **passage Molière**, an enchanting little alley with some quirky shops, such as Des Pieds et des Mains, where you can get a plaster cast made of your hand or foot.

Les Halles

Ⓜ Les-Halles/RER Châtelet-Les-Halles.
Described by Zola as "*le ventre (stomach) de Paris*", Les Halles was Paris's main food market for over eight hundred years until, despite widespread opposition, it was moved out to the suburbs in 1969 and replaced by a large underground shopping and leisure complex, known as the Forum des Halles, as well as a major métro/RER interchange (Ⓜ Châtelet-les Halles). Unsightly, run-down, even unsavoury in parts, the complex is now widely acknowledged as an architectural disaster – so much so that plans are under way to give it a major facelift. The French architect David Mangin, who won the competition to redevelop the site, plans to suspend a vast glass roof over the forum, allowing light to flood in, while also redesigning the gardens and creating a wide promenade on the model of Barcelona's Ramblas. Work is due to start in 2007 and should be complete by 2012.

The Forum des Halles centre stretches underground from the Bourse du Commerce rotunda to rue Pierre-Lescot and is spread over four levels. The overground section comprises aquarium-like arcades of shops, arranged around a sunken patio, and landscaped gardens. The shops are mostly devoted to high-street fashion, though there's also a large FNAC bookshop and the Forum des Créateurs, an outlet for young fashion designers.

Little now remains of the old working-class quarter, but you can still catch a flavour of the old market atmosphere in some of the surrounding bars and bistros and on pedestrianized rue Montorgueil to the north, where traditional grocers, horse butchers and fishmongers still ply their trade, jostling for space with the trendy cafés that have sprung up over the last few years.

St-Eustache

Ⓜ Les-Halles/RER Châtelet-Les-Halles.
For an antidote to the steel and glass troglodytism of Les Halles, head for the soaring vaults of the beautiful church of St-Eustache. Built between 1532 and 1637, it's Gothic in structure, with lofty naves and graceful flying buttresses, and Renaissance in decoration – all Corinthian columns, pilasters and arcades. Molière was baptized here, and Rameau and Marivaux are buried here.

Fontaine des Innocents

Ⓜ Les-Halles/RER Châtelet-Les-Halles.
The Fontaine des Innocents, a fine Renaissance fountain, decorated with bas-reliefs, is Paris's oldest surviving fountain, dating from 1549. It takes its name from the cemetery that used to occupy this site, the Cimetière des Innocents.

▲ LES HALLES

Shops

Agnès b.

2, 3, 6 & 19 rue du Jour. Ⓜ Les-Halles/
RER Châtelet-Les-Halles. Mon–Sat
10am–7pm. Agnès b. pays scant
regard to fashion trends, creating
timeless, understated clothes for
men, women and children. Her
best-known staples are the snap
cardigan and well-made T-shirts
that don't lose their shape.

Comptoir des Ecritures

35 rue Quincampoix. Ⓜ Les-Halles/
RER Châtelet-Les-Halles. Tues–Sat
11am–7pm. A delightful shop
entirely devoted to the art of
calligraphy, with an extensive
collection of paper, pens, brushes
and inks.

Pâtisserie Stohrer

51 rue Montorgueil. Ⓜ Sentier. Daily
7.30am–8pm; closed first two weeks of
Aug. Discover what *pain aux raisins*
should really taste like at Pâtisserie
Stohrer, in business since 1730.

Cafés

Café Beaubourg

43 rue St-Merri. Ⓜ Rambuteau/Hôtel-
de-Ville. Mon–Wed & Sun 8am–1am,
Thurs–Sat 8am–2am. A seat under
the expansive awnings of this
stylish café, bearing the trademark
sweeping lines of designer
Christian Portzamparc, is one of
the best places for people-watching
on the Pompidou Centre's piazza.
It's also good for a relaxed Sunday
brunch – €22 for the full works,
including eggs, hash browns and
sausage. Drinks from €5.

L'Imprévu

7 rue Quincampoix. Ⓜ Châtelet.
Mon–Sat noon–2am, Sun 1pm–2am.
The decor of this arty café-bar
certainly has something of the

imprévu ("unexpected") about it,
with its mishmash of styles, from
cosy tearoom at the front to a
little room at the back done out
like an Arabian tent. There are
plenty of intimate corners where
you can sip tea or reasonably
priced cocktails.

Restaurants

Au Chien qui Fume

33 rue du Pont-Neuf. Ⓜ Châtelet-
Les Halles. ☎01.42.36.07.42.
Mon–Fri noon–1am, Sat & Sun
noon–2am. Named after a local
poodle who allegedly smoked
a cigar, this popular brasserie
has quite literally been around
for centuries. Tuxedoed waiters
serve house favourites like fresh
oysters, *langoustines fricassée volaille*
(prawn fricasée) and *cuisse de
canard en marmite et lentilles* (leg of
duck with lentils). €28 set menu.

Georges

Pompidou Centre, top floor.
Ⓜ Rambuteau/Hôtel-de-Ville.
☎01.44.78.47.99. Daily noon–midnight
except Tues. This cool, ultra-
minimalist restaurant commands
stunning views over the rooftops
of Paris (smoking seats have the
best views). The French-Asian
fusion cuisine is passable though
somewhat overpriced (mains
around €20–30) – but then
that's not really why you come.
Booking advised for dinner.

La Tour de Montlhéry (Chez Denise)

5 rue des Prouvaires. Ⓜ Louvre-
Rivoli/Châtelet. ☎01.42.36.21.82.
Mon–Fri noon–3pm & 7.30pm–5am;
closed mid-July to mid-Aug. An
old-style all-night *bistrot* dating
back to the market days and
serving substantial meaty food,
such as *andouillette* (tripe), offal
and steak, plus the odd fish dish,

accompanied by perfectly cooked chips. Mains cost around €22. Diners sit elbow to elbow at long tables and it's always crowded and smoky. Booking advised.

Au Vieux Molière

Passage Molière, 157 rue Saint-Martin. Ⓜ Etienne-Marcel/Rambuteau/Châtelet. Ⓣ01.42.78.37.87. Mon–Fri noon–2pm & 8–10pm, Sat 8–10pm. French *chansons* playing softly in the background add to the mellow atmosphere of this cosy, candlelit restaurant serving classic French cuisine. Reckon on around €40 a head.

Bars

A la Cloche des Halles

28 rue Coquillière. Ⓜ Châtelet-Les Halles/Louvre. Noon–10pm; closed Sat eve & Sun. The bell hanging over this little wine bar is the one that used to mark the end of trading in the market halls, and the great ambience is due to the local vendors who spend their off-hours here. You are assured of some very fine wines, best sided with the *jambon d'Auvergne* or one of their delectable cheeses, all very reasonably priced.

Kong

5th floor, 1 rue du Pont Neuf. Ⓜ Pont-Neuf. Ⓣ01.40.39.09.00, Ⓦwww.kong.fr. daily 12.30pm–2am, club nights Fri & Sat 11pm–3am. A lift whisks you up to this über-cool, Philippe Starck-designed bar-restaurant atop the flagship Kenzo building. The decor is new Japan meets old: think geisha girls and manga cartoons. Happy hour daily 6–8pm. Drinks €6–11.

Le Petit Marcel

63 rue Rambuteau. Ⓜ Rambuteau. Mon–Fri 7am–2am, Sat & Sun 11am–midnight. Speckled tabletops, mirrors and Art Nouveau tiles, a cracked and faded ceiling and about eight square metres of drinking space, with friendly bar staff and a "local" atmosphere.

Live music

Le Duc des Lombards

42 rue des Lombards. Ⓜ Châtelet. Ⓣ01.42.33.22.88, Ⓦwww.ducdeslombards.com. Mon–Sat 7.30pm–3am. A small, unpretentious jazz bar – the place to hear gypsy jazz, blues, ballads and fusion. Performances at 9pm. Tickets from €16.

Le Sunset & Le Sunside

60 rue des Lombards. Ⓜ Châtelet. Ⓣ01.40.26.46.20, Ⓦwww.sunset-sunside.com. Two clubs in one: *Le Sunside* on the ground floor features mostly traditional jazz; while the downstairs *Sunset* is a venue for electric and fusion jazz. Attracts some big names. Performances daily at 9 or 10pm. Admission €18–25.

▲ LE SUNSET

The Marais

Having largely escaped the attentions of Baron Haussmann and unspoiled by modern development, the Marais is one of the most seductive areas of central Paris, full of splendid Renaissance mansions, narrow lanes and buzzing bars and restaurants. Originally little more than a riverside swamp (*marais*), the area was drained and became a magnet for the aristocracy in the early 1600s after the construction of the place des Vosges – or place Royale, as it was then known. This golden age was relatively short-lived, however, and after the Revolution the mansions became multi-occupied slum tenements and the streets degenerated into unserviced squalor – hard to believe now that the Marais is one of the most desirable areas in the city.

Gentrification proceeded apace from the 1960s, and the quarter is now known for its sophistication and artsy leanings and for being the neighbourhood of choice for gay Parisians. The city's ancient Jewish quarter is also sited here, concentrated on rue des Rosiers.

Prime streets for wandering are rue des Francs-Bourgeois, lined with trendy fashion and interior design boutiques, and rue Vieille-du-Temple and rue des Archives, their lively cafés and bars abuzz at all times of day and night. The quarter also boasts a concentration of superb museums, not least among them the Musée Picasso, the Carnavalet history museum and the Musée d'Art et d'Histoire du Judaïsme, all set in handsome Renaissance mansions.

▼ MUSEE D'ART ET D'HISTOIRE DU JUDAISME

Musée d'Art et d'Histoire du Judaïsme

71 rue du Temple. Ⓜ Rambuteau. ⓦwww.mahj.org. Mon–Fri 11am–6pm, Sun 10am–6pm. €6.80. Housed in the attractively restored Hôtel de Saint-Aignan, the Musée d'Art et d'Histoire du Judaïsme traces Jewish culture and history, mainly in France. The result is a very comprehensive collection, as educational as it is beautiful.

Highlights include a Gothic-

THE MARAIS

SHOPS

Archives de la Presse	a
Bain – Plus Enfants	b
CSAO	c
Librairie Culture	f
Mariage Frères	d
Papier Plus	g
Sacha Finkelsztajn	e

RUE DES GRAVILLIERS

RUE CHAPON

RUE AUX OURS

RUE DU GRENIER-ST-LAZARE

BD DE SEBASTOPOL

RUE QUINCAMPOIX

PGE MOLIERE

RUE ST MARTIN

RUE BRANTOME

BEAUBOURG

RUE DE MONTMORENCY

RUE MICHEL LE COMTE

RUE DU TEMPLE

R DES HAUDRETTES

RUE DES

Musée d'Art et d'Histoire du Judaisme

Atelier Brancusi

Pompidou Centre (Beaubourg)

Ⓜ Rambuteau

RUE RAMBUTEAU

RUE DES 4 FILS

ⓐ **Hôtel Soubise**

RUE

RUE SIMON LE FRANC

PL IGOR STRAVINSKY

RUE ST MERRI

RUE DU RENARD

RUE DU TEMPLE

RUE DES BLANCS MANTEAUX

Les Bains du Marais

ⓑ

Archives Nationales

Notre-Dame des Blancs-Manteaux

ARCHIVES

RUE STE CROIX DE LA BRETONNERIE

Ⓔ

RUE DE LA VERRERIE

Ⓗ

RUE DES

Ⓕ

RUE DU MOUSSY

Ⓘ

RUE VIEILLE DU TEMPLE

Ⓗ

RUE DE RIVOLI

Hôtel de Ville

Ⓜ

Hôtel de Ville Ⓜ

RUE PONT LOUIS PHILIPPE

PL DE L'HÔTEL DE VILLE

Hôtel de Ville

R DU BOURG TIBOURG

ⓓ

Ⓚ Ⓛ

Ⓜ

RUE DE LA

Hôtel de Ville Ⓜ

RUE DE RIVOLI

VERRERIE

RUE VIEILLE DU TEMPLE

ⓔ

RUE DU TRESOR

Ⓜ Ⓩ

R DES ECOUFFES

Ⓠ

Ⓡ

RUE DU ROI

RUE DU ROI

ⓘ

PL ST GERVAIS

R CLOCHE PERCE

RUE DU ROI

RUE DE RIVOLI

RUE FRANCOIS MIRON

Ⓥ

RUE G. L'ASNIER

Maison Européenne de la Photographie

PONT D'ARCOLE

St-Gervais St-Protais

RUE DES BARRES

RUE DE PONT LOUIS PHILIPPE

ⓖ

RUE G. L'ASNIER

R DE FOURCY

QUAI DE L'HOTEL DE VILLE

RUE DE L'HOTEL DE VILLE

Mémorial de la Shoah

R FIGUIER

PONT LOUIS PHILIPPE

Pont Mairie Ⓜ

Notre-Dame

River Seine

Hôtel-de-Sens

QUAI DE BOURBON

PONT MARIE

QUAI DES

RUE ST LOUIS

R DES 2 PONTS EN L'ILE

QUAI D'ANJOU

Ile St Louis

0 ——— 200 m

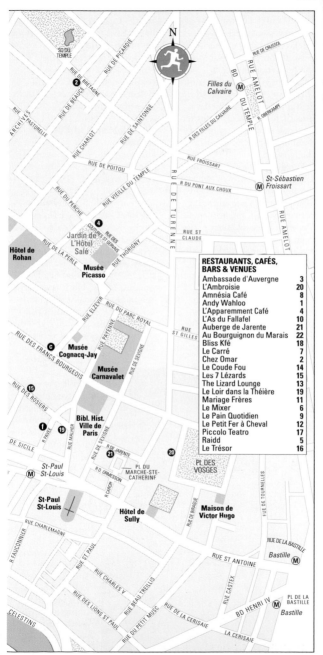

RESTAURANTS, CAFÉS, BARS & VENUES

Ambassade d'Auvergne	3
L'Ambroisie	20
Amnésia Café	8
Andy Wahloo	1
L'Apparrement Café	4
L'As du Fallafel	10
Auberge de Jarente	21
Au Bourguignon du Marais	22
Bliss Kfé	18
Le Carré	7
Chez Omar	2
Le Coude Fou	14
Les 7 Lézards	15
The Lizard Lounge	13
Le Loir dans la Théière	19
Mariage Frères	11
Le Mixer	6
Le Pain Quotidien	9
Le Petit Fer à Cheval	12
Piccolo Teatro	17
Raidd	5
Le Trésor	16

style Hanukkah lamp, one of the very few French Jewish artefacts to survive from the period before the expulsion of the Jews from France in 1394; an Italian gilded circumcision chair from the seventeenth century; and a completely intact late-nineteenth-century Austrian *Sukkah*, a temporary dwelling for the celebration of the harvest.

The museum also holds the Dreyfus archives, with one room devoted to the notorious Dreyfus affair, in which the wrongful conviction of Captain Alfred Dreyfus, a Jew, of treason caused deep divisions in French society, stoking up anticlerical, socialist sympathies on the one hand and conservative, anti-Semitic feelings on the other.

The last few rooms contain a significant collection of paintings and sculpture by Jewish artists – Marc Chagall, Samuel Hirszenberg, Chaïm Soutine and Jacques Lipchitz – who came to live in Paris at the beginning of the twentieth century.

The only reference to the Holocaust is an installation by contemporary artist Christian Boltanski: its very understatement has a powerful impact.

Hôtel Soubise et Hôtel de Rohan

60 rue des Francs-Bourgeois. Ⓜ Rambuteau/St-Paul. Mon & Wed–Fri 10am–12.30pm & 2–5.30pm, Sat & Sun 2–5.30pm. Admission varies.

The entire block enclosed by rue des Quatre Fils, rue des Archives, rue Vieille-du-Temple and rue des Francs-Bourgeois, was once filled by a magnificent early eighteenth-century palace complex. Only half remains today, but it is utterly splendid, especially the grand colonnaded courtyard of the Hôtel Soubise, with its fabulous Rococo interiors and vestigial fourteenth-century towers on rue des Quatre Fils. The *hôtel* houses the city archives and mounts changing exhibitions drawn from its extensive holdings. The adjacent Hôtel de Rohan is also often used for exhibitions from the archives and has more fine interiors, including the Chinese-inspired Cabinet des Singes, whose walls are painted with monkeys acting out various aristocratic scenes.

▲ HOTEL SOUBISE

Musée Picasso

5 rue de Thorigny. Ⓜ Chemin Vert/St-Paul. ⓦwww.musee-picasso.fr. Daily except Tues: April–Sept 9.30am–6pm; Oct–March 9.30am–5.30pm. €9.50, under-18s free, free for everyone first Sun of month. Behind the elegant classical facade of the seventeenth-century Hôtel Salé lies the Musée Picasso. It's the largest collection of Picassos anywhere, representing almost all the major periods of the artist's life from 1905 onwards. Many of the works were owned by Picasso and on his death in 1973 were seized by the state in lieu of taxes owed. The result is an unedited body of work, which, although perhaps not among the most recognizable of Picasso's masterpieces, provides a sense of the artist's development and an insight into the person behind the myth.

Some of the most engaging works on display are his more personal ones – those depicting his wives, lovers and children. Portraits of the artist's lovers, Dora Maar and Marie-Thérèse, exhibited side by side in room 13, show how the two women inspired Picasso in very different ways: they strike the same pose, but Dora Maar is painted with strong lines and vibrant colours, suggesting a passionate, vivacious personality, while Marie-Thérèse's muted colours and soft contours convey serenity and peace.

The museum also holds a substantial number of Picasso's engravings, ceramics and sculpture, reflecting the remarkable ease with which the artist moved from one medium to another. Some of the most arresting sculptures (room 17) are those he created from recycled household objects, such as the endearing *La Chèvre* (*Goat*), whose stomach is made from a basket, and the *Tête de taureau* (*Bull's head*), an ingenious pairing of a bicycle seat and handlebars.

Musée Cognacq-Jay

8 rue Elzévir. Ⓜ St-Paul. Tues–Sun 10am–6pm. Free. The compact Musée Cognacq-Jay occupies the fine Hôtel Donon. The Cognacq-Jay family built up the Samaritaine department store and were noted philanthropists and lovers of European art. Their collection of eighteenth-century pieces on show includes a handful of works by Canaletto, Fragonard, Rubens and Rembrandt, as well as an exquisite still life by Chardin, displayed in beautifully carved wood-panelled rooms filled with Sèvres porcelain and Louis XV furniture.

▲ MUSEE PICASSO

▲ MUSÉE CARNAVALET

Musée Carnavalet

23 rue de Sévigné. Ⓜ St-Paul.
Tues–Sun 10am–6pm. Free. The
fascinating Musée Carnavalet
charts the history of Paris
from its origins up to the
belle époque through an
extraordinary collection of
paintings, sculptures, decorative
arts and archeological finds
– spread over 140 rooms.
The museum's setting in two
beautiful Renaissance mansions,
Hôtel Carnavalet and Hôtel
Le Peletier, surrounded by
attractive gardens, is worth a
visit in itself.

Among the highlights on the
ground floor, devoted largely to
the early history of Paris, is the
orangery housing a significant
collection of Neolithic finds,
including a number of wooden
pirogues unearthed during the
redevelopment of the Bercy
riverside area in the 1990s.

On the first floor, decorative arts
feature strongly, with numerous
re-created salons and boudoirs
full of richly sculpted wood
panelling and tapestries from the
time of Louis XII to Louis XVI,
rescued from buildings that had
to be destroyed for Haussmann's
boulevards. Room 21 is devoted
to the famous letter-writer
Madame de Sévigné, who lived
in the Carnavalet mansion and
wrote a series of letters to her
daughter, which vividly portray
her privileged lifestyle under the
reign of Louis XIV. Rooms 128
to 148 are largely devoted to the
belle époque, evoked through
numerous paintings of the period
and some wonderful Art Nouveau
interiors, among which is the
sumptuous peacock-green interior
designed by Alphonse Mucha for
Fouquet's jewellery shop in the rue
Royal. Also well preserved is José-
Maria Sert's Art Deco ballroom,
with its extravagant gold-leaf
decor and grand-scale paintings,
including one of the Queen of
Sheba with a train of elephants.
Nearby is a section on literary life
at the beginning of the twentieth
century, including a reconstruction
of Proust's cork-lined bedroom
(room 147).

The second floor has rooms full

of mementoes of the French Revolution: original declarations of the Rights of Man and the Citizen, glorious models of the guillotine, crockery with revolutionary slogans and even execution orders to make you shed a tear for the royalists as well.

The Jewish quarter: rue des Rosiers

Ⓜ St-Paul. Crammed with kosher food shops, delicatessens, restaurants and Hebrew bookstores, the narrow, bustling rue des Rosiers has been the heart of the city's Jewish quarter ever since the twelfth century, and remains so, despite incursions by trendy bars and clothes shops. There's also a distinctly Mediterranean flavour to the quarter, as seen in the many falafel stalls, testimony to the influence of the North African Sephardim, who, since the end of World War II, have sought refuge here from the uncertainties of life in the former French colonies.

▲ JEWISH QUARTER DELI

Place des Vosges

Ⓜ St-Paul. A vast square of symmetrical pink brick and stone mansions built over arcades, the place des Vosges is a masterpiece of aristocratic elegance and the first example of planned development in the history of Paris. It was built by Henri IV and inaugurated in 1612 for the wedding of Louis XIII and Anne of Austria; Louis's statue – or, rather, a replica of it – stands hidden by chestnut trees in the middle of the grass-and-gravel gardens at the square's centre.

Through all the vicissitudes of history, the place has never lost its cachet as a smart address. Today, well-heeled Parisians pause in the arcades at art, antique and fashion shops, and lunch alfresco in the restaurants while buskers play classical music. The garden is the only green space of any size in the locality – unusually for Paris, you're allowed to sprawl on the grass.

▼ PLACE DE VOSGES

Maison de Victor Hugo

Ⓜ St-Paul. Tues–Sun 10am–6pm, closed hols. Free. Among the many celebrities who made their homes in place des Vosges was Victor Hugo; his house, at no. 6, where he wrote much of *Les Misérables*, is now a museum, the Maison de Victor Hugo. Hugo's life, including his nineteen years of exile in Jersey and Guernsey, is evoked through a sparse collection of memorabilia, portraits and photographs. What the museum conveys though is an idea of his prodigious creativity: as well as being a prolific writer, he enjoyed drawing and designed his own furniture. Some of his sketches and Gothic-style furniture are on display, and a Chinese-style dining room that he designed for his house in Guernsey is re-created in its entirety.

Hôtel de Sully

62 rue St-Antoine. Ⓜ St-Paul. Tues–Fri noon–7pm, Sat & Sun 10am–7pm. €5. The exquisite Renaissance Hôtel de Sully is the sister site to the Jeu de Paume (see p.84), and mounts temporary photographic exhibitions. The mansion's formal garden, with its orangery and park benches, makes for a peaceful rest stop.

The Quartier St-Paul-St-Gervais

Ⓜ St-Paul. The southern section of the Marais, below rues de Rivoli and St-Antoine, is quieter than the northern part and has some attractive corners, such as cobbled rue des Barres, perfumed with the scent of roses from nearby gardens and the occasional waft of incense from the church of St-Gervais-St-Protais, a late Gothic construction that looks somewhat battered on the

outside owing to a direct hit from a shell fired from a Big Bertha howitzer in 1918. Its interior contains some lovely stained glass, carved misericords and a seventeenth-century organ – Paris's oldest.

Mémorial de la Shoah

17 rue Geoffroy l'Asnier. Ⓜ St-Paul/Pont-Marie. ⓦwww. memorialdelashoah.org. Mon–Fri & Sun 10am–6pm, Thurs until 10pm. Free. Since 1956 this has been the site of the Mémorial du Martyr Juif Inconnu (Memorial to an Unknown Jewish Martyr), a sombre crypt containing a large black marble star of David, with a candle at its centre. In 2005 President Chirac opened a new museum here and unveiled a Wall of Names: four giant slabs of marble engraved with the names of the 76,000 Jews sent to death camps from 1942 to 1944. The weight of all these names is overwhelming.

The new museum gives an absorbing account of the history of Jews in France, especially Paris, during the German occupation. There are last letters from deportees to their families, videotaped testimony from survivors, numerous ID cards and photos.

Maison Européenne de la Photographie

4 rue de Fourcy. Ⓜ St-Paul. ⓦwww. mep-fr.org. Wed–Sun 11am–8pm. €6, free Wed after 5pm. A gorgeous Marais mansion, the early eighteenth-century Hôtel Hénault de Cantobre, has been turned into a vast and serene space dedicated to the art of contemporary photography. Temporary shows combine with a revolving exhibition of the Maison's permanent collection; young photographers and news

photographers get a look-in, as well as artists using photography in multimedia creations or installation art.

Hôtel de Ville

Ⓜ Rambuteau/Hotel-de-Ville. The Hôtel de Ville, the seat of the city's mayor, is a mansion of gargantuan proportions in florid neo-Renaissance style, modelled pretty much on the previous building burned down during the Commune in 1871. The huge square in front of the Hôtel de Ville, a notorious guillotine site during the Revolution, becomes the location of a popular ice-skating rink from December to February; it's free and is particularly magical at night – it's open till midnight at weekends. You can hire skates for around €5.

Shops

Archives de la Presse

51 rue des Archives. Ⓜ Rambuteau. Mon–Sat 10.30am–7pm. A fascinating shop for a browse, trading in old French newspapers and magazines – vintage *Vogues* and the like.

Bain – Plus Enfants

23 rue des Blancs Manteaux. Ⓜ Hotel-de-Ville. Tues–Sat 11am–7.30pm. Aimed at kids up to twelve years old, this stylish shop has

▼ HOTEL DE VILLE

▲ MARAIS CHIC

Mariage Frères

30 rue du Bourg-Tibourg.
Ⓜ Hotel-de-Ville. Shop daily
10.30am–7.30pm. Hundreds of
teas, neatly packed in tins, line
the floor-to-ceiling shelves
of this hundred-year-old
tea emporium and café (see
opposite).

Papier Plus

9 rue du Pont-Louis-Philippe. Ⓜ
Hotel-de-Ville. Mon–Sat noon–
7pm. Fine-quality, colourful
stationery, including
notebooks, photo albums
and artists' portfolios.

Sacha Finkelsztajn

27 rue des Rosiers. Ⓜ Hotel-
de-Ville. Mon & Tues–Sun
10am–2pm & 3–7pm; closed
Aug. Marvellous Jewish deli for
takeaway snacks and goodies:
East European breads, apple
strudel, *gefilte* fish, aubergine
purée, tarama, *blinis* and *borsch*.

an irresistible range of bed and
bath items: chic pyjamas, hooded
robes, fluffy towels and cuddly
bears.

CSAO (Compagnie du Sénégal et de l'Afrique de l'Ouest)

1 & 3 rue Elzévir. Ⓜ St-Paul. Mon–Sat
11am–7pm, Sun 2–7pm. Fairly
traded crafts and artwork from
West Africa, including Malian
cotton scarves in rich, earthy
tones and painted glass from
Senegal.

Librairie Culture

17 bis rue Pavée. Ⓜ
St-Paul. Mon–Sat
10.30am–7pm. A
real Aladdin's
cave, spread over
three floors, with
books piled up
everywhere you
look — mostly
secondhand and
returns, with
some good deals
on art titles.

Hammams

Les Bains du Marais

31–33 rue des Blancs-Manteaux.
Ⓜ Rambuteau/St-Paul. Ⓦwww.
lesbainsdumarais.com. Women only Mon
11am–8pm, Tues 11am–11pm, Wed
10am–7pm; men only Thurs 11am–
11pm, Fri 10am–8pm; mixed sessions

▼ MARIAGE FRERES TEA SHOP

Wed 7–11pm, Sat 10am–8pm, Sun 11am–11pm. Sauna and steam room entry €35. This is as much a posh health club as a *hammam*, with a rather chichi clientele and a glorious interior. It offers facials, massages and haircuts, and you can lounge about in a robe with mint tea and a newspaper. Bring a swimsuit for the mixed sessions.

▲ RUE VIEILLE-DU-TEMPLE

Cafés

L'Apparement Café

18 rue des Coutures-St-Gervais. Ⓜ St-Sébastien-Froissart. Mon–Fri noon–2am, Sat 4pm–2am, Sun 12.30pm–midnight. Chic, cosy café resembling a series of comfortable sitting rooms, with quiet corners and deep sofas. The salads, which you compose yourself by ticking off your chosen ingredients and handing your order to the waiter, are recommended.

L'As du Fallafel

34 rue des Rosiers. Ⓜ St-Paul. Mon–Thurs & Sun noon–midnight. A There's usually a queue outside for these ace falafels; takeaways start at €3.50, or pay a bit more to sit inside.

Le Loir dans la Théière

3 rue des Rosiers. Ⓜ St-Paul. Mon–Fri 11am–7pm, Sat & Sun 10am–7pm. A convivial and trendy *salon de thé,* where you can sink into battered sofas and pit yourself against challenging portions of scrummy, home-made cakes. It's very popular for Sunday brunch (from €15); turn up early or resign yourself to a long wait.

Mariage Frères

30 rue du Bourg-Tibourg. Ⓜ Hôtel-

de-Ville. Daily noon–7pm. A classy, colonial-style *salon de thé* on the ground floor of the Mariages Frères tea emporium, with a choice of over five hundred different brews.

Le Pain Quotidien

18 rue des Archives. Ⓜ Hotel-de-Ville. Daily 8am–8pm. A trendy café-bakery where you have the option of rubbing shoulders with fellow diners at a long, communal *table d'hôte*. It specializes in hearty salads, *tartines* (open sandwiches) and excellent breads, and does a good Sunday brunch (€15).

Restaurants

Ambassade d'Auvergne

22 rue de Grenier St-Lazare. Ⓜ Rambuteau. ☎01.42.72.31.22. Daily noon–2pm & 7.30–10pm; closed last two weeks in Aug. Suited, moustachioed waiters serve scrumptious Auvergnat cuisine that would have made Vercingétorix proud. There's a set menu for €27, but you may well be tempted by some of the house specialities such as the *blanquette d'agneau* (white Roquefort lamb stew, €18).

L'Ambroisie

9 place des Vosges. Ⓜ St-Paul.
☏01.42.78.51.45. Tues–Sat noon–2pm
& 7–10.15pm; closed Aug. Scoring 19
out of 20 in the gourmet's bible
Gault et Millau, *L'Ambroisie* offers
exquisite food in a magnificent
dining room hung with tapestries.
Reckon on upwards of €200 and
book well in advance.

Auberge de Jarente

7 rue Jarente. Ⓜ St-Paul.
☏01.42.77.49.35. Tues–Sat
noon–2.30pm & 7.30–10.30pm;
closed Aug. This friendly Basque
restaurant serves up hearty dishes
of *cassoulet*, hare stew, *magret de
canard*, *pipérade* and the like. Set
menus at €21 and €30.

Au Bourguignon du Marais

52 rue François Miron. Ⓜ St-Paul.
☏01.48.87.15.40. Mon–Fri noon–3pm
& 8–11pm; closed two weeks in Aug.
A warm, relaxed restaurant with
attractive contemporary decor
and tables outside in summer.
Excellent Burgundian cuisine with
carefully selected wines to match.
Mains €15–25, wine from €20.

Chez Omar

47 rue de Bretagne. Ⓜ Temple/Filles-
du-Calvaire. ☏01.42.72.36.26.
Mon–Sat noon–2.30pm & 7–11.30pm,
Sun 7–11.30pm; no credit cards.
A very popular North African
couscous restaurant in a nice old
brasserie. Portions are generous
and the couscous light and fluffy.
The merguez costs €12, or go
all out for the *royal* (€22). No
reservations taken.

Le Coude Fou

12 rue du Bourg-Tibourg. Ⓜ Hôtel-
de-Ville. ☏01.42.77.15.16. Daily
noon–2.45pm & 7.30pm–midnight.
A popular, laidback wine
bistrot, with wooden beams and
brightly painted murals. It serves
traditional and more adventurous

dishes such as *entrecôte au bleu
d'Auvergne* for around €20–30.

Piccolo Teatro

6 rue des Ecouffes. Ⓜ St-Paul.
☏01.42.72.17.79. Tues–Sun noon–
3pm & 7.15–11pm; closed Aug. A
cosy vegetarian restaurant with
low lighting, stone walls and
wooden beams. The speciality is
gratins, with poetic names such as
douceur et tendresse (spinach, mint,
mozzarella and Gruyère). There
are only a few tables, so it's best
to book. Reckon on €15–20
without drinks.

Bars

Amnésia Café

42 rue Vieille-du-Temple. Ⓜ Hotel-de-
Ville/St-Paul. Daily 10am–2am. One
of the more relaxed and friendlier
gay bars in the Marais, with a
predominantly Parisian, fairly
well-heeled clientele lounging
around on the sofas. Low-lit,
cosy and straight-friendly.

Andy Wahloo

69 rue des Gravilliers. Ⓜ Arts-
et-Métiers. Mon–Sat noon–2am.
This popular bar, decked out
in original Pop Art-inspired
decor, and playing a wide range
of dance music, gets packed to
the gills at weekends. Cocktails
cost around €10 and delicious
meze appetizers are served until
midnight.

Bliss Kfé

30 rue du Roi de Sicile. Ⓜ Hotel-de-
Ville/St-Paul–St-Louis. Daily 5pm–2am.
This appealingly scruffy lesbian
bar squats in a former *boulangerie*
in the heart of the pink triangle.
The regulars are mostly young
and fairly trendy women, but
gay men are welcome too.
On Thursday, Friday and
Saturday nights DJs turn up the

temperature, but it's always a warm and laidback address.

Le Carré

18 rue du Temple. Ⓜ Hotel-de-Ville. Daily 10am–4am. Big, stylish, designer café with good food, comfortable chairs, ultra-cool lighting and an excellent *terrasse* on the street. Mostly full of sophisticated, good-looking Parisians, with a loyal, local gay clientele.

The Lizard Lounge

18 rue du Bourg-Tibourg. Ⓜ Hôtel-de-Ville/St-Paul. Daily noon–2am. A loud, lively, stone-walled bar on two levels; American-run and popular with young expats. Choose from around fifty reasonably priced cocktails.

Le Mixer

23 rue Ste-Croix de la Bretonnerie. Ⓜ Hôtel-de-Ville. Daily 5pm–2am. A popular and crowded Marais bar, raising the pulse of gay and straight pre-clubbers with its pounding techno and house soundtrack.

Le Petit Fer à Cheval

30 rue Vieille-du-Temple. Ⓜ St-Paul. Mon–Fri 9am–2am, Sat & Sun 11am–2am; food served noon–midnight. A very attractive small *bistrot*-bar with original fin-de-siècle decor.

You can snack on sandwiches or light meals in the little back room furnished with old wooden métro seats.

Raidd

23 rue du Temple. Ⓜ Hotel-de-Ville. Daily 5pm–2am. The city's premier gay bar, famous for its sculpted, topless waiters, go-go boys' shower shows and everlasting good-times. Straights and non-beautiful people need not apply.

Le Trésor

7 rue Trésor. Ⓜ St-Paul. Daily 9am–2am. This long-standing bar-restaurant, patronized by a hip, young crowd, has been stylishly revamped – with lots of luminous colours, velvet fabrics, concave mirrors and cosy nooks. Real live goldfish in the toilet cisterns will make you wonder if you've had one too many drinks, but it's ok, you can't flush them away.

Live music

Les 7 Lézards

10 rue des Rosiers. Ⓜ St-Paul. ☎01.48.87.08.97, ⓦwww.7lezards. com. Daily until 2am; concerts 7 & 10pm. €10–18. A cosy and intimate jazz club, attracting international and local acts. Also hosts the odd world music gig, and there's a decent restaurant, too.

▼ LE PETIT FER A CHEVAL

The Quartier Latin

The Quartier Latin has been associated with students ever since the Sorbonne was established in the thirteenth century. The odd name derives from the Latin spoken at the medieval university, which perched on the slopes of the Montagne Ste-Geneviève. Many colleges remain in the area to this day, along with some fascinating vestiges of the medieval city, such as the Gothic church of St-Séverin and the Renaissance Hôtel de Cluny, site of the national museum of the Middle Ages. Some of the quarter's student chic may have worn thin in recent years – notably around the now too-famous place St-Michel – and high rents have pushed scholars and artists out of their garrets, but the quarter's cafés, restaurants and arty cinemas are still packed with young people, making this one of the most relaxed areas of Paris for going out.

The Huchette quarter

Ⓜ St-Michel. The touristy bustle is at its worst around rue de la Huchette, just east of the place St-Michel, but look beyond the cheap bars and overpriced Greek seafood-and-disco tavernas and you'll find some evocative remnants of medieval Paris. Connecting rue de la Huchette to the riverside is the incredibly narrow rue du Chat-qui-Pêche, a tiny slice of how Paris looked before Baron Haussmann flattened the old alleys to make room for his wide boulevards.

The mainly fifteenth-century church of **St-Séverin** (Mon–Sat 11am–7.15pm, Sun 9am–8.30pm) is one of the city's more intense churches. Its Flamboyant choir rests on a spiralling central pillar – a virtuoso piece of stonework—

and its windows are filled with edgy stained glass by the modern French painter Jean Bazaine. The flame-like carving that gave the Flamboyant (blazing) style its name flickers in the window arch above the entrance, while inside, the first three pillars of the nave betray the earlier, thirteenth-century origins of the church.

▲ FLAMBOYANT VAULT AT ST-SEVERIN

The riverbank

Ⓜ St-Michel. The riverbank quais east of place St-Michel are ideal for wandering, and you can browse among the books, postcards, prints and assorted goods on sale from the *bouquinistes*, who display their wares in green, padlocked boxes hooked onto the parapet. There are wonderful views of Notre-Dame across the Seine, especially from square Viviani – a welcome patch of grass with an ancient, broken-down tree, reputed to be Paris's oldest, a false acacia brought over from Guyana in 1680. The mutilated church behind is **St-Julien-le-Pauvre** (daily 9.30am–12.30pm & 3–6.30pm), which used to be the venue for university assemblies until rumbustious students tore it apart in 1524. For the most dramatic view of Notre-Dame of all, walk along the riverbank as far as the tip of the Ile St-Louis and the Pont de Sully.

Institut du Monde Arabe

1 rue des Fossés St-Bernard. Ⓜ Jussieu. ⊚www.imarabe.org. Tues–Sun 10am–6pm. Museum €5. Many visitors come to the Institut du Monde Arabe (IMA) just to admire its stunning design – the work of a group of architects, among them the fashionable Jean Nouvel. On the outside, the IMA is a bold slice of glass and steel that betrays Nouvel's obsession with light – its rectangular southern facade comprises thousands of tiny light-sensitive shutters that modulate the light levels inside while simultaneously mimicking a *moucharabiyah* (traditional Arab latticework balcony).

Inside, it's a cultural centre designed to further national understanding of the Arab world. There are good temporary exhibitions on Arab and Islamic art and culture, and regular films and concerts, often featuring leading performers from the Arab world. But the heart of the institute is its sleek **museum**, which traces the evolution of Islamic art and civilization. Brass celestial globes, astrolabes, compasses and sundials illustrate cutting-edge Arab medieval science, while exquisitely crafted ceramics, metalwork and carpets from all over the Muslim world cover the artistic side. Up on the ninth floor, the terrace has brilliant views over the Seine towards the apse of Notre-Dame, and a café-restaurant (see p.128).

Musée National du Moyen Age

Entrance at 6 place Paul-Painlevé. Ⓜ Cluny–La Sorbonne. ⊚www. musee-moyenage.fr. Mon & Wed–Sun 9.15am–5.45pm. €6.50, €4.50 on Sun. Concerts Fri 12.30pm & Sat 4pm. The Hôtel de Cluny, an attractive sixteenth-century mansion built by the abbots of the powerful Cluny monastery as their Paris pied-à-terre, now

▲ INSTITUT DU MONDE ARABE

The Quartier Latin

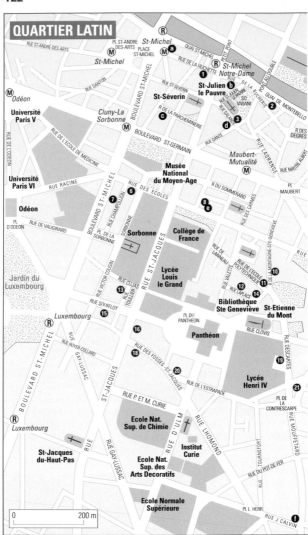

QUARTIER LATIN

houses the richly rewarding Musée National du Moyen Age. The museum is an amazing ragbag of tapestries, carved choir stalls, altarpieces, ivories, stained glass, illuminated Books of Hours, games, brassware and all manner of precious *objets d'art*. The greatest wonder of

the collection is the exquisitely executed late-fifteenth-century tapestry series known as the *Lady with the Unicorn*, displayed in a specially darkened, chapel-like chamber on the first floor. Even if you don't immediately grasp the tapestries' allegorical meaning – they represent the five senses

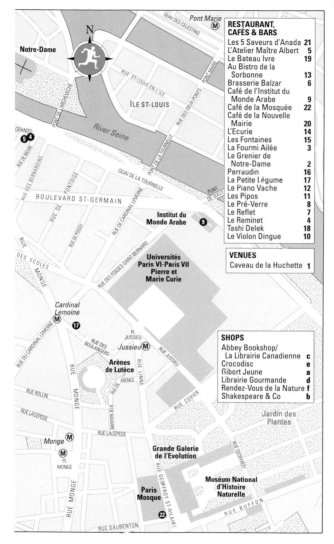

RESTAURANT, CAFÉS & BARS

Les 5 Saveurs d'Anada	21
L'Atelier Maître Albert	5
Le Bateau Ivre	19
Au Bistro de la Sorbonne	13
Brasserie Balzar	6
Café de l'Institut du Monde Arabe	9
Café de la Mosquée	22
Café de la Nouvelle Mairie	20
L'Ecurie	14
Les Fontaines	15
La Fourmi Ailée	3
Le Grenier de Notre-Dame	2
Perraudin	16
La Petite Légume	17
Le Piano Vache	12
Les Pipos	11
Le Pré-Verre	8
Le Reflet	7
Le Reminet	4
Tashi Delek	18
Le Violon Dingue	10

VENUES

Caveau de la Huchette	1

SHOPS

Abbey Bookshop/ La Librairie Canadienne	c
Crocodisc	e
Gibert Jeune	a
Librairie Gourmande	d
Rendez-Vous de la Nature	f
Shakespeare & Co	b

– it's hard not to be blown away by the sheer wealth of detail and richness of colour. The meaning of the sixth and final tapestry is something of a mystery: the scene is of a woman putting away her necklace into a jewellery box held out by her servant, captioned with the words *A Mon Seul Désir* ("To My Only Desire").

The building itself is part of the attraction of the visit: some rooms are decorated in the original style, and the Flamboyant Gothic chapel preserves its remarkable vault splaying out from a central pillar.

▲ MUSEE DU MOYEN AGE ENTRANCE

You can also explore the remains of Paris's third-century Roman baths, the **Thermes de Cluny**, whose characteristic rounded arches and stripey brickwork can also be seen from the boulevard St-Michel.

It's worth timing your visit to coincide with one of the excellent concerts of medieval music, held twice a week inside the museum.

Place de la Sorbonne

Ⓜ Cluny–La Sorbonne / RER Luxembourg.

The traffic-free place de la Sorbonne is a great place to sit back and enjoy the Quartier Latin atmosphere, with its lime trees, fountains, cafés and book-toting students. Frowning over it, however, are the high walls of the **Sorbonne**, which was once the most important of the medieval colleges huddled on the top of the Montagne Ste-Geneviève. More recently it was a flashpoint in the student riots of 1968 – and again in the spring of 2006. The frontage is dominated by the Chapelle Ste-Ursule, built in the 1640s by the great Cardinal Richelieu, whose tomb it contains. A building of enormous influence in Paris for its unabashed emulation of the Roman Counter-Reformation style, it also helped establish a trend for domes, many more of which mushroomed over the city's skyline in the latter part of the seventeenth century.

The Panthéon

Ⓜ Cardinal Lemoine/RER Luxembourg. Daily: April–Sept 10am–6.30pm; Oct–March 10am–6pm. €7.50.

Crowning the very top of the Montagne Ste-Geneviève, the largest and most visible of Paris's domes graces the bulky Panthéon,

▲ CHAPELLE STE-URSULE SORBONNE

Louis XV's thank-you to Sainte Geneviève, patron saint of Paris, for curing him of illness. The building was completed only in 1789, whereupon the Revolution promptly transformed it into a mausoleum, emblazoning the front with the words "*Aux grands hommes la patrie reconnaissante*" ("The nation honours its great men") underneath the pediment of the giant portico. Down in the vast, barrel-vaulted crypt, you can visit the tombs of French cultural icons such as Voltaire, Hugo and Zola, along with more recent arrivals Marie Curie – the only woman – and Alexandre Dumas, author of *The Three Musketeers* (moved here in 2002).

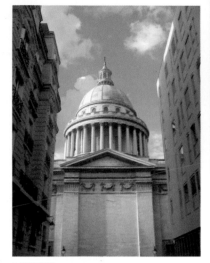

▲ PANTHEON

In the nave, you can also see a working model of Foucault's Pendulum swinging from the dome. French physicist Léon Foucault devised the experiment, conducted here in 1851, to demonstrate that while the pendulum appeared to rotate over a 24-hour period, it was in fact the earth beneath it turning.

St-Etienne-du-Mont

Ⓜ Cardinal Lemoine. The remains of two seventeenth-century literary giants, Pascal and Racine, lie in the church of St-Etienne-du-Mont, alongside a few relics of Paris's early patron, Ste-Geneviève, housed in a luxuriously appointed chapel. The main attraction, however, is the fabulously airy interior, formed of a Flamboyant Gothic choir joined to a Renaissance nave,

the two parts linked by a sinuous catwalk that runs right round the interior, arching across the width of the nave in the form of a carved rood screen – an extremely rare survival, as most French screens fell victim to Protestant iconoclasts, reformers or revolutionaries.

▲ ST-ETIENNE-DU-MONT

Place de la Contrescarpe and rue Mouffetard

Ⓜ Cardinal Lemoine/Monge.
Encircled by cafés, tiny place de la Contrescarpe is the focal point for the student nightlife of the Quartier Latin, and it's a pleasant spot to have a drink or a coffee during the day.

Stretching downhill from the square, the narrow, medieval rue Mouffetard – rue Mouff' to locals – may not be the quintessentially Parisian market street it once was but it still offers an honest local ambience, lined with clothes and shoe shops, a giant health-food centre, and lots of unpretentious bars and restaurants. The lower half of the street maintains a few grocers' stalls, butchers and speciality cheese shops, with a fruit-and-veg market on Tuesday and Saturday mornings.

The Paris mosque

Entrance on rue Daubenton, southeast corner of the mosque. Ⓜ Jussieu/ Censier–Daubenton. Daily except Fri & Muslim hols 9am–noon & 2–6pm. €3. Even in this quiet, residential area, the Paris mosque feels like an oasis of serenity behind its high, crenellated walls. You can walk in the sunken garden and patios with their north-African-style polychrome tiles and carved ceilings, but non-Muslims are asked not to enter the prayer room – though no one seems to mind if you watch from a discreet distance during prayers.

The Paris mosque's hammam

39 rue Geoffrey-St-Hilaire. Ⓜ Jussieu/ Censier–Daubenton. Women Mon, Wed, Thurs & Sat 10am–9pm, Fri 2–9pm; men Tues 2–9pm, Sun 10am–9pm. €15, towels extra. The excellent *hammam* in the Paris mosque, entered via the gate in the southeast corner, is one of the most atmospheric baths in the city, with its vaulted cooling-off room and marble-lined steam chamber. It's usually quiet inside, the clients focused on washing and simply relaxing, so the atmosphere shouldn't feel intimidating, even if you've never taken a public bath before. You can also have a reasonably priced massage and *gommage* – a kind of rubber-gloved rub-down for

▲ RUE MOUFFETARD MARKET STALL

exfoliating. Afterwards, slip into the lovely, gardened tearoom (open to all, even if you haven't used the *hammam*; see p.129).

Jardin des Plantes

Entrances at the corners of the park and opposite rue Jussieu. Ⓜ Jussieu/Censier–Daubenton. Daily: summer 8am–7.30pm; winter 8am–dusk. The magnificent, varied floral beds of the Jardin des Plantes were founded as a medicinal herb garden in 1626 and gradually evolved into Paris's botanical gardens, with hothouses, shady avenues of trees, lawns, a brace of museums and a zoo.

The gardens make a pleasant place to while away the middle of a day. Near the rue Cuvier entrance opposite rue Jussieu stands a fine cedar of Lebanon, planted in 1734 and raised from seed sent over from the Botanical Gardens in Oxford. There's also a slice of an American sequoia more than 2000 years old, with the birth of Christ and other historical events marked on its rings. On a cold day there's no better place to warm up than the hot and humid **winter garden**, a greenhouse filled with palms, cacti and chattering birds.

Grande Galerie de l'Evolution

Muséum National d'Histoire Naturelle, Jardin des Plantes. Ⓜ Censier-Daubenton/Gare d'Austerlitz. Ⓦwww.mnhn.fr. Mon & Wed–Sun 10am–6pm. €8. Part of the Muséum National d'Histoire Naturelle, and by far its most impressive section, is the Grande Galerie de l'Evolution. It occupies the nineteenth-century Galerie de Zoologie, an enormous, dark space surrounded by tier upon tier of glass and iron balconies, dramatically lit by glowing spotlights. The museum tells the story of evolution and the relations between human beings and nature with the aid of a huge cast of life-size animals that parade across the central space. The wow-factor may initally grab children's attention, but you'll have to look out for the translation placards to make the most of the visit.

The Ménagerie

Northeast corner of the Jardin des Plantes. Ⓜ Jussieu. Summer Mon–Sat 9am–6.30pm, Sun 9am–6pm; winter Mon–Sat 9am–5.30pm, Sun 9am–5pm. €7. The Ménagerie is France's oldest zoo – and feels it. The iron cages of the big cats' *fauverie*, the stinky vivarium and the glazed-in primate house are distinctly old-fashioned, though most of the rest of the zoo is pleasantly park-like, given over to deer, antelope, goats, buffaloes and other marvellous beasts that seem happy enough in their outdoor enclosures.

Arènes de Lutèce

Ⓜ Jussieu. The Arènes de Lutèce is an unexpected and peaceful backwater hidden from the streets. Once a Roman amphitheatre seating ten thousand, it is now the only structure from that period left in Paris besides the Gallo-Roman baths (see p.124). A few ghostly rows of stone seats now look down on boules players, while benches, gardens and a kids' playground stand behind.

Shops

Abbey Bookshop/La Librairie Canadienne

29 rue de la Parcheminerie. Ⓜ St-Michel. Mon–Sat 10am–7pm. A Canadian bookshop with lots of secondhand British and North American fiction, plus knowledgeable and helpful staff – and free coffee.

Crocodisc

40–42 rue des Ecoles. Ⓜ Maubert-Mutualité. Tues–Sat 11am–7pm. Folk, Oriental, Afro-Antillais, raï, funk, reggae, salsa, hip-hop, soul and country music, both new and secondhand, at some of the best prices in town.

Gibert Jeune

10 place St-Michel & 27 quai St-Michel. Ⓜ St-Michel. Mon–Sat 9.30am–7.30pm. The biggest of the Quartier Latin student and academic bookshops with a vast selection of French books. There's a fair English-language and discounted selection at its other branch, Gibert Joseph, 26 boulevard St-Michel. An institution.

Librairie Gourmande

4 rue Dante. Ⓜ Maubert-Mutualité. Daily 10am–7pm. The very last word in books on cookery and food in general, with a decent English-language selection.

Rendez-Vous de la Nature

96 rue Mouffetard. Ⓜ Cardinal-Lemoine. Tues–Sat 9.30am–7.30pm, Sun 9.30am–1pm. One of the city's most comprehensive health-food stores, with everything from organic produce to herbal teas.

Shakespeare & Co

37 rue de la Bûcherie. Ⓜ Maubert-Mutualité. Daily noon–midnight. A cosy, American-run literary haunt, with the biggest selection of secondhand English books in town – and a few beds upstairs for starving American writers willing to man the tills. Also holds poetry readings and the like.

Cafés

Café de l'Institut du Monde Arabe

Institut du Monde Arabe. Ⓜ Jussieu. Tues–Sun 10am–6pm. Amazing rooftop café-restaurant where you can drink mint tea and nibble on cakes in the sunshine. Inside the building, the self-service cafeteria *Moucharabiyah* offers a good plate of lunchtime couscous and the chance to marvel at the aperture action of the windows.

▲ GIBERT JEUNE

▲ SHAKESPEARE & CO

Café de la Mosquée

39 rue Geoffroy-St-Hilaire. Ⓜ
Jussieu/Censier–Daubenton. Daily
9am–midnight. Drink mint tea and
eat sweet cakes beside a fountain
and assorted fig trees in the
courtyard of this Paris mosque
– a delightful haven of calm.
The salon has a beautiful Arabic
interior, while full meals are
served in the adjoining restaurant.

Café de la Nouvelle Mairie

19 rue des Fossés-St-Jacques. Ⓜ
Cluny–La Sorbonne/RER Luxembourg.
Mon, Wed & Fri 9am–10pm, Tues &
Thurs 9am–11pm. Sleek café-wine
bar with a relaxed feel generated
by its older, university-based
clientele. Serves good, reasonably
priced food such as *curry d'agneau*,
linguine and salads, and you can
drink at the outside tables on
sunny days.

La Fourmi Ailée

8 rue du Fouarre, on sq Viviani. Ⓜ
Maubert-Mutualité. Daily noon–
midnight. This former bookshop
has been transformed into a
relaxed place to eat or linger over
a coffee. The high ceiling, painted
with a lovely mural, open fire
(in winter) and book-filled wall
contribute to the atmosphere.
Serves decent *plats du jour* for
around €8–15.

Le Reflet

6 rue Champollion. Ⓜ Cluny–La
Sorbonne. Daily 10am–2am. This
artsy cinema café has a strong
flavour of the *nouvelle vague*, with
its scruffy black paint scheme,
lights rigged up on a gantry
overhead and rickety tables
packed with arty film-goers
and chess players. Good steaks,
quiches, salads and the like from a
short list of blackboard specials.

Restaurants

Les 5 Saveurs d'Anada

72 rue Cardinal-Lemoine. Ⓜ Cardinal-
Lemoine. ☎01.43.29.58.54. Daily
Noon–2.30pm & 7.30–10.30pm. Airy
and informal restaurant serving
delicious, reasonably priced
organic vegetarian food. Salads
are good, or you could try one
of the creative meat-substitute
dishes (around €12), such as tofu

soufflé, confit of tempeh with ginger, or seitan with celeriac and basil.

L'Atelier Maître Albert

1 rue Maître Albert. Ⓜ Maubert-Mutualité. ☎01.56.81.30.01. Daily noon–2.30pm & 7–11pm. This classy *rôtisserie* is decorated like a designer's take on a medieval château. It's a fitting look for the speciality of spit-roast meats, though you can also find lighter, more modern dishes on the menu such as pan-fried red mullet with penne gratin. Lunch *menu* at €23, or roughly double for *à la carte*.

Au Bistro de la Sorbonne

4 rue Toullier. RER Luxembourg. ☎01.43.54.41.49. Daily noon–2.30pm & 7–11pm. Traditional French and delicious North African food served at reasonable prices to a crowd of locals and students. The muralled interior is attractively bright.

Brasserie Balzar

49 rue des Ecoles. Ⓜ Maubert-Mutualité. ☎01.43.54.13.67. Daily 8am–11.30pm. This mirrored, high-ceilinged brasserie is festooned with pot plants in the classic style. Earlier on, the atmosphere can be quite touristy, but if you choose to eat late it becomes almost intimidatingly Parisian – which about fits the decor and the menu. Eating *à la carte* will cost around €35 a head.

L'Ecurie

58 rue de la Montagne Ste-Geneviève, cnr rue Laplace. Ⓜ Maubert-Mutualité/ Cardinal-Lemoine. ☎01.46.33.68.49. Mon–Sat noon–3pm & 7pm–midnight, Sun 7pm–midnight. Shoehorned into a former stables on a particularly lovely corner of the Montagne Ste-Geneviève, this small, family-run restaurant is bustling and very loveable.

Expect well-cooked, inexpensive meat dishes (mostly under €15) served without flourishes.

Les Fontaines

9 rue Soufflot. RER Luxembourg. ☎01.43.26.42.80. Mon–Sat noon–3pm & 7.30–10.30pm. The brasserie decor looks unpromising from the outside, but the welcome inside this family-owned place is warm and genuine, and the cooking is in the same spirit, with honest French meat and fish dishes, or game in season, all at reasonable prices.

Le Grenier de Notre-Dame

18 rue de la Bûcherie. Ⓜ Maubert-Mutualité. ☎01.43.29.98.29. Mon–Sat noon–2.30pm & 6.30–10pm. This cramped, unpretentious vegetarian restaurant serves substantial traditional French fare made with tofu and other meat substitutes, such as a hearty vegetarian cassoulet for €10. Coloured lanterns help warm up the slightly wholesome atmosphere.

Perraudin

157 rue St-Jacques. RER Luxembourg. ☎01.46.33.15.75. Mon–Fri noon–2pm & 7.30–10.15pm; closed last fortnight in Aug. One of the classic *bistrots* of the Left Bank. The atmosphere is thick with Parisian chatter floating above the brightly lit, packed-in tables. Solid cooking, with moderately priced menus. No reservations.

La Petite Légume

36 rue Boulangers. Ⓜ Jussieu. ☎01.40.46.06.85. Mon–Sat noon–2.30pm & 7.30–10pm. A health-food grocer's that doubles as a vegetarian restaurant and tearoom, serving homely, inexpensive organic *plats*, along with fresh-tasting organic Loire wines.

Le Pré-Verre

8 rue Thénard. Ⓜ Maubert-Mutualité.
☎01.43.54.59.47. Tues–Sat noon–2pm
& 7.30–10.30pm; closed three weeks
in Aug. This sleek, modern,
slightly posey *bistrot à vins* has a
great wine list, while blackboard
lists are dotted with unusual
ingredients and spices – swordfish
on a bed of quinoa grain, wild
boar ragout with quince, or roast
bananas with mango mousse
and chilli syrup. Evening *menu*
at €25.

Le Reminet

3 rue des Grands Degrés. Ⓜ
Maubert-Mutualité. ☎01.44.07.04.24.
Mon & Thurs–Sun noon–2.30pm &
7.30–11pm; closed two weeks in
Aug. Snowy-white tablecloths
and fancy chandeliers add a
touch of class to this little bistro-
restaurant, and imaginative sauces
grace high-quality traditional
French ingredients. By no means
a budget bistro, but excellent
value all the same.

Tashi Delek

4 rue des Fossés-St-Jacques. RER
Luxembourg. ☎01.43.26.55.55. Mon–
Sat noon–2.30pm & 7–11pm; closed
two weeks in Aug. Elegantly styled
Tibetan restaurant serving hearty,
warming noodle soups and the
addictive, ravioli-like *momok*.
There is even yak-butter tea, a
salty, soupy concoction that's an
acquired taste. You can eat well
for remarkably little money.

Bars

Le Bateau Ivre

40 rue Descartes. Ⓜ Cardinal-
Lemoine. Daily 6pm–2am. Small,
dark and ancient, this studenty
bar is just clear of the Mouffetard
tourist hotspot, though it attracts

a fair number of "Anglos" in the
evenings, especially after about
10pm. If it's packed out, the *Pub
River* next door is less appealing
but more spacious.

Le Piano Vache

8 rue Laplace. Ⓜ Cardinal-Lemoine.
Mon–Fri noon–2am, Sat & Sun 9pm–
2am. Venerable bar crammed with
students drinking at little tables,
with French rock or dance-based
music on the CD player and a
laidback, grungey atmosphere.

Les Pipos

2 rue de l'Ecole-Polytechnique. Ⓜ
Maubert-Mutualité. Mon–Sat 8am–
1am; closed two weeks in Aug. Old,
carved wooden bar in a long-
established position opposite the
gates of the former *grande école*.
Serves well-priced wines along
with simple plates of Auvergnat
charcuterie, cheese and the like.

Le Violon Dingue

46 rue de la Montagne Ste-Geneviève.
Ⓜ Maubert-Mutualité. Daily 6pm–
2.30am. A long, dark student pub
that's also popular with young
travellers. Noisy and friendly,
with English-speaking bar staff
and cheap drinks. The cellar bar
stays open until 4.30am on busy
nights.

Live music

Caveau de la Huchette

5 rue de la Huchette. Ⓜ St-
Michel. ☎01.43.26.65.05, ⓦwww.
caveaudelahuchette.fr. Daily
9.30pm–2am. Entrance around €13.
A wonderful slice of old Parisian
life in an otherwise touristy
area. Live jazz, usually trad and
big band, to dance to on a floor
surrounded by tiers of benches.
Best at weekends.

St-Germain

St-Germain, the westernmost section of Paris's Left Bank, has long been famous as the haunt of bohemians and intellectuals. A few well-known cafés preserve a strong flavour of the old times, but the dominant spirit these days is elegant, relaxed and seriously upmarket. At opposite ends of the quarter are two of the city's busiest and best-loved sights: to the east, bordering the Quartier Latin, spread the exquisite lawns of the Jardin du Luxembourg, while to the west stands the Musée d'Orsay, a converted railway station with a world-beating collection of Impressionist paintings. Between the two, you can visit the churches of St-Sulpice and St-Germain-des-Prés, or intriguing museums dedicated to the artists Delacroix and Maillol, but really, shopping is king. The streets around place St-Sulpice swarm with international fashion brands, while on the north side of boulevard St-Germain, antique shops and art dealers dominate. Between shopping sprees, you can explore the *quartier*'s excellent cafés and bars, among which you'll find some Parisian classics.

Pont des Arts

The delicate and much-loved Pont des Arts was installed in Napoleon's time. It offers a classic upstream view of the Ile de la Cité, and also provides a grand entrance to St-Germain under the watchful eye of the Institut de France, an august academic institution whose members are known as "Immortals".

Jardin du Luxembourg

Ⓜ Odéon & RER Luxembourg. Daily dawn to dusk. Fronting onto rue de Vaugirard, Paris's longest street, the Jardin du Luxembourg is the chief lung of the Left Bank. Its atmosphere is a beguiling mixture of formal and utterly relaxed. At the park's centre, the perfectly round pond and immaculate floral parterres are overlooked by the haughty Palais du Luxembourg, the seat of the French Senate. Elsewhere, students sprawl about on the garden's famous metal chairs, children sail toy yachts, watch the puppets at the *guignol*, or run about in the playgrounds, and old men gather to play

▲ JARDIN DU LUXEMBOURG

boules or chess. In summer, the most contested spots are the shady Fontaine de Médicis in the northeast corner, and the lawns of the southernmost strip – one of the few areas where you're allowed to lie out on the grass. The quieter, wooded southwest corner is dotted with the works of famous sculptors, and ends in a miniature orchard of elaborately espaliered pear trees.

Musée du Luxembourg

19 rue de Vaugirard. Ⓜ St-Sulpice. ☎01.42.34.25.95, ⓦwww. museeduluxembourg.fr. The Musée du Luxembourg lies at the top end of rue de Vaugirard, backing onto the park. It holds temporary art exhibitions that rank among the most ambitious in Paris – recent shows have included twentieth-century self-portraits and "profane" Veronese, Raphael, Gauguin, Modigliani and Botticelli. Check for opening hours.

Place St-Germain-des-Prés

Ⓜ St-Germain-des-Prés. The hub of the *quartier* is place St-Germain-des-Prés, with the famous café *Les Deux Magots* on one corner, and *Café Flore* and *Brasserie Lipp* just a stone's throw away (see pp.139 & 140). All three are renowned for the number of intellectual and literary backsides that have shined their seats, and are expensive and extremely crowded in summer.

St-Germain-des-Prés

place St-Germain-des-Prés. Ⓜ St-Germain-des-Prés. Daily 7.30am–7.30pm. The ancient tower overlooking place St-Germain-des-Prés opposite *Les Deux Magots* is all that remains of a once-enormous Benedictine monastery. Inside the adjoining church of St-Germain-des-

Prés, the transformation from Romanesque nave to early Gothic choir is just about visible under the heavy green and gold nineteenth-century paintwork. The last chapel on the south side contains the tomb of the philosopher René Descartes, while in the corner of the churchyard by rue Bonaparte, a little Picasso sculpture of a woman's head is dedicated to the poet Apollinaire.

Musée Delacroix

6 rue de Furstenberg. Ⓜ Mabillon. ⓦwww.musee-delacroix.fr. Daily except Tues 9.30am–5pm. €5. The Musée Delacroix occupies the house where the artist lived and worked from 1857 until his death in 1863, and still displays his paintbox alongside other curiosities and personal effects. Although Delacroix's major work is exhibited permanently at the Louvre (see p.74) and the Musée d'Orsay (see p.136), this museum displays a refreshingly intimate collection of small-scale paintings, watercolours, drawings and frescoes, and holds good temporary exhibitions on Delacroix and his contemporaries.

▼ ST-GERMAIN STREET SCENE

St-Germain **PLACES**

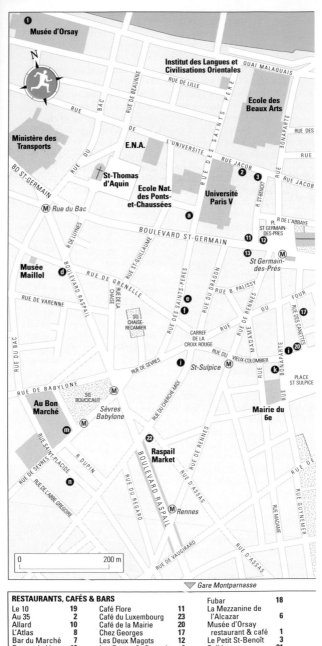

Gare Montparnasse

RESTAURANTS, CAFÉS & BARS

Le 10	19	Café Flore	11	Fubar	18
Au 35	2	Café du Luxembourg	23	La Mezzanine de	
Allard	10	Café de la Mairie	20	l'Alcazar	6
L'Atlas	8	Chez Georges	17	Musée d'Orsay	
Bar du Marché	7	Les Deux Magots	12	restaurant & café	1
Brasserie Lipp	13	Les Etages St-Germain	9	Le Petit St-Benoît	3
				Polidor	21

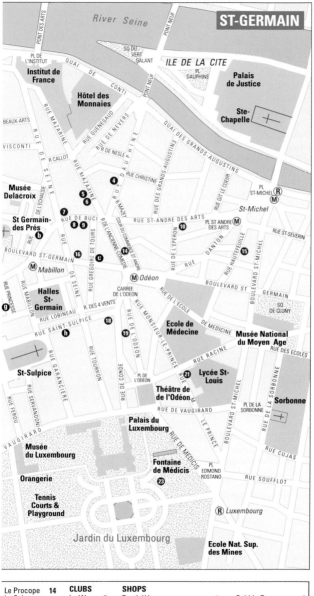

		CLUBS		SHOPS				
Le Procope	14	Le Wagg	5	Barthélémy	d	Sabbia Rosa	f
Le Salon				Au Bon Marché	m	Sonia/Sonia Rykiel	e
d'Hélène	22			Comptoir des Cotonniers	b & i	Vanessa Bruno	h
La Taverne				Debauve & Gallais	a	Village Voice	g
de Nesle	4			Le Mouton à Cinq Pattes	c & n	Zadig & Voltaire	k
La Tourelle	15			Poilâne	j		
Vagenende	16						

St-Sulpice

place St-Sulpice. Ⓜ St-Sulpice. Daily
7.30am–7.30pm. It took over
a hundred years to build the
enormous church of St-Sulpice,
and it remains incomplete,
with uncut masonry blocks still
protruding from the south tower,
awaiting the sculptor's chisel. The
facade is rather overpoweringly
classical, but any severity is
softened by the chestnut trees and
fountain of the peaceful place
St-Sulpice, and the crowds at the
outside tables of the *Café de la
Mairie* (see p.139), on the sunny
side of the square. The best thing
about the gloomy interior is the
three Delacroix murals, including
one of St Michael slaying a
dragon, in the first chapel on the
right.

The rue Mabillon grid

Ⓜ Mabillon. The miniature group
of streets immediately north of
St-Sulpice – rue des Canettes,
rue Princesse and rue Mabillon
– is particularly glossy, with
lots of rather expensive *bistrot*
restaurants, little boutiques and
bars packed into the pretty old
houses. The main attraction,
however, is the array of fashion
boutiques, which start with
Agnès b and the very elegant
Yves Saint Laurent Rive Gauche
on the corner of place St-Sulpice
itself, and spread west from there.

Boulevard Raspail Marché "Bio"

Boulevard Raspail. Ⓜ Sèvres-
Babylone/Rennes. Sun roughly
9am–2pm. Between rue du
Cherche Midi and rue de
Rennes, the central reservation
in the middle of broad boulevard
Raspail is entirely taken over by
food stalls every Tuesday and
Friday morning. The best day
to come, however, is Sunday for
the celebrated "Marché Bio" or
organic food market. Even if
you're not shopping for fine fruit
and veg, you can find superb
cheeses and cold meats to take
home, as well as various herbal
products, wheatgrass juices, oils
and the like.

Musée Maillol

61 rue de Grenelle. Ⓜ Rue du Bac.
ⓌWwww.museemaillol.com. Daily except
Tues 10am–6pm. €8. An outwardly
inconspicuous eighteenth-
century house is now the home
of the Musée Maillol, its interior
bursting with Aristide Maillol's
buxom sculptures of female
nudes, of which the smoothly
curvaceous *Mediterranean* is his
most famous. Other rooms house
drawings by Matisse, Dufy and
Bonnard, humorously erotic
paintings by Bombois, and the
odd Picasso, Degas, Gauguin and
Kandinsky. The museum also
organizes excellent exhibitions
of twentieth-century art – recent
ones have included Frida Kahlo
and Diego Rivera.

Musée d'Orsay

1 rue de la Légion d'Honneur. Ⓜ
Solferino & RER Musée d'Orsay.
Ⓦwww.musee-orsay.fr. Tues–Sun
9.30am–6pm, Thurs until 9.45pm.
Mon–Sat €7.50, Sun €5.50, free
for under-18s and on first Sun of the
month. Down on the riverfront,
just west of St-Germain, the
Musée d'Orsay dramatically
fills a former railway station
with paintings and sculptures
dating from between 1848 and
1914, including an unparalleled
Impressionist and Post-
Impressionist collection. The
museum's **ground floor**, spread
out under the giant glass arch,
is devoted to pre-1870 work,
contrasting Ingres, Delacroix and
other serious-minded painters
with the relatively wacky works
of Puvis de Chavannes, Gustave

Moreau and the younger Degas. On the other side of the tracks, as it were, the Barbizon school and the Realists prepare the ground for Impressionism, along with Monet's violently light-filled *Femmes au Jardin* (1867) and Manet's provocative *Olympia* (1863), which heralded the arrival of the new school.

Impressionism proper packs the attic-like **upper level**, with famous images such as Monet's *Poppies* and *Femme à l'Ombrelle*, Manet's *Déjeuner sur l'Herbe*, Degas' *L'Absinthe* and Renoir's *Bal du Moulin de la Galette*. You'll also find some of Degas' wonderful sculptures of ballet-dancers and a host of small-scale landscapes and outdoor scenes by Renoir, Sisley, Pissarro and Monet that owed much of their brilliance to the novel practice of setting up easels in the open. More heavyweight masterpieces can be found by Monet and Renoir in their middle and late periods, Van Gogh and Cézanne, as well as a dimly lit section devoted to pastels by Degas, Redon, Manet, Mondrian and others. The final suite of rooms on this level begins with Rousseau's dreamlike *La Charmeuse de Serpent* (1907) and continues past Gauguin's Tahitian paintings to Pointillist works by Seurat, Signac and others, ending with Toulouse-Lautrec at his caricaturial nightclubbing best.

Down on the **middle level** is a disparate group of paintings, including the Art Nouveau Nabis, notably Bonnard and Vuillard, some international Symbolist paintings, and lots of late-nineteenth-century painting from the naturalist schools.

Bridging the parallel sculpture terraces, the **Rodin terrace** puts almost everything else to shame. Finally, try to spare some energy for the half-dozen adjacent rooms filled with superb Art Nouveau furniture and *objets d'art*. Look out too for the temporary exhibitions, including major shows of Impressionist and post-Impressionist artists.

Shops

Barthélémy

51 rue de Grenelle. Ⓜ Rue du Bac. Tues–Sat 8am–1pm & 4–7.15pm; closed Aug. Purveyors of cheeses to the rich and powerful. Madame Bathélémy herself is on hand in the mornings to offer expert advice on choosing and caring for your cheese.

▲ MUSEE D'ORSAY

Au Bon Marché

38 rue de Sèvres. Ⓜ Sèvres-Babylone. Mon–Wed & Fri 9.30am–7pm, Thurs 10am–9pm, Sat 9.30am–8pm. The oldest department store in Paris, founded in 1852, and one of its most upmarket – in fact, it's famous for having a name meaning the opposite of what it really is (*bon marché* in French means "cheap"). The food hall is legendary and there's an excellent kids' department.

Comptoir des Cotonniers

30 rue de Buci & 58 rue Bonaparte. Ⓜ Mabillon/St-Germain-des-Prés. Mon 11am–7pm, Tues–Sat 10am–7.30pm. Utterly reliable little chain stocking comfortable, well-cut women's basics that nod to contemporary fashions without being modish. Trousers, shirts and dresses for around €100. It has around twenty branches in Paris.

Debauve & Gallais

30 rue des Sts-Pères. Ⓜ St-Germain-des-Prés. Ⓦ www.debauve-et-gallais.com. Mon–Sat 9.30am–7pm; closed Aug. This beautiful, ancient shop specializes in exquisite, expensive dark chocolates. Open since 1800, it now offers an online-shopping service.

Le Mouton à Cinq Pattes

Men and women 138 bd St-Germain & 18 rue St-Placide; women 8 rue St-Placide. Ⓜ Odéon. ☎01.43.26.49.25. Mon–Sat 10am–7pm. A classic bargain clothing address, with racks upon racks of end-of-line and reject clothing from designer names both great and small. You might find a shop-soiled Gaultier classic (if you can recognize it without the label); you might find nothing. At these prices, it's worth the gamble.

Poilâne

8 rue du Cherche-Midi. Ⓜ Sèvres-Babylone. Mon–Sat 6.15am–8.15pm. This extremely classy bakery is the ultimate source of the famous "Pain Poilâne", and a great place for other bakery treats, too.

Sabbia Rosa

71–73 rue des Saints-Pères. Ⓜ St-Germain-des-Près. Mon–Sat 10am–7pm. Supermodels' knickers – literally, they all shop here – at supermodel prices. Beautiful lingerie creations in silk, fine cotton and Calais lace. An ensemble will cost around €150, and you could pay three times that.

Sonia/Sonia Rykiel

61 rue des Saints-Pères. Ⓜ Sèvres-Babylone. Mon–Sat 10.30am–7pm. Sonia Rykiel has been a St-Germain institution almost since her shop opened at 175 bd St-Germain in spring 1968. Since then, her daughter Nathalie has started up this younger, more exciting and less expensive offshoot of the Rykiel brand.

Vanessa Bruno

25 rue St-Sulpice. Ⓜ Odéon. Mon–Sat 10.30am–9.30pm. Bright, breezy and effortlessly beautiful women's fashions

▲ POILANE BAKERY

– trainers, dresses and bags – with a hint of updated hippy chic.

Village Voice

6 rue Princesse. Ⓜ Mabillon. Mon 2–7.30pm, Tues–Sat 10am–7.30pm, Sun 1–6pm. A welcoming re-creation of an American neighbourhood bookstore, with a good selection of contemporary fiction and nonfiction, and a decent list of British and American poetry and classics.

Zadig & Voltaire

1 & 3 rue du Vieux Colombier. Ⓜ St-Sulpice. Mon–Sat 10am–7pm. The women's clothes at this small, moderately expensive Parisian chain are pretty and feminine. In style it's not a million miles from Agnès b – and her shop's just opposite – only with a more wayward flair. There are branches all over the city.

Cafés

Bar du Marché

75 rue de Seine. Ⓜ Mabillon. Daily 7am–2am. Humming café where the waiters are funkily kitted out in flat caps and bright aprons, although you pay a little extra for the location near the rue de Buci market.

Café Flore

172 bd St-Germain. Ⓜ St-Germain-des-Prés. Daily 7am–1.30am. The great rival and immediate neighbour of *Les Deux Magots*. Sartre, de Beauvoir and Camus used to hang out here, and it keeps up a fashionable, vaguely intellectual reputation. Best enjoyed in the late-afternoon sunshine, or upstairs among the regulars. Beware of the prices.

Café du Luxembourg

Hours vary according to park opening times. This delightful, tree-shaded *buvette* serves hot and cold drinks right through the day. Situated northeast of the pond, in the heart of the Jardin du Luxembourg. Prices are high, but not unfairly so.

Café de la Mairie

Place St-Sulpice. Ⓜ St-Sulpice. Mon–Sat 7am–2am. Situated on the north side of the square, this not unduly pricey café is famous for the beautiful people sun-seeking on the outdoor *terrasse*.

Les Deux Magots

170 bd St-Germain. Ⓜ St-Germain-des-Prés. Daily 7.30am–1am. Right on the corner of place St-Germain-des-Prés, this expensive café is the victim of its own reputation as the historic hang-out of Left Bank intellectuals, but it's still great for people-watching.

Musée d'Orsay Restaurant and Café

Musée d'Orsay, Upper Level. Ⓜ Solferino & RER Musée d'Orsay. Mon–Wed & Fri–Sun 10.30am–5pm, Thurs 10.30am–9pm. The upper-level café in the Musée d'Orsay has a summer terrace and a wonderful view of Montmartre through the giant railway clock. The main restaurant – once that of the railway hotel – is worth it for the

▼ LES DEUX MAGOTS

ornate decor alone. Both serve good afternoon tea and cakes.

Le Procope

13 rue de l'Ancienne-Comédie. Ⓜ Odéon. Daily noon–1am. Opened in 1686 as the first establishment to serve coffee in Paris, it is still a great place to enjoy a cup and bask in the knowledge that over the years Voltaire, Benjamin Franklin, Rousseau, Marat and Robespierre, among others, have done the very same thing. Decent but rather overpriced meals are served, too.

Restaurants

Au 35

35 rue Jacob. Ⓜ St-Germain-des-Prés. ☎01.42.60.23.24. Mon–Fri noon–2.30pm & 7.30–11pm, Sat 7.30–11pm. This *bistrot* is adorably intimate, but the food's the thing – from a perfect duck breast to an exotic, rich *pastilla* of lamb with honey and spices. Count on around €30 without wine.

Allard

41 rue St-André-des-Arts. Ⓜ Odéon. ☎01.43.26.48.23. Mon–Sat noon–2.30pm & 7.30–11pm. The menu at this proudly unreconstructed Parisian restaurant is meaty and rich rather than sophisticated or imaginative. The atmosphere is impeccably antique: if it wasn't for the international clientele, you could be dining in another century. From around €30.

L'Atlas

11 rue de Buci. Ⓜ Mabillon. ☎01.40.51.26.30. Daily 6.30am–1am. Despite a few Art Deco details, the decor at *l'Atlas* is functional rather than classic, but that's half the charm of this unpretentious market brasserie. Good seafood, and simple, meaty main dishes at around €17.

Brasserie Lipp

151 bd St-Germain. Ⓜ St-Germain-des-Prés. ☎45.48.53.91. Daily 9am–12.45am. One of the most celebrated of all the classic Paris brasseries, and still the haunt of the successful and famous, with a wonderful 1900s wood-and-glass interior. *Plats du jour*, including the famous sauerkraut, are decent and not overpriced at under €20, but ordering on the full menu can get expensive. Meals served from noon daily; no reservations, so be prepared to wait.

Le Petit St-Benoît

4 rue St-Benoît. Ⓜ St-Germain-des-Prés. ☎01.42.60.27.92. Mon–Sat noon–2.30pm & 7–10.30pm. Another of the tobacco-stained St-Germain institutions, all rickety wooden tables and brass train-carriage-style coat racks. Serves the sort of homely, meaty, comfort food your *grand-mère* would cook, at reasonable prices.

Polidor

41 rue Monsieur-le-Prince. Ⓜ Odéon. ☎01.43.26.95.34. Mon–Sat noon–2.30pm & 7pm–12.30am, Sun noon–2.30pm & 7–11pm. Eating at *Polidor* is a classic of Left Bank life. A bright, noisy traditional *bistrot*, open since 1845, it's packed until late with regulars and tourists alike enjoying meaty Parisian classics on the good-value *menus* (€20 and €30, or just €12 for a weekday lunch). No bookings; just turn up and wait.

Le Salon d'Hélène

4 rue d'Assas. Ⓜ St-Sulpice/Sèvres-Babylone. ☎01.42.22.00.11. Tues 7.30–10.15pm, Wed–Sat 12.30–2.15pm & 7.30–10.15pm; closed Aug. Underneath celebrity chef Hélène Darroze's gastronomic restaurant, the trendier and more relaxed ground-floor *bistrot*-tapas bar offers imaginative (but very

expensive) dishes drawing on her native Basque cuisine. Count on €100 a head, without wine. Book well in advance.

La Tourelle

5 rue Hautefeuille. Ⓜ St-Michel. ☎01.46.33.12.47. Mon–Fri 12.15–2.15pm & 7–10pm, Sat 7–10pm; closed Aug. This splendidly convivial, almost medieval little bistro offers fresh, simple and largely meaty cuisine. Excellent service and even better value. No bookings are taken, so you'll just have to turn up and wait.

Vagenende

142 bd St-Germain. Ⓜ Mabillon. ☎01.43.26.68.18. Daily noon–1am. The marvellous Art Nouveau interior is registered as a historic monument. The food can't quite match up, but is enjoyable if you stick to the straightforward brasserie dishes (mains around €20) or seafood specials.

Bars

Le 10

10 rue de l'Odéon. Ⓜ Odéon. Daily 6pm–2am. Classic Art Deco-era posters line the walls of this small dark bar, and the theme is continued in the atmospheric cellar bar, with a studenty and international crowd.

Chez Georges

11 rue des Canettes. Ⓜ Mabillon/St-Germain-des-Prés. Tues–Sat noon–2am; closed Aug. Deeply old-fashioned, tobacco-stained wine bar with its old shop front still in place. The downstairs bar attracts a younger, beery crowd that stays lively well into the small hours. Relatively inexpensive for the area.

Les Etages St-Germain

5 rue de Buci. Ⓜ Mabillon. Daily 11am–2am. Outpost of boho trendiness at the edge of the rue de Buci market, with a certain trashy glamour. The downstairs café-bar is open to the street, and in the evenings you can lounge around upstairs with a cocktail.

Fubar

5 rue St-Sulpice. Ⓜ Odéon. Daily 5pm–2am. Relaxed lounge bar with a young, international crowd drinking well past the last métro. The upstairs room is very cosy, with soft armchairs and deep red walls.

La Mezzanine de l'Alcazar

62 rue Mazarine. Ⓜ Odéon. Daily 7pm–2am. The decor is *très design* at this cool cocktail bar, set on a mezzanine level overlooking Conran's *Alcazar* restaurant. Expensive but exquisite – much like the clientele. DJs Wed–Sat.

La Taverne de Nesle

32 rue Dauphine. Ⓜ Odéon. Mon–Thurs & Sun 6pm–4am, Fri & Sat 6pm–5am. Full of local night owls fuelled by happy-hour cocktails (at around €7) and beers (just over €3). It gets busier during student terms, especially at weekends when DJs take to the decks.

Clubs

Le Wagg

62 rue Mazarine. Ⓜ Odéon. Ⓦwww.wagg.fr. Fri & Sat 11.30pm–dawn, Sun 5pm–midnight. Entry €15, free on Sun. This intimate, Conran-owned and designed club sits in an ancient, stone-vaulted cellar. International St-Germain yuppie-types lounge around on designer furnishings, drink cocktails and dance to UK-influenced house and disco-funk – or seventies classics on the Friday Carwash nights.

The Eiffel Tower area

Between St-Germain and the Eiffel Tower, the atmosphere of the Left Bank changes. Gone are the little boutique bars and bistro-restaurants, and in their place are elegant aristocratic mansions and some of the city's most magnificent public monuments. The Eiffel Tower dominates the entire area, its giant scale matched by the sweeping lawns of the Champs de Mars, the 109-metre arch of the Pont Alexandre III and the great military edifices of Les Invalides and the Ecole Militaire. But it's not all inhuman in scale. Right at the foot of the Tower is the village-like oasis of shops, cafés and restaurants around the rue Cler market.

The Eiffel Tower

RER Champ de Mars–Tour Eiffel.
Ⓦwww.tour-eiffel.fr. Daily: mid-June to Aug 9am–midnight; Sept to mid-June 9.30am–11pm. Top level €11; second level €7.70, or €3.80 by stairs (access closes 6pm); first level €4.20.

It's hard to believe that the Eiffel Tower, the quintessential symbol both of Paris and the brilliance of industrial engineering, was designed to be a temporary structure for a fair, the 1889 Exposition Universelle. When completed, the 300-metre tower was the tallest building in the world. Outraged critics protested against this "grimy factory chimney", though Eiffel himself (not surprisingly) thought it was beautiful in its sheer structural efficiency: "To a certain extent," he wrote, "the tower was formed by the wind itself."

Unless you get there ahead of the opening times, or go on a cloudy or rainy day, you're bound to queue at the bottom, for lifts at the changeovers and again when descending. It's absolutely worth it, however, not just for the view, but for the sheer exhilaration of being inside the structure. The views are usually clearer from the second level, but there's something irresistible about taking the lift all the way up

▲ THE EIFFEL TOWER

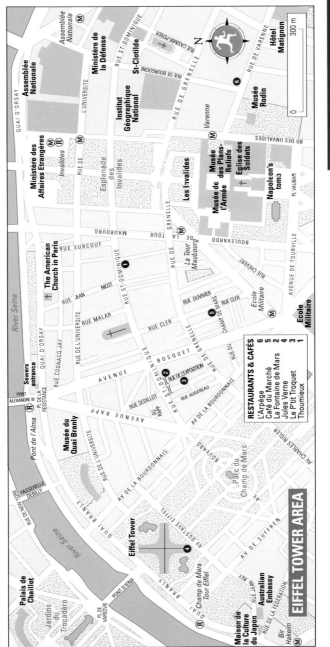

EIFFEL TOWER AREA

N

300 m

0

RESTAURANTS & CAFÉS

L'Arpège	6
Café du Marché	5
La Fontaine de Mars	2
Jules Verne	4
Le P'tit Troquet	3
Thoumieux	1

Palais de Chaillot

Jardins du Trocadéro

Maison de la Culture du Japon

Australian Embassy

River Seine

Rive Seine

RUE DE NEW YORK

PASSERELLE DEBILLY

PONT ALEXANDRE III

Sewers entrance

PONT D'IÉNA

Eiffel Tower

Tour Eiffel

Champ de Mars

Parc du Champ de Mars

Musée du Quai Branly

The American Church in Paris

Ministère des Affaires Étrangères

Assemblée Nationale

Ministère de la Défense

St-Clotilde

Institut Géographique National

Musée Rodin

Hôtel Matignon

Esplanade des Invalides

Les Invalides

Musée de l'Armée

Musée des Plans-Reliefs

Église des Soldats

Napoleon's tomb

Musée des Plans-Reliefs

Ecole Militaire

La Tour Maubourg

QUAI D'ORSAY

QUAI D'ORSAY

QUAI BRANLY

RUE DE L'UNIVERSITÉ

AVENUE RAPP

AVENUE BOSQUET

RUE ST-DOMINIQUE

RUE DE GRENELLE

RUE SURCOUF

RUE JEAN NICOT

RUE MALAR

RUE COGNACQ JAY

RUE SÉDILLOT

RUE AUGEREAU

RUE DE L'EXPOSITION

RUE CLER

RUE DUVIVIER

AV DE LA BOURDONNAIS

AV DE SUFFREN

AVENUE DE LA MOTTE-PICQUET

BOULEVARD DE LA TOUR MAUBOURG

BD DES INVALIDES

AVENUE DE TOURVILLE

RUE CHEVERT

PL VAUBAN

RUE DE GRENELLE

RUE DE VARENNE

RUE CASIMIR-PÉRIER

RUE DE BOURGOGNE

L'UNIVERSITÉ

RUE DE L'UNIVERSITÉ

PL DE LA RÉSISTANCE

Bir Hakeim

RUE DE LA FÉDÉRATION

RUE DE VARSOVIE

PONT DE L'ALMA

(though be sure to arrive well before 10.30pm, when access to the lifts is closed; note too that the stairs to the second level close at 6pm from September to mid-June). Paris looks surreally microscopic from the top, the boulevards like leafy canyons and the parks and cemeteries like oases of green. The paint scheme may now be dull brown, but the lighting is more spectacular than ever. The dramatic sweeping searchlight that originally crowned the top has been restored, and for the first ten minutes of every hour from dusk until 2am (1am in winter), thousands of miniature lamps flicker and strobe, making the whole structure sparkle with light.

Musée du Quai Branly

Quai Branly. RER Pont de l'Alma/Ⓜ Place d'Iéna. Check Ⓦwww.quaibranly. fr for opening hours and prices. A short distance upstream from the Eiffel Tower, and facing the Palais de Tokyo across the river, the extravagant new Musée du Quai Branly reflects President Jacques Chirac's private passion for non-European art, and his desire to leave a lasting landmark of his troubled presidency. The museum gathers together France's magnificent collections of non-European art – sometimes called *arts primitifs* or *arts premiers* – under one extremely showy architectural roof. Architect Jean Nouvel's futuristic design featuring a glazed, curving edifice on stilts is well worth seeing in its own right. Setting aside the rather dubious politics of excluding Western art, the objects themselves are as fascinating as they are beautiful, and the museum has gone to some length to

explain their cultural, and often ritual, contexts. Four separate areas are devoted to Asia, Africa, the Americas and the Pacific ("Oceania").

The Sewers

RER Pont de l'Alma/Ⓜ Place d'Iéna. Mon–Wed, Sat & Sun: May–Sept 11am–5pm; Oct–April 11am–4pm. €4. On the northeast side of the busy junction of place de la Résistance is the entrance to one of Paris's more unusual attractions – a small, visitable section of the sewers, or *les égouts*. Once you're underground it's dark, damp and noisy with gushing water, but children may be disappointed to find that it's not too smelly. The main part of the visit runs along a gantry walk poised above a main sewer, displaying photographs, lamps, specialized sewermen's tools and other antique flotsam and jetsam, which turn the history of the city's water supply and waste management into a surprisingly fascinating topic. What the display doesn't tell you is that the work isn't quite finished. Around thirty times a year parts of the system get overloaded with rainwater, and

▲ RUE ST-DOMINIQUE

the sewermen have to empty the excess – waste and all – straight into the Seine.

Rue Cler and around

A little further upstream, the American Church on quai d'Orsay, together with the American College nearby at 31 avenue Bosquet, is a central point in the well-organized life of Paris's large American community, its noticeboard usually plastered with job and accommodation offers and requests.

Just to the south, and in stark contrast to the austerity of much of the rest of the quarter, is the attractive, villagey wedge of early nineteenth-century streets between avenue Bosquet and the Invalides. Chief among them is rue Cler, whose food shops act as a kind of permanent market. The cross-streets, rue de Grenelle and rue St-Dominique, are full of neighbourhood shops, posh *bistrots* and little hotels.

Les Invalides

Hôtel des Invalides. Ⓜ Varenne/La Tour-Maubourg Ⓦ www.invalides. org. There's no missing the overpowering facade of the Hôtel des Invalides, topped by its resplendently gilded dome. It was built on the orders of Louis XIV as a home for wounded soldiers, and part of the building is still used as a hospice. The rest houses Napoleon's tomb, in the Eglise du Dôme, and a suite of museums, the most interesting of which are detailed separately below.

Musée de l'Armée

Daily: April–Sept 10am–6pm; Oct–March 10am–5pm. €7.50, including Musée des Plans-Reliefs and Napoleon's tomb. The most fascinating section of this vast national army museum is

devoted to World War II. The battles, the resistance and the slow liberation are documented through imaginatively displayed war memorabilia combined with gripping reels of contemporary footage, many of which have an English-language option. You'll leave shocked, stirred, and with the distinct impression that Général de Gaulle was personally responsible for the liberation of France. The beautiful collection of medieval and Renaissance armour in the west wing of the royal courtyard is well worth admiring, but the core of the museum, dedicated to the history of the French army from Louis XIV up to the 1870s, is closed for restoration until at least 2008.

Musée des Plans-Reliefs

Same hours and ticket as Musée de l'Armée. Up under the roof of the east wing, the Musée des Plans-Reliefs displays an extraordinary collection of super-scale models of French ports and fortified

▲ LES INVALIDES

cities, created in the seventeenth and eighteenth centuries to aid military planning. With the eerie green glow of their landscapes only just illuminating the long, tunnel-like attic, the effect is distinctly chilling.

Eglise des Soldats

Daily: April–Sept 10am–6pm; Oct–March 10am–5pm. Free. The lofty "Soldiers' Church" is the spiritual home of the French army, its proud simplicity standing in stark contrast to the lavish Eglise du Dôme, which lies on the other side of a dividing glass wall – a design innovation that allowed worshippers to share the same high altar without the risk of coming into social contact. The walls are hung with almost one hundred enemy standards captured on the battlefield, the rump of a collection of some three thousand that once adorned Notre-Dame.

Napoleon's tomb

Same hours and ticket as Musée de l'Armée; also open mid-June to mid-Sept till 7pm. Some visitors find the Eglise du Dôme gloriously sumptuous, others think it's supremely pompous. Either way, it's overwhelming. Once

the Eglise Royale, it is now a monument to Napoleon. Sunk into the floor at the centre is the megalomaniac emperor's tomb, a giant red porphyry sarcophagus, enclosed within a gallery emblazoned with Napoleonic quotations of awesome but largely truthful conceit. When Napoleon was finally interred here, on a freezing cold day in 1840, half a million Parisians came to watch his last journey. Victor Hugo commented: "It felt as if the whole of Paris had been poured to one side of the city, like liquid in a vase which has been tilted."

Musée Rodin

79 rue de Varenne. Ⓜ Varenne. Ⓦ www.musee-rodin.fr. Tues–Sun: April–Sept 9.30am–5.45pm, garden closes 6.45pm; Oct–March 9.30am–4.45pm, garden closes 5pm. €6 or €7 during exhibitions; €1 for garden only. The captivating Musée Rodin is housed in the eighteenth-century mansion where the sculptor died in November 1917. Bronze versions of major projects like *The Burghers of Calais*, *The Thinker* and *The Gate of Hell* are exhibited in the garden, while smaller-scale works are housed indoors, their raw energy offset by the hôtel's elegant wooden panelling, tarnished mirrors and chandeliers.

The museum is usually very crowded with visitors eager to see well-loved works such as *The Hand of God* and *The Kiss*, but it's well worth lingering by the vibrant, impressionistic clay and plaster works, small studies done from life by Rodin's own hand – after completing his apprenticeship Rodin rarely picked up a chisel, in keeping with the nineteenth-century practice of artists delegating the task of working up stone and bronze versions to assistants. On

▲ NAPOLEON'S TOMB

▲ MUSEE RODIN

the ground floor a room is devoted to Camille Claudel, Rodin's pupil, model and lover – look out for the sculpture *The Age of Maturity*, which symbolizes Rodin's ultimate rejection of her.

Cafés

Café du Marché

38 rue Cler. Ⓜ La Tour-Maubourg. ☏01.47.05.51.27. Mon–Sat noon–11pm. This big, busy café-brasserie in the bustling heart of the rue Cler market serves inexpensive, market-fresh *plats du jour*.

Restaurants

L'Arpège

84 rue de Varenne. Ⓜ Varenne. ☏01.45.05.09.06. Mon–Fri noon–2.30pm & 8–11pm. Elite chef Alain Passard has shocked the gastronomic establishment at his Michelin-starred restaurant by making vegetables the highlight of his cuisine. Exhilarating cooking in a (relatively) relaxed, plain setting. Budget on €100 as a bare minimum, and book well in advance.

La Fontaine de Mars

129 rue St-Dominique. Ⓜ La Tour-Maubourg. ☏01.47.05.46.44. Daily noon–3pm & 7.30–11pm. Almost entirely decked out in genteel pinks – tablecloths, napkins, gingham café-curtains – this local restaurant is formal but friendly, and there's a wonderful summer *terrasse* under a stone arcade that's perfect for lunch (€16 *menu*).

Jules Verne

South Pillar, Eiffel Tower Ⓜ Ecole Militaire. ☏01.45.55.61.44. Daily 12.15–1.45pm & 7.15–9.45pm. Genuinely haute cuisine – served in the second-floor restaurant of the Eiffel Tower in a moodily designed, modern space with lots of romantic corners. Book three months in advance for the exceptional, highly adventurous cuisine and, of course, the views. Lunch *menu* at €49 (weekdays only), evening *menus* from €114.

Le P'tit Troquet

28 rue de l'Exposition. Ⓜ Ecole Militaire. ☏01.47.05.80.39. Mon 7.30–10pm, Tues–Sat 12.30–2.30pm & 7.30–10pm. Decked out like an elegant antiques shop, this tiny family restaurant is a very discreet place, serving refined cuisine to the diplomats and politicians of the *quartier*. Expect to pay upwards of €30.

Thoumieux

79 rue St-Dominique. Ⓜ La Tour-Maubourg. ☏01.47.05.49.75. Daily noon–3.30pm & 6.30pm–midnight. This cavernous, traditional brasserie is replete with mirrors, carved wood, hat stands and bustling, black-and-white-clad waiters. It's popular with a smart local clientele for the carefully prepared classic dishes, many from the southwest of France. The basic lunch menu is inexpensive, but you'll pay over €30 in the evening.

Montparnasse

Montparnasse has been Paris's place of play for centuries. The entertainments today are mostly glitzy cinemas and late-opening restaurants, but between the wars the celebrated cafés on boulevard du Montparnasse were filled with fashionable writers and artists such as Picasso, Matisse, Man Ray, Modigliani, Giacometti and Chagall. The most animated stretch of the boulevard begins at the ugly brown skyscraper, the Tour Montparnasse, and ends at boulevard Raspail, where Rodin's hulking statue of Balzac broods over the traffic. You can climb the tower for fantastic views or, for a complete contrast, descend into the grisly catacombs in the old quarries of Denfert-Rochereau. To hunt down Montparnasse's artistic past, visit the excellent, intimate museums dedicated to the sculptors Zadkine and Bourdelle, or the old studios that now house the gallery and exhibition space of the Musée de Montparnasse. Modern art – not to mention modern architecture – has its own cool venue, the superb Fondation Cartier, while the Fondation Cartier-Bresson puts on photography exhibitions.

▲ TOUR MONTPARNASSE

The Tour Montparnasse

33 av du Maine. Ⓜ Montparnasse-Bienvenüe. Ⓦ www. tourmontparnasse56.com. April–Sept daily 9.30am–11pm; Oct–March Mon–Thurs & Sun 9.30am–10pm, Fri & Sat 9.30am–11pm. €8.70. The two-hundred-metre-tall Tour Montparnasse may be one of the city's least-liked landmarks, but it offers fabulous views from the top – though its most vehement opponents say this is only because the tower you're standing on doesn't spoil the view. Carping aside, the panorama is arguably better than the one from the Eiffel Tower – after all, it has the Eiffel Tower in it, plus it also costs less to ascend and there are no queues. Sunset is the best time for the trip, and you could always treat yourself to a pricey drink in the 56th-storey bar.

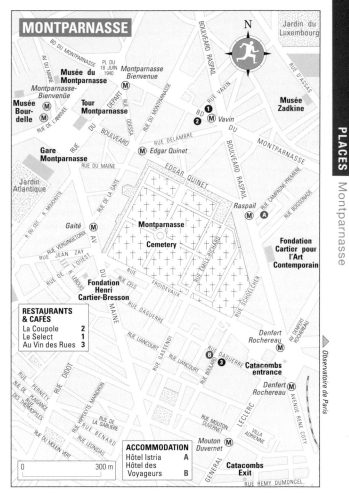

MONTPARNASSE

Jardin du Luxembourg

N

Musée du Montparnasse
Ⓜ *Montparnasse Bienvenue*
PL DU 18 JUIN 1940

BD DU MONTPARNASSE
AV DU MAINE

Montparnasse-Bienvenüe

Musée Bourdelle Ⓜ

Tour Montparnasse
RUE DE L'ARRIVÉE

RUE DU DÉPART
RUE DU MONTPARNASSE
RUE D'ODESSA
BD DU MONTPARNASSE

BOULEVARD RASPAIL
RUE VAVIN
RUE D'ASSAS

Musée Zadkine

Ⓜ ❶ ❷ Ⓜ *Vavin*
BD

Gare Montparnasse
RUE DU MAINE
RUE DELAMBRE
Ⓜ *Edgar Quinet*

BOULEVARD DU MONTPARNASSE
BOULEVARD RASPAIL

Jardin Atlantique

R DU CDT. R. MOUCHOTTE
RUE DE LA GAÎTÉ

EDGAR QUINET

Gaîté Ⓜ
R. DU MAINE
RUE VERCINGÉTORIX
RUE JEAN ZAY
RUE DE L'OUEST
RUE DE LIÉBOURS

AV DU MAINE

Montparnasse Cemetery

RUE CELS
RUE FROIDEVAUX

RUE ÉMILE RICHARD
RUE CAMPAGNE-PREMIÈRE
RUE BOISSONADE

Raspail Ⓜ Ⓐ

Fondation Cartier pour l'Art Contemporain

RUE SCHOELCHER

Fondation Henri Cartier-Bresson

RUE DAGUERRE

RESTAURANTS & CAFÉS
La Coupole 2
Le Select 1
Au Vin des Rues 3

RUE LIANCOURT
RUE DAGUERRE

Denfert Rochereau Ⓜ

AV. DENFERT ROCHEREAU

RUE GASSENDI
RUE LIANCOURT
RUE BOULARD
RUE DAGUERRE
Ⓑ ❸ **Catacombs entrance**

Denfert Rochereau Ⓜ

AVENUE RENÉ COTY
LECLERC
VILLA ADRIENNE

RUE BERNETY
RUE DE PLAISANCE
RUE DES THERMOPYLES
RUE DIDOT
RUE HIPPOLYTE MAINDRON
RUE DE LA SABLIÈRE
RUE BÉNARD
RUE DU MOULIN VERT
RUE LÉONIDAS

RUE MOUTON DUVERNET

Mouton Duvernet Ⓜ

ACCOMMODATION
Hôtel Istria A
Hôtel des Voyageurs B

Catacombs Exit
GÉNÉRAL
RUE RÉMY DUMONCEL

0 ——— 300 m

PLACES Montparnasse

▶ *Observatoire de Paris*

Jardin Atlantique

Access by lifts on rue Cdt. R. Mouchotte and bd Vaugirard, or by the stairs alongside platform #1 in Montparnasse station. Ⓜ Montparnasse-Bienvenüe. Open daily dawn to dusk.

Montparnasse station was once the great arrival and departure point for travellers crossing the Atlantic, and for Bretons seeking work in the capital. The connection is commemorated in the

▲ JARDIN ATLANTIQUE

extraordinary Jardin Atlantique, a sizeable park that the city planners have actually suspended on top of the train tracks, between cliff-like, high-rise apartment blocks. The park's design is a classic example of Parisian flair, with a field of Atlantic-coast grasses, wave-like undulations in the lawn, whimsical, electronically controlled fountains and sculptural areas hidden among trees.

Musée du Montparnasse

21 avenue du Maine. Ⓜ Montparnasse-Bienvenüe. Tues–Sun noon–7pm. €5. Picasso, Léger, Modigliani, Chagall, Braque and other members of the Montparnasse group of artists from the first half of the twentieth century used to dine at what was then the *Cantine des Artistes*, a canteen and studio run by Marie Vassilieff. The venue now hosts the Musée du Montparnasse, which displays exhibitions of work by Montparnasse artists, past and present. The gallery lies at the end of a secretive, ivy-clad alley, an attractive remnant of the interwar years that is still used for studio space – though mostly by expensive architects nowadays.

Musée Bourdelle

16–18 rue A. Bourdelle. Ⓜ Montparnasse-Bienvenüe. Ⓦwww. bourdelle.paris.fr. Tues–Sun 10am–6pm. €4.50. Large-scale, heroic-looking modern sculptures loom over the small, street-front courtyard of the Musée Bourdelle, providing a good taste of what's inside. The museum was created around the former *atelier* of the early twentieth-century sculptor, Antoine Bourdelle, and the highlight of the visit is the artist's atmospheric old studio, littered with half-

complete works and musty with the smells of its ageing parquet floor. The rest of the museum is more conventional, a showpiece for Bourdelle's half-naturalistic, half-geometrical style – he was Rodin's pupil and Giacometti's teacher, after all.

Musée Zadkine

100 bis rue d'Assas. Ⓜ Vavin/ RER Port-Royal. Ⓦwww.zadkine.paris. fr. Tues–Sun 10am–6pm. Free. The cottage-like home and garden studios of Cubist sculptor Ossip Zadkine, where he lived and worked from 1928 to 1967, are now overshadowed by tall buildings on all sides, and occupied by the tiny but satisfying Musée Zadkine. A mixture of slender, elongated figures and blockier, harder-edged works are displayed in just a handful of intimate rooms, while the sculptor's Cubist bronzes are scattered about the minuscule garden, sheltering under trees or emerging from clumps of bamboo. The site is low-key, but invites contemplative lingering.

Fondation Cartier pour l'Art Contemporain

261 bd Raspail. Ⓜ Raspail. Ⓦwww. fondation.cartier.fr. Tues–Sun noon–8pm. €6.50. The Fondation Cartier pour l'Art Contemporain is a stunningly translucent construction designed by Jean Nouvel in 1994. A bold wall of glass follows the line of the street, attached by thin steel struts to the building proper, which is also built almost entirely of glass. All kinds of contemporary art – installations, videos, multimedia pieces – often by foreign artists little known in France, are shown in temporary exhibitions that use the building's light and very generous spaces to maximum

advantage. Photographer Herb Ritts' work has been showcased here, Issey Miyake has experimented with fabric designs, and a group of artists and photographers has collaborated on an exhibition inspired by the Amazonian Yanomami people.

Montparnasse cemetery

Boulevard Edgar Quinet. Ⓜ Raspail/ Gaîté/Edgar Quinet. 16 March–5 Nov Mon–Fri 8am–6pm, Sat 8.30am–6pm, Sun 9am–6pm; 6 Nov–15 March closes 5.30pm. Fascinating rather than gloomy, Montparnasse cemetery is filled with ranks of miniature temples whose architecture ranges from the austere to the utterly sentimental. There are plenty of illustrious names to chase up, too.

To the right of the main entrance on boulevard Edgar Quinet, by the wall, is the unembellished joint grave of Jean-Paul Sartre and Simone de Beauvoir – Sartre lived out the last few decades of his life just a few metres away on boulevard Raspail. Down avenue de l'Ouest, which follows the western wall of the cemetery, you'll find the tombs of Baudelaire, the painter Soutine, Dadaist Tristan Tzara, Zadkine, and the Fascist Pierre Laval, a member of Pétain's government who, after the war, was executed for treason, not long after a suicide attempt. As an antidote, you can pay homage to Proudhon, the anarchist who coined the phrase "Property is theft!"; he lies in Division 1, by the Carrefour du Rond-Point.

In the southwest corner of the cemetery is an old windmill, which housed a famously raucous tavern in the seventeenth century.

Across rue Emile-Richard,

in the eastern section of the cemetery, lie car-maker André Citroën, Guy de Maupassant, César Franck, and the celebrated victim of French anti-Semitism at the end of the nineteenth century, Captain Dreyfus. Hidden away in the northern corner is a tomb crowned with a version of Brancusi's sculpture, *The Kiss* – an utterly poignant statement of grief.

Fondation Henri Cartier-Bresson

Impasse Lebouis. Ⓜ Gaîté. Ⓦwww. henricartierbresson.org. Tues–Fri & Sun 1–6.30pm, Wed until 8.30pm, Sat 11am–6.45pm; closed Aug. €5; free Wed 6.30–8.30pm. Old-fashioned networks of streets still exist in the Pernety and Plaisance *quartiers*, immediately south of Montparnasse cemetery. It's an appropriately atmospheric location for the Fondation Henri Cartier-Bresson, which puts on excellent photography exhibitions, often focusing on celebrated, individual photographers, alternating with shows of the work of the great Parisian photojournalist himself. Check in advance what's on, as the museum is closed between exhibitions.

PLACES Montparnasse

▲ MONTPARNASSE CEMETERY

The Catacombs

Place Denfert-Rochereau. Ⓜ Denfert-Rochereau. ⓦ www.catacombes.paris.fr. Tues–Sun 10am–4pm. €5. Paris's catacombs are frankly weird. The entrance in the middle of busy place Denfert-Rochereau – formerly place d'Enfer, or "Hell Square" – takes you down into what was once an underground quarry, but is now a series of tunnels lined with seemingly endless heaps of human bones. It's estimated that the remains of six million Parisians are interred here, which is more than double the population of the modern city (not counting the suburbs). The bones originally came from Paris's old charnel houses and cemeteries, which had become overstocked health hazards and were cleared between 1785 and 1871. The fact that the long femurs and skulls are stacked in elaborate geometric patterns makes the effect bizarre rather than spooky, and some visitors find the experience genuinely unsettling. Older children often love it, but there are a good couple of kilometres to walk, and it can quickly become claustrophobic, not to mention cold and gungy underfoot.

▲ CATACOMBS

Cafés

Le Select

99 bd du Montparnasse. Ⓜ Vavin. Mon–Thurs & Sun till 3am, Fri & Sat till 4.30am. Perhaps not quite as famous as its immediate neighbours – the *Dôme*, the *Rotonde* and the other Montparnasse cafés frequented by Picasso, Modigliani, Cocteau and the rest – but much less spoilt, distinctly less expensive and infinitely more satisfying. Perfect for a coffee or just possibly a Cognac.

Restaurants

La Coupole

102 bd du Montparnasse. Ⓜ Vavin. ☏ 01.43.20.14.20. Daily 8.30am–1am. The largest and perhaps the most enduring arty-chic Parisian hang-out for dining, dancing and debate. The place buzzes with conversation and clatter from the diners packed in tightly under the high, chandeliered roof. The menus are moderately priced at lunch, becoming more expensive in the evening at around €35 and up; if you can wait until 10.30pm you'll be able to take advantage of their great-value late-night menu for under €25.

Au Vin des Rues

21 rue Boulard. Ⓜ Denfert-Rochereau. ☏ 01.43.22.19.78. Mon–Sat noon–3pm & 7.30–11pm, Sun 7.30–11pm. This utterly traditional French wine bar and *bistrot* was once photographer Robert Doisneau's favourite, and still seems to have the same rickety wooden chairs. It serves satisfyingly unreconstructed classic meals for around €30 a head.

Southern Paris

You might not think of venturing into the relatively amorphous swathe of southern Paris, but there are some beguiling, untouched pockets of the old city to explore, as well as an excellent flea market, the Puces de Vanves. Some of the city's loveliest public parks are found on the southernmost fringes of the city, too: the Parc Montsouris has been imaginatively landscaped while the futuristic Parc André-Citroën has its own giant helium balloon, offering fantastic views. There are few sights as such, though you could make the pilgrimage to the Bibliothèque Nationale de France, the gargantuan, hyper-modern national library. In the evening, Chinatown has obvious culinary attractions, while the Butte-aux-Cailles, one of southern Paris's most characterful quarters, offers lots of excellent, relaxed restaurants and bars.

Allée des Cygnes

Ⓜ Bir-Hakeim. Of all the oddball sights in southern Paris, the allée des Cygnes is probably the most eccentric. It might not sound promising – the "alley" is basically a narrow, embanked concrete avenue lined with trees – but once you've strolled down from the double-decker road and rail bridge, the Pont de Bir-Hakeim, taken in the views of the Eiffel Tower, admired the passing coal barges and visited the small-scale version of the Statue of Liberty at the southern tip of the island, you might just share Samuel Beckett's opinion of the place – it was one of his favourite spots in Paris.

Parc André-Citroën

quai André-Citroën. Ⓜ Lourmel/Javel-André-Citroën/RER bd Victor. Mon–Fri 8am–dusk, Sat & Sun 9am–dusk. Balloon rides daily 9am to 40min before park closure; call to check weather conditions on the day ℡01.44.26.20.00. Mon–Fri

€10, under-12s €5; Sat & Sun €12, under-12s €6. The riverfront south of the Eiffel Tower bristles with office blocks and miniature skyscrapers, but at the southwestern extreme of the city limits lies the open, landscaped space of the Parc André-Citroën. It's not a park for traditionalists: there is a central grassy area, but elsewhere are concrete terraces and walled gardens with abstract themes, hothouses and a large platform sprouting a capricious set of automated fountain jets, luring children and occasionally adults to dodge the sudden spurts of water. Best of all is the tethered balloon, which rises and sinks regularly on calm days, taking small groups up for great views of the city.

Puces de Vanves

av Marc-Sangnier & av Georges-Lafenestre. Ⓜ Porte de Vanves. Sat & Sun 7am–1pm. For original finds, the city's best flea market is the Puces de Vanves. It starts

RESTAURANTS, CAFÉS & BARS
Le Bambou	5
Le Café du Commerce	1
L'Entrepôt	4
L'Os à Moëlle	2
Tricotin	6

CLUBS
Batofar	3

ACCOMMODATION
Hôtel de la Loire	D
Hôtel Port-Royal	B
Hôtel Printemps	A
Hôtel Tolbiac	E
Résidence des Gobelins	C

SOUTHERN PARIS

at daybreak at weekends, when endless stalls selling trinkets, knick-knacks and miscellaneous collectables are set up in a long line down avenues Marc-Sangnier and Georges-Lafenestre. It's well worth the long haul out to the city's southern edge – take métro line 13 to Porte de Vanves and

follow the signs – for an excellent morning's curiosity-shopping.

Parc Montsouris

RER Cité-Universitaire. At the southern limits of the city lies the Parc Montsouris. It's a pleasant place to wander, with its winding, contouring paths, its waterfall above the lake and the RER train tracks cutting right through. More surprising features include a meteorological office, a marker of the old meridian line, near boulevard Jourdan, and, by the southwest entrance, a kiosk run by the French Astronomy Association. For a longer walk, you could explore the artistic associations of the immediate neighbourhood. Le Corbusier built the studio at 53 avenue Reille, which runs along the north side of the park, while just off rue Nansouty, the road that follows the park's western edge, lies the secretive and verdant

▲ PUCES DE VANVES

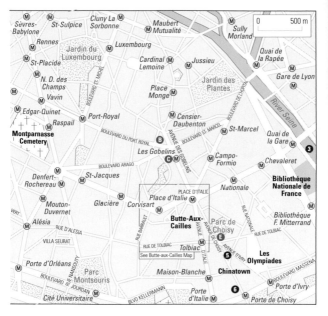

square du Montsouris, and Georges Braque's home on rue Georges Braque. Five minutes' walk to the north, Dalí, Lurçat, Miller and Durrell once lived in the tiny cobbled street of Villa Seurat, off rue de la Tombe-Issoire.

The Butte-aux-Cailles

Ⓜ Corvisart/Place d'Italie. The almost untouched quartier of the Butte-aux-Cailles, with its little streets and cul-de-sacs of prewar houses and studios, is typical of pre-1960s Paris. The rue de la Butte-aux-Cailles itself is the animated heart of the area, lined with trendy but laidback bars and restaurants, most of which stay open till the early hours.

Chinatown

Ⓜ Tolbiac. You can find Paris's best southeast Asian cuisine in the area that's known as Chinatown, despite the presence of several

other east Asian communities. Chinese, Lao, Cambodian, Thai and Vietnamese shops and restaurants fill avenue d'Ivry and avenue de Choisy all the way down to the city limits. The strangest section of the quarter, known as Les Olympiades, is an elevated platform hidden away between giant tower blocks and accessed by escalators from the streets around – rue Nationale, rue de Tolbiac and avenue d'Ivry. At 66 avenue d'Ivry, an escalator climbs up next door to a sliproad leading down to an underground car park; halfway down this access road lurks a tiny Buddhist temple and community centre, advertised by a pair of red Chinese lanterns dimly visible in the gloom.

Bibliothèque Nationale de France

Quai de la Gare. Ⓜ Quai de la Gare/ Bibliothèque François Mitterrand.

BUTTE-AUX-CAILLES

N

PLACE D'ITALIE
Place d'Italie

BLANQUI

Corvisart

AUGUSTE

BUTTE-AUX-CAILLES ❶

BOBILLOT

R. SIMONETTE

RUE

RUE BARRAULT

RUE DE LA BUTTE

❷

❸

AUX

❹

CAILLES

❺

AVENUE DE CHOISY

RUE VANDRENNE

AVENUE D'ITALIE

RUE DU MOULIN

Jardin de la Montgolfière

Tolbiac

RUE DE TOLBIAC

0   100 m

RESTAURANTS, CAFÉS BARS & CLUBS

L'Avant Goût	1
Chez Gladines	2
La Folie en Tête	5
Le Merle Moqueur	4
Le Temps des Cerises	3

ⓦ www.bnf.fr. Tues–Sat 9am–7pm, Sun 1–7pm. €3.30 for a day pass. Architect Dominique Perault's Bibliothèque Nationale de France dominates this heavily modernized section of the riverbank with four enormous L-shaped towers. These are supposed to mimic open books, reflecting what's inside them – the national library. They look down on a huge sunken pine wood, with glass walls that filter light into the floors below your feet. There are occasional exhibitions inside, and the reading rooms on the "haut-jardin" level are open to everyone over 16.

Cafés

L'Entrepôt

7–9 rue Francis-de-Pressensé. Mon–Sat noon–2am. This arts cinema has a spacious, relaxed café with a conservatory area, and outside seating in the courtyard. There are moderately priced, tasty *plats* and an excellent Sunday brunch, while regular live music and arts events keep the place humming.

▲ BIBLIOTHEQUE NATIONALE DE FRANCE

Restaurants

L'Avant Goût

37 rue Bobillot. Ⓜ Place d'Italie. ☎01.45.81.14.06. Tues–Sat noon–2.30pm & 7.30–11pm; closed three weeks in Aug. Small neighbourhood restaurant with a big reputation for exciting modern French cuisine, and wines to match. The contemporary decor, with its red banquettes, and the stylishly presented dishes are distinctly cool. There's a superb-value lunch menu for less than €15, and you won't pay over the odds in the evening either – around €30–45, plus wine.

Le Bambou

70 rue Baudricourt. Ⓜ Tolbiac. ☎01.45.70.91.75. Tues–Sun noon–3pm & 7–10.30pm. Tiny Chinatown bistro crammed with punters tucking into sublimely fresh-tasting, inexpensive Vietnamese food. They serve giant, powerfully flavoured *pho* soups, packed with beef and noodles (choose the large version only if you really mean it), a full menu of specialities and their addictive Vietnamese coffee, made with condensed milk.

Le Café du Commerce

51 rue du Commerce. Ⓜ Emile Zola. ☎01.45.75.03.27. Daily noon–midnight. This deeply old-fashioned brasserie has a dramatic, buzzing setting around a central atrium, with tables on the balconies at three levels. The menu lists all the classics, with a strong emphasis on high-quality meat. Lunch menus are splendidly inexpensive, but prices rise somewhat in the evening, though the bill is never excessive.

Chez Gladines

30 rue des Cinq-Diamants. Ⓜ Corvisart. ☎01.45.80.70.10. Mon & Tues noon–3pm & 7pm–midnight, Wed–Sun noon–3pm & 7pm–1am. This tiny corner bistro is always warm and cosy, with a young clientele packed in on rickety tables between the bar and the windows. Serves excellent wines and hearty Basque and southwest dishes such as *magret de canard* or a giant, warm salad with saucisson and egg. Filling and excellent value.

Le Merle Moqueur

11 rue de la Butte-aux-Cailles. Ⓜ Place d'Italie/Corvisart. Daily 5pm–2am. Tiny bar with a distressed chic ambience, serving up chilled-out music and home-made flavoured rums to young Parisians.

L'Os à Moëlle

3 rue Vasco de Gama. Ⓜ Lourmel. ☎01.45.57.27.27. Tues–Sat noon–2pm & 7pm–midnight; closed Aug. On the southwestern edge of the city, chef Thierry Faucher's relaxed neighbourhood *bistrot* offers superb French cuisine at reasonable prices (evening

▲ L'OS A MOELLE

menu at €38). His *Cave de l'Os à Moëlle* (☎01.45.57.28.88), across the road, is a friendly wine bar with two big communal tables groaning with the same exciting dishes as the *bistrot*. For a mere €20 you just help yourself...

Le Temps des Cerises

18–20 rue de la Butte-aux-Cailles. Ⓜ Place d'Italie/Corvisart. ☎01.45.89.69.48. Mon–Fri noon–2.15pm & 7.30–11.45pm, Sat 7.30pm–midnight. Truly welcoming restaurant – it's run as a workers' co-op – with elbow-to-elbow seating and a different daily choice of imaginative dishes. Inexpensive lunch and evening *menus*, though there are opportunities to splash out a little too.

Tricotin

15 av de Choisy. Ⓜ Porte-de-Choisy. ☎01.45.85.51.52 & t01.45.84.74.44. Daily 9am–11.30pm. Glazed in like a pair of overgrown fish tanks, the twin *Tricotin* restaurants are just set back from the broad avenue de Choisy, at the south end of Chinatown (next to the Chinese-signed *McDonald's*). Both cover much the same ground, and cover it well and inexpensively. Restaurant no. 1 (closed Tues) specializes in Thai and grilled dishes, while no. 2 has a longer list of Vietnamese, Cambodian and steamed foods.

Bars

La Folie en Tête

33 rue de la Butte-aux-Cailles. Ⓜ Place d'Italie/Corvisart. Mon–Sat 5pm–2am. This is the classic Butte-aux-Cailles address, a laidback and alternative-spirited bar playing world music and modern French *chanson* and serving beers and coffees to a young, lefty clientele. Cheap drinks and snacks are available in the daytime.

Clubs

Batofar

Quai de la Gare. Ⓜ Quai de la Gare. Daily 9pm–3am. Admission €10–12. This old lighthouse boat moored at the foot of the Bibliothèque Nationale is an excellent bet for a not-too-expensive night out, with a kooky, slightly grungy atmosphere, an eclectic music policy and a diverse clientele. If you don't like the music you hear from the quay, you can also check *Péniche Makara*, or *La Guinguette Pirate*, adjacent.

Montmartre and northern Paris

One of the most romantic quarters in Paris, **Montmartre** is principally famous for being the home, place of work and playpen of artists such as Renoir, Degas, Picasso and Toulouse-Lautrec. For most of its history, Montmartre was a hilltop village outside the city walls, and today the steep streets around the **Butte Montmartre**, Paris's highest point, preserve an attractively village-like atmosphere – although the very crown of the hill, around **place du Tertre**, is overrun with tourists. The Butte is topped by the church of **Sacré-Cœur** whose bulbous white domes are visible all over the city. As Montmartre becomes ever more gentrified, brassy **Pigalle** still laps up against the foot of the Butte, its boulevards buzzing with nightspots, ethnic fast-food outlets, cabarets, clubs and, of course, brothels. South again, and in complete contrast, is the genteel and handsome **9e arrondissement**, with its two elegant museums: the **Musée de la Vie Romantique** and the **Musée Moreau**. On the northern edge of the city limits, the mammoth **St-Ouen market** hawks everything from extravagant antiques to the cheapest flea-market hand-me-downs.

The Butte Montmartre

Ⓜ Anvers/Abbesses. The name "Montmartre" is probably a corruption of Mons Martyrum – the Martyrs' Hill – but its origins may lie further back with Mons Martis, a Roman shrine to Mars. You can get a dim sense of this pagan past if you stand on top of the Butte Montmartre, the highest point in Paris at 130m, and look down on the sun falling across the valley of the Seine. The quickest way up is by the funicular, which is part of the city's métro system, so passes or métro tickets can be used. You can also go straight up the steps from square Willette, directly below Sacré-Cœur, but it's more fun to make up a route through the winding streets of Montmartre, a few steps to the west.

Place des Abbesses

Ⓜ Abbesses. Postcard-pretty place des Abbesses has one of the only two original Guimard Art-Nouveau métro entrances that survive intact. The streets immediately around the square are relatively chichi for Montmartre, with lots of boutique clothing shops – this is a good area for fashion exploration if you're after one-off outfits and accessories. From here you can head up rue de la Vieuville, from where the stairs in rue Drevet lead to the minuscule place du Calvaire, which has a lovely view back over the city.

CLUBS & VENUES

Le Divan du Monde	16
Elysée Montmartre	15
Folies Pigalle	18
Le Lapin Agile	1
New Morning	20

RESTAURANTS, CAFÉS & BARS

Le Bar du Relais	5	Julien	23
Café des Deux Moulins	8	Le Martel	19
Chez Camille	6	Le Mono	7
Chez les Fondus	12	A la Pomponnette	2
L'Eté en Pente Douce	4	Pooja	22
La Famille	9	Le Progrès	14
Flo	21	Le Relais Gascon	13
La Fourmi Café	17	Le Sancerre	10
Au Grain de Folie	11	Au Virage Lepic	3

MONTMARTRE & NORTHERN PARIS

0   300 m

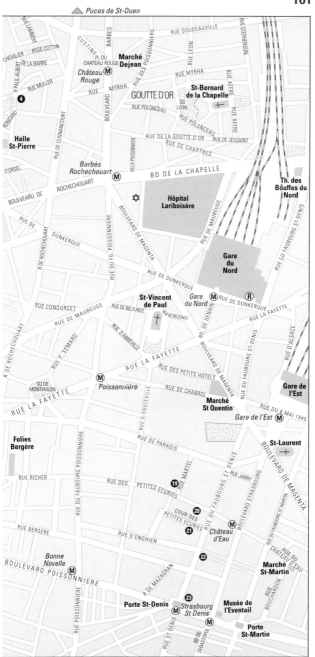

Puces de St-Ouen

RUE LAMBERT
RUE LETORT
CHEVALIER PSGE COTTIN
R PAUL ALBERT
RUE DE LA BARRE
RONSARD
RUE MULLER

CUSTINE
BARBES
PL DU CHATEAU ROUGE
Marché Dejean
Château Rouge (M)
RUE
MYRHA
BOULEVARD
GOUTTE D'OR
RUE DES POISSONNIERS
RUE LEON
RUE DOUDEAUVILLE
RUE MYRHA
RUE STEPHENSON
St-Bernard de la Chapelle
RUE AFFRE
SQ LEON
RUE POLONCEAU
RUE POLONCEAU
RUE DE LA GOUTTE D'OR
RUE DE JESSAINT
RUE DE CHARTRES
RUE AFFRE

❹

Halle St-Pierre
D'ORSEL
BOULEVARD DE
RUE DE
DUNKERQUE
RUE CONDORCET
R DE ROCHECHOUART

RUE DE CLIGNANCOURT
Barbès Rochechouart (M)
ROCHECHOUART
✡
VILLA POISSONNIÈRE
BD DE LA CHAPELLE
Hôpital Lariboisère
RUE DE MAUBEUGE
BOULEVARD DE MAGENTA
RUE DE DUNKERQUE

Th. des Bouffes du Nord

RUE DU FG. POISSONNIÈRE

Gare du Nord
RUE LU FAUBOURG ST-DENIS

RUE DE MAUBEUGE
RUE DE BELZUNCE
St-Vincent de Paul
RUE DE BELZUNCE
RUE D'ABBEVILLE
Gare du Nord (M) RUE DE DUNKERQUE (R)
BD DE DENAIN
RUE LA FAYETTE
RUE D'ALSACE

RUE P. SEMARD
RUE LA FAYETTE
Poissonnière (M)
RUE DES PETITS HOTELS
RUE DE CHABROL
BOULEVARD DE MAGENTA
RUE DU FAUBOURG ST-DENIS
Marché St Quentin
Gare de l'Est
RUE DU 8 MAI 1945
Gare de l'Est (M)

SQ DE MONTHOLON
RUE LA FAYETTE

Folies Bergère
RUE RICHER
RUE BERGERE
RUE DU FAUBOURG POISSONNIÈRE
RUE DE PARADIS
RUE DE HAUTEVILLE
RUE DES PETITES ECURIES
RUE MARTEL
St-Laurent ✚
BOULEVARD DE MAGENTA
BOULEVARD STRASBOURG
RUE JARRY

❶❾
❷⓿
COUR DES PETITES ECURIES
❷❶
Château d'Eau (M)
RUE DU FAUBOURG ST-DENIS
RUE DU FAUBOURG ST MARTIN
RUE DU CHATEAU D'EAU
Marché St-Martin

❷❷

Bonne Novelle (M)
BOULEVARD POISSONNIERE
R DE MAZAGRAN
❷❸
Porte St-Denis
Strasbourg St Denis (M)
Musée de l'Eventail
Porte St-Martin
RUE ST DENIS
BD DE SEBASTOPOL
RUE BOUCHARDON

Moulin de la Galette

Ⓜ Abbesses/Lamarck–Caulaincourt.
On rue Lepic stands the
imposing, wooden Moulin de
la Galette. This is one of only
two survivors of Montmartre's
forty-odd windmills, and once
held fashionable dances – as
immortalized by Renoir in his
Bal du Moulin de la Galette, which
hangs in the Musée d'Orsay.

Place Emile-Goudeau

Ⓜ Abbesses/Anvers. Halfway up
steep, curving rue Ravignan is
tiny place Emile-Goudeau, where
Picasso, Braque and Juan Gris
initiated the Cubist movement
in an old piano factory known as
the Bateau-Lavoir. The current
building is actually a faithful
reconstruction, but it's still
occupied by studios. With its
bench and little iron fountain,
the *place* is a lovely spot to draw
breath on your way up the Butte.

Place du Tertre and St-Pierre-de-Montmartre

Ⓜ Abbesses. The bogus heart of
Montmartre, the place du Tertre,
is photogenic but jammed with
sightseers, overpriced restaurants
and artists selling lurid oils of
Paris landmarks. At the east
end of the *place*, however,
stands the serene church of
St-Pierre-de-Montmartre, the
oldest in Paris, along with St-
Germain-des-Prés. Although
much altered since it was built
as a Benedictine convent in the
twelfth century, the church
still retains its Romanesque and
early Gothic character. The four
ancient columns inside – two by
the door and two in the choir
– are probably leftovers from the
Roman shrine that stood on the
hill, and their capitals date from
Merovingian times, as does the
cemetery outside.

Sacré-Cœur

Ⓜ Anvers/Abbesses.
Daily 6am–10.15pm.
Dome daily: April–Sept
8.30am–7pm; Oct–March
9am–6pm. €5 for the
dome. Crowning the
Butte, Sacré-Cœur
is a weird pastiche
of Byzantine-style
architecture whose
white tower and ice-
cream-scoop dome
has nevertheless
become a much-loved
part of the Paris
skyline. Construction
was started in the
1870s on the initiative
of the Catholic
Church to atone
for the "crimes" of
the revolutionary
Commune, which
first attempted to
seize power by
dominating the

▲ ABBESSES METRO

heights of Montmartre. There's little to see in the oversized and soulless interior, but climbing up the dome gets you almost as high as the Eiffel Tower. The view from the top is fantastic, but best enjoyed early in the morning or later in the afternoon if you don't want to look straight into the sun.

Musée de Montmartre

12 rue Cortot. Ⓜ Lamarck–Caulaincourt. ⓦ www.museedemontmartre.fr. Tues–Sun 10am–6pm. €5.50. This pretty, old Montmartre house, occupied at various times by Renoir, Dufy, Suzanne Valadon and her son Utrillo, is now the low-key Musée de Montmartre, where posters, paintings and mock-ups of various period rooms attempt to recall the atmosphere of Montmartre's pioneering heyday. There's a magnificent view from the back over the hilly northern reaches of the city and the tiny Montmartre vineyard, and the shop usually has a few bottles of the rather acid - but nevertheless eminently collectable – Montmartre wine, which they sell for around €40.

Montmartre vineyard area

Ⓜ Lamarck–Caulaincourt. The streets falling away to the north of the Butte are among the quietest and least touristy in Montmartre, and a good bet for a romantic stroll. Head down past the Montmartre vineyard, which produces some 1500 bottles a year, and the St-Vincent cemetery. From rue du Mont Cenis, just east of the museum, there's a particularly picturesque view north of some typical Montmartre steps, complete with their double handrail running down the centre, and lampposts between.

Montmartre cemetery

Entrance on av Rachel, underneath rue Caulaincourt. Ⓜ Blanche/Place de Clichy. March 16–Nov 5 Mon–Fri 8am–6pm, Sat from 8.30am, Sun from 9am; Nov 6 to March 15 closes 5.30pm. Tucked down below street level in the hollow of an old quarry is Montmartre cemetery, a tangle of trees and funerary pomposity that feels more intimate and less melancholy than Père-Lachaise or Montparnasse. The illustrious dead at rest here include Stendhal, Berlioz, Degas, Nijinsky and François Truffaut, as well La Goulue, the dancer at the Moulin Rouge immortalized by Toulouse-Lautrec. Zola's grave, with its recumbent figure of a corpse, is another fascinating one to look out for, though his remains have been transferred to the Panthéon. There's also a large Jewish section by the east wall. By the entrance, look out for a curious, antique cast-iron poor-box (*Tronc pour les Pauvres*).

Puces de St-Ouen

Ⓜ Porte de Clignancourt. Mon, Sat & Sun 9am–6.30pm weather dependent; many stands closed Mon. The Puces de St-Ouen spreads beyond the *périphérique* ring road, at the northern edge of the city, between the Porte de St-Ouen and the Porte de Clignancourt. It's often called the largest flea market in the world, though it's predominantly a proper antiques market, selling mainly furniture but also such fashionable junk as old café counters, telephones, traffic lights, posters, jukeboxes and petrol pumps. Although it's great fun wandering around this section, don't expect any bargains. Each of the twelve official markets within the complex has a slightly different character. Marché Biron is the poshest – Marché Cambo,

Marché Antica and Marché Malassis all sell serious and expensive antique furniture. Marché Vernaison – the oldest – has the most diverse collection of old and new furniture and knick-knacks, while Marché Serpette and Marché des Rosiers concentrate on twentieth-century decorative pieces. The relatively new and swish Marché Dauphine has mostly expensive furniture and furnishings, while Marché Paul-Bert offers all kinds of furniture, china, and the like. Marché Malik stocks mostly discount and vintage clothes, as well as some high-class couturier stuff. Finally, there are Marché Jules-Vallès and Marché Lécuyer-Vallès, which are the cheapest, most junk-like – and most likely to throw up an unexpected treasure.

If you get hungry, make for the classic *restaurant-buvette* in the centre of Marché Vernaison, *Chez Louisette*, where the great gypsy jazz guitarist, Django Reinhardt, sometimes played. The livelier, more rough-and-ready market area is strung out along rue J.H. Fabre and rue du Dr Babinski, under the flyover of the *périphérique* and beyond the boundaries of the market proper. This area is alive with vendors selling cheap clothing and pirated DVDs and endless leather jackets.

Pigalle

Ⓜ Pigalle. The southern slopes of Montmartre are bordered by the broad, busy boulevards de Clichy and de Rochechouart.

The area where the two roads meet, around place Pigalle, has long been a byword for sleaze, with sex shows, sex shops and prostitutes vying for custom. In recent years, however, a resurgence of trendy bars, clubs and music venues have helped rescue Pigalle's reputation.

The Moulin Rouge

82 bd de Clichy. Ⓜ Blanche. ☎01.53.09.82.82, ⓦwww.moulinrouge.fr. The Moulin Rouge is probably the most famous of Paris's cabaret theatres. In the days when Toulouse-Lautrec immortalized it in his cabaret paintings, it was one of a number of bawdy, populist places of entertainment – as depicted in the blockbuster film. Nowadays, an evening at the cabaret consists of an extremely expensive (€150) Vegas-style dinner-and-show formula that attracts coachloads of package-tourists to see the glitz, the special effects and the original feathery cancans. For a show without dinner, you can get away with €97 a head at 9pm, or €87 at 11pm. Book well in advance.

Musée de l'Erotisme

72 bd de Clichy. Ⓜ Pigalle. Daily 10am–2am. €8. Appropriately placed amongst all the sex shops and shows of Pigalle, the Musée de l'Erotisme is testament to its owner's fascination with sex as

▲ ST-OUEN FLEA MARKET

expressed in folk art. The place is awash with model phalluses, fertility symbols and intertwined figurines from all over Asia, Africa and pre-Columbian Latin America, as well as lots of naughty pictures and statuettes from around Europe. Visiting the museum is by turns an instructive, seedy or hilarious experience, but it's rarely particularly erotic.

Musée de la Vie Romantique

16 rue Chaptal. Ⓜ St-Georges/ Blanche/Pigalle. Ⓦ www.vie-romantique.paris.fr. Tues–Sun 10am–6pm, closed public hols. €7 during exhibitions, otherwise free. The Musée de la Vie Romantique sets out to evoke the era when this quarter was the home of Chopin, Delacroix, Dumas and other prominent figures in the Romantic movement. The house itself, set off a surprising cobbled courtyard, once belonged to the painter Ary Scheffer. George Sand used to visit, and the ground floor consists mainly of bits and pieces associated with her, including jewels, locks of hair and a cast of her lover Chopin's surprisingly small hand. Upstairs are a number of Scheffer's sentimental aristocratic portraits.

Musée Moreau

14 rue de La Rochefoucauld. Ⓜ St-Georges/Trinité. Daily except Tues 10am–12.45pm & 2–5.15pm. €4. The bizarre and little-visited museum dedicated to the fantastical, Symbolist works of Gustave Moreau was conceived by the artist himself, to be carved out of the house he shared with his parents for many years – you can visit their tiny, stuffy apartments, crammed with furniture and trinkets. Connected by a beautiful spiral staircase, the two huge, studio-like spaces are no less cluttered: Moreau's canvases hang cheek by jowl, every surface crawling with figures and decorative swirls – literally crawling in the case of *The Daughters of Thespius* – or alive with deep colours and provocative symbolism, as in the museum's *pièce de résistance*, *Jupiter and Séméle*.

Marché Dejean

Rue Dejean. Ⓜ Château Rouge Tues–Sat roughly 9am–2pm. The gritty swathe of Paris north of the Gare du Nord has been known as the Goutte d'Or, or "drop of gold", ever since there were vineyards here. Nowadays, it's the heart of African Paris, the earlier North African immigrants having mostly given way to West Africans from the Francophone countries. The heart of the quarter is the African market filling the little urban canyon of rue Dejean, which heaves with imported groceries, exotic fish and halal meat, and thrums with shoppers. You can try African drinks and snacks, or explore the adjacent streets for CDs or perhaps colourful Senegalese fabrics.

▲ MUSEE MOREAU

Cafés

Café des Deux Moulins

15 rue Lepic. Ⓜ Blanche. Daily 7am–2am. Having seen its heyday of fans on the trawl of *Amélie* lore (she waited tables here in the film), this diner-style café is back to what it always was: a down-to-earth neighbourhood hangout, preserved in a bright, charming 1950s interior. Sunday brunch is popular.

L'Eté en Pente Douce

23 rue Muller, cnr rue Paul-Albert. Ⓜ Anvers/Château Rouge. Daily noon–midnight. Pure Montmartre atmosphere, with chairs and tables set out beside the long flight of steps that leads up to Sacré-Cœur from the eastern side. Serves decent, fairly inexpensive traditional French *plats*.

Le Progrès

1 rue Yvonne Le Tac. Ⓜ Abbesses/ Anvers. Daily 9am–2am. This café is something of a lighthouse for the young *bobos* (bohemian-bourgeoises) of Montmartre. By day a simple, relaxed café serving reasonably priced meals and salads (€12–15), at night it turns into a lively bar. The café *Le Carrousel*, opposite, boasts a south-facing *terrasse* for sunny days.

Le Sancerre

35 rue des Abbesses. Ⓜ Abbesses. Daily 7am–2am. A fashionable hangout under the southern slope of Montmartre, with a row of outside tables that's perfect for watching the world go by. The food can be disappointing, so go for a drink, or just the atmosphere on sunny days.

Restaurants

Chez les Fondus

17 rue des Trois Frères. Ⓜ Abbesses. ☎01.42.55.22.65. Daily 5pm–2am. The €15 menu gets you a hearty fondue – Bourguignonne (meat) or Savoyarde (cheese) – and your personal *biberon*, or baby bottle of wine. It's unflaggingly popular with a raucous young Parisian crowd, who squeeze onto the banquette tables between the zanily graffitied walls.

La Famille

41 rue des Trois-Frères. Ⓜ Abbesses. ☎01.42.52.11.12. Tues–Sat 9–11.15pm; closed three weeks in Aug. *La Famille* gets its name from the big table that you share with the other customers – trendy, local and thirty-something for the most part. The decor is relaxed but designer, and the adventurous menu (around €30) features zingy, constrasting flavours.

Flo

7 cours des Petites-Ecuries (off rue du Faubourg-St Denis). Ⓜ Château d'Eau. ☎01.47.70.13.59. Daily noon–3pm & 7pm–1am. Dark, handsome old-time brasserie where you eat elbow to elbow at long tables, served by waiters in ankle-length aprons. Fish and seafood are the specialities, but the food generally is excellent, as is the atmosphere. It's not cheap, but good value for the quality, especially at lunchtime, or if you have the *menu* including wine.

Au Grain de Folie

24 rue La Vieuville. Ⓜ Abbesses. ☎01.42.58.15.57. Mon–Sat 12.30–2.30pm & 7–10.30pm, Sun 12.30–10.30pm. Tiny, colourfully dilapidated vegetarian place. The food is inexpensive and organic and there's always a vegan option.

Julien

16 rue du Faubourg-St Denis. Ⓜ Strasbourg St-Denis. ☏01.47.70.12.06. Daily noon–3pm & 7pm–1am. Part of the same enterprise as *Flo*, with an even more splendid decor, all globe lamps, hat stands, white linen, brass and polished wood. Serves the same good traditional French cuisine as *Flo*, at the same prices, and it's just as crowded.

Le Martel

3 rue Martel. Ⓜ Château d'Eau. ☏01.47.70.67.56. Mon–Fri noon–2.30pm & 7.30–11pm, Sat 7.30pm–11pm. A smart, trendy Moroccan-French *bistrot* with polished wood banquettes and dark cream walls. Ultra-low lighting and soft, trancey music adds a stylish touch. The menu is pricey for North African food: the couscous is good but the savoury-sweet pastilla and the tajines are more worth the thirty-odd euros you'll pay for a meal.

Le Mono

40 rue Véron. Ⓜ Abbesses. ☏01.46.06.99.20. Daily except Wed noon–2.30pm & 7.30–11pm. Welcoming, family-run Togolese restaurant. Mains (around €10) are mostly grilled fish or meat served with sour, hot sauces. Enjoyable atmosphere, with Afro-print tablecloths, *soukous* on the stereo and Togolese carvings on the walls.

A la Pomponnette

42 rue Lepic Ⓜ Blanche/Abbesses. ☏01.46.06.08.36. Tues–Thurs noon–2.30pm & 7–11pm, Fri & Sat noon–2.30pm & 7pm–midnight. A genuine old Montmartre *bistrot*, complete with posters, drawings, zinc-top bar and nicotine stains. The traditional French food is reliably good, but expect to pay a little extra for the location and adorable atmosphere.

Pooja

91 passage Brady (off rue du Faubourg-St Denis). Ⓜ Strasbourg–St Denis/Château d'Eau. ☏01.48.24.00.83. Mon 6–11pm, Tues–Sun noon–3pm & 6–11pm. Located in a glazed *passage* that is Paris's own slice of the Indian subcontinent, *Pooja* is slightly pricier and sometimes slightly more elaborate than its many inexpensive neighbours, so it probably has the edge – unless you feel like exploring.

Le Relais Gascon

6 rue des Abbesses ☏01.42.58.58.22. Daily 10am–2am. An excellent, welcoming lunch-stop for hearty, inexpensive Gascon *plats* and enormous hot salads.

Au Virage Lepic

61 rue Lepic. Ⓜ Blanche/Abbesses. ☏01.42.52.46.79. Daily except Tues 7pm–2am. The pink gingham napkins draped over the lamps and camp 1970s tracks quietly playing are clues that this isn't quite the classic old bistro it otherwise appears to be. The warm welcome is old-fashioned, however, as are the cosy atmosphere (tables are very close together) and satisfying, reasonably priced *cuisine bourgeoise*.

Bars

Le Bar du Relais

12 rue Ravignan. Ⓜ Abbesses. Mon–Thurs 3pm–2am, Fri–Sun noon–2am. The decor is quaint and romantic, as is the location just under the Butte, with tables out on the little square. It's perfect for an early evening glass of wine, while later on, especially at weekends, the music gets cooler and dance-oriented, and crowds gather outside for cocktails and chatter.

Chez Camille

8 rue Ravignan. Ⓜ Abbesses. Tues–Sat

9am–2am, Sun 9am–8pm. A cosy little bar on the slopes of the Butte, full of trendy-grungy media types chatting over drinks. Relaxing earlier on, fairly hectic towards the end of the night

La Fourmi Café

74 rue des Martyrs. Ⓜ Pigalle/ Abbesses. Mon–Thurs 8am–2am, Fri & Sat 8am–4am, Sun 10am–2am. Trendy but relaxed, this high-ceilinged café-bar, on a street packed with gourmet food shops, has a warm, distressed-bistro decor. It's full of conscientiously beautiful young Parisians drinking coffee by day and beers and cocktails at night.

Clubs

Elysée Montmartre

72 bd de Rochechouart. Ⓦwww. elyseemontmartre.com. A historic Montmartre club that pulls in a young, excitable crowd with its up-tempo nights, held under the huge, arching roof from around 11pm. Panik is a popular electro night on Fridays, and every other Saturday sees a cheesy, school-disco-style party, *Le Bal*, with live rock and dance acts and DJs playing 1980s French pop tunes. Frequent gigs midweek.

Folies Pigalle

11 place Pigalle. Ⓜ Pigalle. Ⓦwww.

folies-pigalle.com. Tues–Sat midnight–dawn, Sun dawn–midnight. Famed for its sleazy past, and only slightly less sleazy present, the *Folies* is a club-scene landmark for its house nights and gay-trash "after" events early Saturday morning and right through Sunday.

Live music

Le Divan du Monde

75 rue des Martyrs. Ⓜ Anvers. ☏01.44.92.77.66, Ⓦwww. divandumonde.com. The regulars at this deeply famous old café once included Toulouse-Lautrec. Now it's a youthful venue with one of the city's most diverse and exciting programmes, ranging from "photo concerts" and contemporary *chanson* nights to Balkan gypsy music and Congolese rumba. There are frequent *apéro* events from around 8pm, and dancing from midnight till dawn on weekend nights with themes such as "ethno groove".

Le Lapin Agile

22 rue des Saules. Ⓜ Lamarck–Caulaincourt. ☏01.46.06.85.87, Ⓦwww. au-lapin-agile.com. Tues–Sun 9pm–2am. This old Montmartre artists' haunt features nights of mixed cabaret (largely incomprehensible to non-Parisians), poetry and *chanson* nights. Sometimes touristy – it's fairly pricey – but often excellent.

New Morning

7–9 rue des Petites-Ecuries ☏01.45.23.51.41, Ⓦwww.newmorning. com. One of the most exciting venues in Paris, and *the* place to catch big international names in jazz and major world music acts. There are seats, and a spacious bar area behind, but it's usually standing room only in front of the stage.

Bastille and Bercy

Now one of Paris's nightlife hotspots, the lively Bastille quarter used to be a working-class district, but with the construction of the opera house, the glass-fronted Opéra Bastille, it soon became a magnet for artists and young people. Much has changed, too, in nearby Bercy. Once the largest wine market in the world, Bercy's warehouses have been stylishly converted into restaurants and bars. Other imaginative developments in the area include the Viaduc des Arts, an old railway viaduct whose arches now house a wonderful variety of craft and workshops, while the disused railway running above has been turned into a delightful green walkway, stretching all the way to the Bois de Vincennes on the city's outskirts.

Place de la Bastille

Ⓜ Bastille. The huge and usually traffic-clogged place de la Bastille is where Parisians congregate to celebrate Bastille Day on July 14, though hardly anything survives of the prison – the few remains have been transferred to square Henri-Galli at the end of boulevard Henri-IV. At the centre of the *place* is a column (Colonne de Juillet) surmounted by a gilded *Spirit of Liberty*, erected to commemorate not the surrender of the prison, but the July Revolution of 1830 that replaced the autocratic Charles X with the "Citizen King" Louis-Philippe.

Rue de Lappe

Ⓜ Bastille. One of the liveliest night-time spots in Paris is rue de Lappe, crammed with animated, young bars, full to bursting at weekends. *Balajo* (see p.175) is one remnant of a very Parisian tradition: the *bals musettes*, or music halls of 1930s Paris, frequented between wars by Piaf, Jean Gabin and Hayworth. Hip cafés and

bars have also sprung up in the surrounding streets, elbowing their way in among the fashion boutiques and wacky interior designers on rue de Charonne and the alternative, hippy outfits on rues Keller and de la Roquette.

▲ PLACE DE LA BASTILLE COLUMN

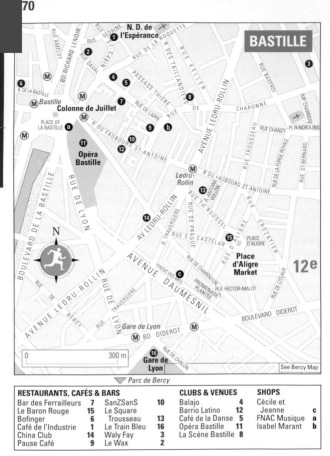

BASTILLE

Colonne de Juillet

Opéra
Bastille

Ledru-
Rollin

Place
d'Aligre
Market

12e

Gare de Lyon

Gare de
Lyon

Parc de Bercy

RESTAURANTS, CAFÉS & BARS				CLUBS & VENUES		SHOPS	
Bar des Ferrailleurs	7	SanZSanS	10	Balajo	4	Cécile et	
Le Baron Rouge	15	Le Square		Barrio Latino	12	Jeanne	c
Bofinger	6	Trousseau	13	Café de la Danse	5	FNAC Musique	a
Café de l'Industrie	1	Le Train Bleu	16	Opéra Bastille	11	Isabel Marant	b
China Club	14	Waly Fay	3	La Scène Bastille	8		
Pause Café	9	Le Wax	2				

Place d'Aligre market

Ⓜ Ledru-Rollin. Tues–Sun 7.30am–
1pm. The place d'Aligre market,
between avenue Daumesnil and
rue du Faubourg St-Antoine, is a
lively, raucous affair, particularly
at weekends. The square itself is
given over to clothes and bric-a-
brac stalls, selling anything from
old gramophone players to odd
bits of crockery. It's along the
adjoining rue d'Aligre where
the market really comes to life,
though, with the vendors, many
of Algerian origin, doing a
frenetic trade in fruit and veg.

The Promenade Plantée

Ⓜ Bastille. The Promenade
Plantée is an excellent way to see
a little-visited part of the city
– and from an unusual angle.
This stretch of disused railway
line, much of it along a viaduct,
has been ingeniously converted
into an elevated walkway and
planted with a profusion of
trees and flowers. The walkway
starts near the beginning of
avenue Daumesnil, just south of
the Bastille opera house, and is
reached via a flight of stone ste▪
– or lifts – with a number of

similar access points all the way along. It takes you to the Parc de Reuilly, then descends to ground level and continues nearly as far as the *périphérique*, from where you can follow signs to the Bois de Vincennes. The whole walk is around 4.5km long, but if you don't feel like doing the whole thing you could just walk the first part – along the viaduct – which also happens to be the most attractive stretch, running past venerable old mansion blocks and giving you a bird's eye view of the street below.

The Viaduc des Arts

Ⓜ Bastille. The arches of the Promenade Plantée's viaduct itself have been converted into attractive spaces for artisans' studios and craft shops, collectively known as the Viaduc des Arts, and include furniture and tapestry restorers, interior designers, cabinet-makers, violin- and flute-makers, embroiderers and fashion and jewellery designers; a full list and map is available from no. 23 avenue Daumesnil.

The Bois de Vincennes

Ⓜ Château de Vincennes. Daily dawn till dusk. The Bois de Vincennes is one of the largest green spaces that the city has to offer. Unfortunately it's so crisscrossed with roads that countryside sensations don't stand much of a chance. There are some pleasant corners however, including Paris's best gardens, the **Parc Floral** (daily: Nov–Jan 9.30am–5pm; Feb & Oct 9.30am–6pm; March & April 9.30am–7pm; May–Sept 9.30am–8pm; €1; Ⓦwww.parcfloraldeparis.com; Ⓜ Château-de-Vincennes, then bus #112 or a fifteen-minute walk). Flowers are always in bloom in its **Jardin des Quatre Saisons**, and you can picnic beneath pines, then wander through concentrations of camellias, rhododendrons, cacti, ferns, irises and bonsai trees. Between April and September there are art and horticultural exhibitions in several pavilions, free jazz and classical music concerts, an adventure ground for children and a mini-golf of Parisian monuments.

PLACES Bastille and Bercy

▲ PROMENADE PLANTEE

If you just feel like a lazy day out in the park, you could go boating on the **Lac Daumesnil**, near the Porte Dorée entrance and métro station (line 8). Just north of the Lac Daumesnil, at 53 avenue de St-Maurice, is the city's largest **zoo** (April–Sept Mon–Sat 9am–6pm, Sun 9am–6.30pm; Oct–March closes one hour earlier; €5), one of the first to replace cages with trenches and use landscaping to give the animals room to exercise. The animals are at their most animated during the feeding times scheduled throughout the afternoon.

Château de Vincennes

Ⓜ Château-de-Vincennes. Daily 10am–noon & 1.15–6pm. Guided tours daily: 1hr 15min €6.10; 40min €4.60. On the northern edge of the *bois* is the Château de Vincennes – erstwhile royal medieval residence, then state prison, porcelain factory, weapons dump and military training school. Highlight of the tour is the flamboyant Gothic Chapelle Royale, completed in the mid-sixteenth century and decorated with superb Renaissance stained-glass windows.

Bercy Village

Ⓜ Cour St-Emilion. Bercy village is a complex of rather handsome old wine warehouses stylishly converted into shops, restaurants and, appropriately enough, wine bars – popular places to come before or after a film at the giant Bercy multiplex cinema at the eastern end of Cour Saint Emilion.

Parc de Bercy

Ⓜ Bercy/Cour St-Emilion. The contemporary-style Parc de Bercy incorporates elements of the old warehouse site, such as disused railway tracks and cobbled lanes. The western section of the park is a fairly unexciting expanse of grass, but the area to the east has arbours, rose gardens, lily ponds and an orangerie.

La Cinémathèque Française

51 rue de Bercy. Ⓜ Bercy. Ⓦwww.cinematheque.fr. Transferred here in 2005, the Cinémathèque seems to be settling nicely into its new home, the former American centre designed by Bilbao Guggenheim architect Frank O. Gehry. On site there's a huge archive of films dating back to the earliest days of cinema, and regular retrospectives of French and foreign films are screened in its four cinemas. It also has an engaging museum (Mon & Wed–Fri noon–7pm, Thurs till 10pm, Sat & Sun 10am–8pm; €4), with lots of early cinematic equipment and silent-film clips.

Shops

Cécile et Jeanne

49 av Daumesnil. Ⓜ Gare-de-Lyon. Mon–Fri 10am–7pm, Sat & Sun 2–7pm. Reasonably priced and innovative jewellery in one of the Viaduc des Arts showrooms.

FNAC Musique

4 place de la Bastille. Ⓜ Bastille.

▲ LE BARON ROUGE

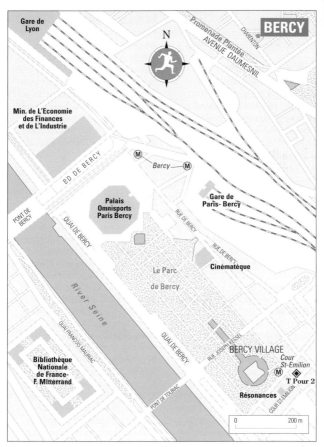

Ⓦwww.fnac.fr. Mon–Sat 10am–8pm,
Wed & Fri until 10pm. A stylish shop
in black, grey and chrome with
computerized catalogues, every
variety of music, books, and a
concert booking agency.

Isabel Marant

16 rue de Charonne. Mon–Sat
10.30am–7.30pm. Marant has
established an international
reputation for her feminine
and flattering clothes in quality
fabrics such as silk and cashmere.
Prices are above average, but not
exorbitant.

Résonances

9 Cour Saint Emilion. Ⓜ Cour St-Emilion.
Daily 11am–9pm. Stylish kitchen
and bathroom accessories, with
an emphasis on French design.
Covetable items include elegant
wine decanters and a white
porcelain hot-chocolate maker.

Cafés

Le Baron Rouge

1 rue Théophile-Roussel. Ⓜ Ledru-
Rollin. Tues–Fri 10am–2pm & 5–10pm,
Sat 10am–10pm, Sun 10.30am–
3.30pm. This *bar à vins* is as close

as you'll find to the spit-on-the-floor, saloon stereotype of the old movies; *verres* start at €1.30.

Café de l'Industrie

16 rue St-Sabin. Ⓜ Bastille. Daily 10am–2am. One of the best Bastille cafés, packed out every evening. Rugs on the floor around solid old wooden tables, mounted rhinoceros heads, old black-and-white photos on the walls and an unpretentious crowd enjoying the comfortable absence of minimalism.

Pause Café

41 rue de Charonne, cnr rue Keller. Ⓜ Ledru-Rollin. Tues–Sat 8am–2am, Sun to 9pm. A traditional café popular with the *quartier*'s young and fashionable, especially at aperitif time.

T pour 2

Bercy village, 23 Cour Saint Emilion. Ⓜ Cour Saint-Emilion. Mon–Thurs 10am–midnight, Fri–Sun 11am–2am. The old stone walls of this coolly converted wine warehouse in Bercy combine with contemporary furnishings to create an attractive and relaxed space. You can choose from a wide variety of teas and coffees by day and flavoured vodkas and rums (€9–11) by night.

Restaurants

Bofinger

7 rue de la Bastille ☎01.42.72.87.82. Daily noon–3pm & 6.30pm–1am. The popular *fin-de-siècle* brasserie, with its splendid, perfectly preserved decor, is always crowded with Bastille opera-goers and tourists. Set menu €30–50.

Le Square Trousseau

1 rue Antoine Vollon. Ⓜ Ledru-Rollin. ☎01.43.43.06.00. Tues–Sat noon–2pm & 8pm–11.30pm; closed Aug. A handsome belle époque brasserie serving old stand-bys like *pot-au-feu* and *steak au poivre*, as well as more creative dishes. Lunch *menu* for €20, evening is *à la carte* – around €35 excluding wine. Booking recommended.

Le Train Bleu

Gare de Lyon. Ⓜ Gare de Lyon. ☎01.43.43.09.06. Daily 11.30am–3pm & 7–11pm. The *Train Bleu*'s decor is straight out of a bygone golden era – everything drips with gilt, and chandeliers hang from frescoed ceilings. The traditional French cuisine is good, if a tad overpriced. The set menu costs €43, including half a bottle of wine; for *à la carte* reckon on €70.

Waly Fay

6 rue Godefroy-Cavaignac. Ⓜ Charonne/Faidherbe-Chaligny. ☎01.40.24.17.79. Mon–Sat noon–2pm & 7.30–11pm; closed last two weeks of Aug. A West African restaurant with a cosy, stylish atmosphere. Smart, young black and white Parisians come here to dine on perfumed, richly spiced stews and other West African delicacies at a moderate cost (mains €12.50).

Bars

Bar des Ferrailleurs

18 rue de Lappe. Ⓜ Bastille. Daily 5pm–2am. Dark and stylishly sinister, with rusting metal decor, an eccentric owner and a relaxed and friendly crowd.

China Club

50 rue de Charenton. Ⓜ Bastille/Ledru-Rollin. Ⓦ www.chinaclub. cc. Daily 7pm–2am, Fri & Sat until

3am; happy hour 7–9pm; closed Aug.
Packed at the weekends with a
vibrant, mixed crowd propping
up the long mahogany bar or
sipping cocktails (€6 during
happy hour, otherwise €8.50) on
comfy chesterfield sofas. Spread
over three floors, with a jazz club
downstairs and quieter space
upstairs for tête-à-têtes.

SanZSanS

49 rue du Faubourg St-Antoine. Ⓜ
Bastille. Daily 9am–2am. Gothic
decor of red velvet, oil paintings
and chandeliers, and a young
crowd in the evening. Drinks and
food reasonably priced. DJs every
evening.

Le Wax

15 rue Daval. Ⓜ Bastille. Fri & Sat
10pm–5am, Tues–Thurs 10pm–2am.
Lose yourself in the huge pod
chairs at this popular bar with
great early-1970s interior. Full
of happy young locals and
foreigners dancing to the soul,
house and electronica DJs.

Clubs

Balajo

9 rue de Lappe. Ⓜ Ledru-Rollin/
Bastille. ☎01.47.00.07.87, ⓦwww.
balajo.fr. Thurs–Sat 11pm–5am, Wed
9pm–3am. A 1930s *guinguette*
reworked into a dance club, and
still sporting its original kitsch
decor. The Sunday afternoon
tea dance (3–7pm €8 including
first drink) manages to recapture
something of the Paris of Edith
Piaf and Maurice Chevalier,
while the themed music nights,
such as R'n'B on Friday and
Saturday and rock'n'roll or salsa
on Wednesday, are a bit more run
of the mill (€12–20 including
first drink).

Barrio Latino

46–48 rue du Faubourg St-Antoine. Ⓜ
Bastille. ☎01.55.78.84.75. Mon–Thurs
& Sun 11am–2am, Fri & Sat until 3am.
Entry Thurs–Sat €8, other days free.
Tremendously popular Latin
club with dancing every night.
Cocktails €9.50.

La Scène Bastille

2 bis rue des Taillandiers. Ⓜ Bastille.
☎01.48.06.50.70, ⓦwww.la-scene.
com. Concerts Mon–Sat 8–10.45pm;
club Thurs–Sat midnight–6am; gay
tea dance Sun 6pm–2am. A club
and concert venue in a snazzily
converted warehouse. The
eclectic music policy embraces
rock, Afro-beat, funk and
reggae, although the emphasis at
weekends is on electro, techno
and house, with gay-friendly
nights most Fridays. Entry
around €12–15.

Live music

Café de la Danse

5 passage Louis-Philippe. Ⓜ Bastille.
☎01.47.00.57.59, ⓦwww.chez.com/
cafedeladanse. Open nights of concerts
only. Rock, pop, world and folk
music played in an intimate and
attractive space.

Opéra Bastille

120 rue de Lyon. Ⓜ Bastille.
☎08.36.69.78.68, ⓦwww.opera-
de-paris.fr. Opened in 1989 to a
rather mixed reception – one
critic described the amorphous
glass and steel building as a
hippopotamus in a bathtub – the
new opera house still inspires
a fair amount of controversy,
but its performances are nearly
always a sell-out. For programme
and booking details consult their
website or phone the box office.
Tickets start from as little as
€5, but most are in the €40–90
range.

Eastern Paris

Traditionally a working-class area, with a history of radical and revolutionary activity, eastern Paris is nowadays one of the most diverse and vibrant parts of the city, home to sizeable ethnic populations, as well as students and artists, drawn by the area's low rents. The area's most popular attractions are Père-Lachaise cemetery, the final resting place of many well-known artists and writers; the Canal St-Martin, with its trendy cafés and bars; and the vast, postmodern Parc de la Villette. Visiting the Parc de Belleville and the bucolic Parc des Buttes-Chaumont reveals the east's other chief asset – fantastic views of the city.

The Canal St-Martin

Built in 1825 to enable river traffic to shortcut the great western loop of the Seine around Paris, the Canal St-Martin possesses a great deal of charm, especially along its southern reaches: plane trees line the cobbled *quais,* and elegant, high-arched footbridges punctuate

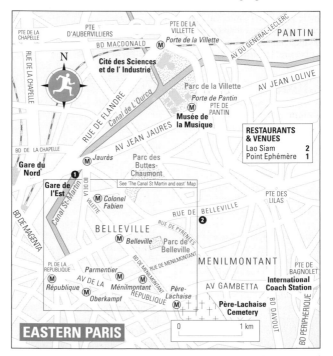

the spaces between the locks, from where you can still watch the odd barge slowly rising or sinking to the next level. In the last decade or so the area has been colonized by the new arty and media intelligentsia, bringing in their wake trendy bars, cafés and boutiques. The area is particularly lively on Sunday afternoons when the *quais* are closed to traffic, pedestrians, cyclists and rollerbladers take over the streets, and people hang out along the canal's edge, drinking beers or strumming guitars.

The Parc de la Villette

Ⓜ Porte-de-Pantin/Porte-de-la-Villette. Ⓦwww.villette.com. Daily 6am–1am. Free. Built in 1986 on the site of what was once Paris's largest abattoir and meat market, the Parc de la Villette's landscaped grounds include a state-of-the-art science museum, a superb music museum, a series of themed gardens and a number of jarring, bright-red "follies". The effect of these numerous, disparate elements can be quite disorienting – all in line with the creators' aim of eschewing meaning and "deconstructing" the whole into its parts. All very

well, but on a practical level you'll probably want to pick up a map at the information centre at the southern entrance to help you make sense of it all.

The extensive park grounds contain ten themed gardens, aimed mainly at children. In the Jardin des Miroirs, for example, steel monoliths hidden amongst the trees and scrub cast strange reflections, while, predictably, dune-like shapes, sails and windmills make up the Jardin des Dunes (for under-13s only and accompanying adults). Also popular with children is the eighty-metre-long Dragon Slide.

In front of the Cité des Sciences floats the Géode (hourly shows: Tues–Sat 10.30am–9.30pm, Sun 10.30am–7.30pm; €9), a bubble of reflecting steel that looks as though it's been dropped from an intergalactic boules game into a pool of water. Inside is a screen for Omnimax films, not noted for their plots, but a great visual experience.

Cité des Sciences et de l'Industrie

Parc de la Villette. Ⓜ Porte-de-la-Villette. Ⓦwww.cite-sciences.fr. Tues–Sat 10am–6pm, Sun 10am–7pm. €7.50. Planetarium shows 11am, noon, 2pm, 3pm, 4pm & 5pm; 35min; €2.50. Cité des Enfants ☎08.92.69.70.72; sessions Tues, Thurs & Fri 9.45am, 11.30am, 1.30pm & 3.15pm; Wed, Sat & Sun 10.30am, 12.30pm, 2.30pm & 4.30pm; €5. The Cité des Sciences et de l'Industrie is one of the world's finest science museums, set in a huge building four times the size of the Pompidou Centre. Its giant walls are made of glass and the centre of the museum is left open to the full extent of the roof, 40m high. An excellent programme of temporary exhibitions complements the permanent

▲CANAL ST-MARTIN

Eastern Paris **PLACES**

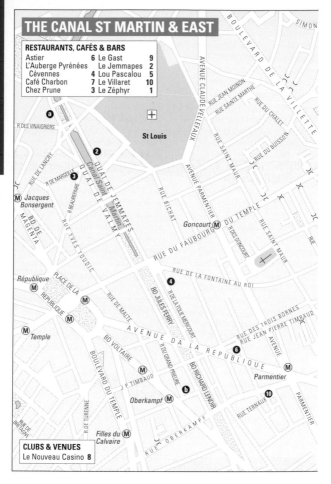

THE CANAL ST MARTIN & EAST

RESTAURANTS, CAFÉS & BARS

Astier	**6**	Le Gast	**9**
L'Auberge Pyrénées		Le Jemmapes	**2**
Cévennes	**4**	Lou Pascalou	**5**
Café Charbon	**7**	Le Villaret	**10**
Chez Prune	**3**	Le Zéphyr	**1**

St Louis

Ⓜ Jacques Bonsergent

République Ⓜ

Ⓜ

Ⓜ

Ⓜ Temple

Goncourt Ⓜ

Parmentier Ⓜ

Oberkampf Ⓜ

Filles du Ⓜ Calvaire

CLUBS & VENUES
Le Nouveau Casino **8**

▼ CITE DES SCIENCES

exhibition, called Explora, covering subjects such as sound, robotics, energy, light, ecology, maths, medicine, space and language. As the name suggests, the emphasis is on exploring, and there are numerous interactive computers, videos, holograms, animated models and games. You can have your head spun further by a session in the planetarium.

The Cité has a special section for children called the Cité des Enfants, with areas for 3- to

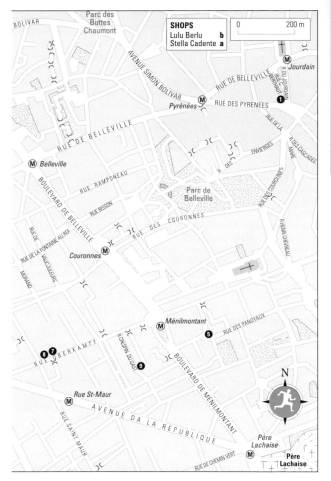

SHOPS	
Lulu Berlu	b
Stella Cadente	a

5-year-olds and 6- to 12-year-olds; all children have to be accompanied by an adult and a session lasts ninety minutes. Among the numerous engaging activities, children can play about with water, construct buildings on a miniature construction site (complete with cranes, hard hats and barrows), experiment with sound and light and manipulate robots.

Musée de la Musique

Cité de la Musique complex, Parc de la Villette. Ⓜ Porte-de-Pantin. Ⓦwww.cite-musique.fr. Tues–Sat noon–6pm, Sun 10am–6pm. €7. The Musée de la Musique presents the history of music from the end of the Renaissance to the present day, both visually, exhibiting some 4500 instruments, and aurally, via headsets (available in English; free). Glass case after glass case holds gleaming,

▲ CITE DE LA MUSIQUE

beautiful instruments: jewel-inlaid crystal flutes and a fabulous lyre-guitar are some impressive examples. The instruments are each presented in the context of a key work in the history of Western music: as you step past each case, the headphones are programmed to emit a short scholarly narration, followed by a delightful concert.

Père-Lachaise cemetery

Main entrance on bd de Ménilmontant.
Ⓜ Père-Lachaise/Philippe Auguste.
Mon–Fri 8am–5.30pm, Sat 8.30am–5.30pm, Sun 9am–5.30pm. Free.
Final resting place of a host of French and foreign notables, Père-Lachaise covers some 116 acres, making it one of the world's largest cemeteries. Size aside, it's surely also one of the most atmospheric – an eerily beautiful haven, with terraced slopes and magnificent old trees that spread their branches over the moss-grown tombs. Free plans are given out at the entrance, though it's worth buying a slightly more detailed plan, as it's tricky tracking down some of the graves; the best is the one published by Editions Métropolitain Paris (around €2), usually available in the newsagents and florists near the main entrance.

Père-Lachaise was opened in 1804 to ease the strain on the city's overflowing cemeteries and churchyards. The civil authorities had Molière, La Fontaine, Abélard and Héloïse reburied here, and to be interred in Père-Lachaise quickly acquired cachet. Among the most visited graves is that of Chopin (Division 11), often attended by Poles bearing red-and-white wreaths and flowers. Fans also flock to the ex-Doors lead singer Jim Morrison (Division 6), who died in Paris at the age of 28. You can tell when you're getting near his grave: messages in praise of love and drugs are scribbled on nearby trees and tombs.

Femme fatale Colette's tomb, close to the main entrance in Division 4, is very plain, though always covered in flowers. The same holds true for Sarah Bernhardt's (Division 44) and the great *chanteuse* Edith Piaf's (Division 97). Marcel Proust lies in his family's black-marble, conventional tomb (Division 85).

Cutting a rather romantic figure, French president Félix Faure (Division 4), who died in the arms of his mistress in the Elysée palace in 1899, lies draped

▲ OSCAR WILDE'S GRAVE, PERE-LACHAISE

in a French flag, his head to one side. One of the most impressive of the individual tombs is Oscar Wilde's (Division 89), topped with a sculpture by Jacob Epstein of a mysterious Pharaonic winged messenger (sadly vandalized of its once prominent member, last seen being used as a paper weight by the director of the cemetery).

On a much more sombre note, in Division 97, you'll find the memorials to the victims of the Nazi concentration camps and executed Resistance fighters. Marking one of the bloodiest episodes in French history is the Mur des Fédérés (Division 76), the wall where the last troops of the Paris Commune were lined up and shot in the final days of the battle in 1871.

▲ PARC DES BUTTES-CHAUMONT

Parc des Buttes-Chaumont

Ⓜ Buttes-Chaumont/Botzaris. The Parc des Buttes-Chaumont was constructed under Haussmann in the 1860s to camouflage what until then had been a desolate warren of disused quarries, rubbish dumps and shacks. Out of this rather unlikely setting, a fairy-tale-like park was created – there's a grotto with a cascade and artificial stalactites, and a picturesque lake from which a huge rock rises up, topped with a delicate Corinthian temple. From the temple you get fine views of the Sacré-Cœur and beyond, and you can also go boating on the lake in summer.

Belleville

Ⓜ Belleville/Pyrénées. Absorbed into Paris in the 1860s and subsequently built up with high-rise blocks to house migrants from rural areas and the ex-colonies, Belleville might not be exactly "belle", but it's worth seeing for another side to the city. The main street, rue de Belleville, abounds with Vietnamese, Thai and Chinese shops and restaurants, which spill south along boulevard de Belleville and rue du Faubourg-du-Temple. African and Oriental fruits, spices, music and fabrics attract shoppers to the boulevard de Belleville market on Tuesday and Friday mornings. From the Parc de Belleville, with its terraces and waterfalls, you get great views across the city, especially at sunset.

▲ PARC DE BELLEVILLE

Ménilmontant

Ⓜ Ménilmontant. Ménilmontant has a similar history to that of Belleville, and aligns itself along one straight, steep, long street, the rue de Ménilmontant and its lower extension rue Oberkampf. Although run-down in parts, its popularity with students and artists has brought a cutting-edge vitality to the area. Alternative shops and trendy bars and restaurants have sprung up among the grocers and cheap hardware stores, especially along rue Oberkampf, one of the city's premier after-dark hangouts.

Shops

Lulu Berlu

27 rue Oberkampf. Ⓜ Oberkampf. Mon–Sat 11.30am–7.30pm. This shop is crammed with twentieth-century toys and curios, most with their original packaging.

Stella Cadente

93 quai de Valmy. Ⓜ Jacques-Bonsergent. Daily 10am–7.30pm. Soft and feminine clothes, such as floaty chiffon dresses, from designer Stanislassia Klein.

Cafés

Chez Prune

36 rue Beaurepaire. Ⓜ Jacques-Bonsergent. ☎01.42.41.30.47. Mon–Sat 8am–2am, Sun 10am–2am. A laidback café, with smiley waiting staff and pleasant outdoor seating facing the canal. Lunchtime dishes cost around €12; evening snacks like platters of cheese or charcuterie are around €8; cocktails €7.

Restaurants

Astier

44 rue Jean-Pierre-Timbaud. Ⓜ Jacques-Bonsergent. ☎01.43.57.16.35. Mon–Fri noon–2pm & 8–11pm; closed Aug, plus a fortnight in May. A popular restaurant with simple decor, unstuffy atmosphere and food renowned for its freshness and refinement. Outstanding selection of perfectly ripe cheeses. Lunch €21, dinner set menu €26. Booking advised.

L'Auberge Pyrénées Cévennes

106 rue de la Folie Méricourt. Ⓜ République. ☎01.43.57.33.78. Mon–Fri noon–2pm & 7–11pm, Sat 7–11pm. Make sure you come hungry to this homely little place serving hearty portions of country cuisine. Highly recommended are the garlicky *moules marinières* for starters and the superb *cassoulet*, served in its own copper pot. Around €30 a head *à la carte*.

Lao Siam

49 rue de Belleville. Ⓜ Belleville. ☎01.40.40.09.68. Mon–Fri noon–3pm & 6–11.30pm, Sat & Sun noon–12.30am. The surroundings are nothing special, but the excellent Thai and Lao food, popular with locals, makes up for it. Dishes start at €7.

▼ CAFE CHARBON

Le Villaret

19 rue Ternaux. Ⓜ Parmentier.
☎01.43.57.89.76. Mon–Fri
noon–2pm & 7.30pm–midnight, Sat
7.30pm–midnight. This slightly
out-of-the-way place does some
of the best creative *bistrot* cuisine
in the capital. Typical dishes
are roasted country chicken in
Arbois wine sauce and there's an
exceptional wine list, with bottles
from €14. Lunchtime *formule*s
at €20 and €23, or go all out
for the €50 five-course *menu
dégustation* in the evening; *à la
carte* €30–50. Booking essential.

Le Zéphyr

1 rue Jourdain. Ⓜ Jourdain.
☎01.46.36.65.81. Daily noon–3pm &
7–11pm. Buzzy 1930s Art Deco-
style *bistrot*, with mirrors, frescoes
and dark-red leather benches at
closely packed tables. You'll pay
around €13 for lunch, double
that in the evenings, for fine
traditional cooking.

Bars

Café Charbon

109 rue Oberkampf. Ⓜ Saint-Maur/
Parmentier. ☎01.43.57.55.13. Daily
9am–2am, DJ Thurs, Fri & Sat eves
10pm–2am, live music Sun from
8.30pm. A very successful and
attractive resuscitation of an early
twentieth-century café, popular
with a young crowd.

Le Gast

5 rue Crespin-du-Gast. Ⓜ
Ménilmontant. Mon–Sat 5pm–2am.
Almost exclusively Parisian
hipsters nod their heads to goateed
drum-and-bass DJs at this small
bar, just off the Oberkampf main
drag.

Le Jemmapes

82 Quai de Jemmapes. Ⓜ Jacques
Bonsergent. ☎01.40.40.02.35. Daily
11am–2am. In the summer this
neighbourhood resto-bar and bobo
(bourgeois-bohemian) hangout is
well-known for letting its patrons
cross the road to sip at their drinks
along the banks of the canal. The
standard French cuisine is good,
but the lure here is the atmosphere.

Lou Pascalou

14 rue des Panoyaux. Ménilmontant.
Daily 9am–2am. Trendy but
friendly place with a zinc bar.
Wide range of cocktails (from
€5) and beers bottled and on tap.

Live Music

Point Ephémère

200 quai de Valmy. Ⓜ Jaurès/Louis
Blanc. ☎01.40.34.02.48. Daily
1pm–2am or later if there's live music.
A great energetic atmosphere
pervades this creative space for
music, dance and visual arts. Set
in a dilapidated canal boathouse,
the rotating art exhibitions range
from the quotidian to the abstract,
while the frequent concerts
feature cutting-edge rock and
electronica bands. The bar serves
beer and finger food, and you
can even get a decent order of
steak-frites in the ad-hoc restaurant
looking out onto the canal.

Clubs

Le Nouveau Casino

109 rue Oberkampf. Ⓜ Parmentier.
☎01.43.57.57.40, ⓦwww.
nouveaucasino.net. Tues & Wed
9pm–2am, Thurs–Sat midnight–5am.
Entry around €10–15. Right behind
Café Charbon (see above) lies this
excellent venue. An interesting,
experimental line-up of live gigs
makes way to a relaxed, dancey
crowd later on, with music
ranging from electro-pop or
house to rock.

Western Paris

Commonly referred to as the Beaux Quartiers, Paris's well-manicured western arrondissements, the 16e and 17e, are mainly residential with few specific sights, the chief exception being the Musée Marmottan, with its dazzling collection of late Monets. The most rewarding areas for exploration are the old villages of Auteuil and Passy, which were incorporated into the city in the late nineteenth century. They soon became very desirable districts, and well-to-do Parisians commissioned houses here. As a result, the area is rich in fine examples of architecture, notably by Hector Guimard and Le Corbusier. Running all the way down the west side of the 16e is the Bois de Boulogne, with its trees, lakes, cycling trails and the beautiful floral displays of the Parc de Bagatelle. Further west, modern architecture comes bang up to date with the gleaming skyscrapers of the purpose-built commercial district of La Défense, dominated by the enormous Grande Arche.

Auteuil

Ⓜ Michel-Ange-Auteuil. The Auteuil district is now an integral part of the city, but there's still a village-like feel about its streets, and it has some attractive *villas* and leafy lanes of old houses, fronted with English-style gardens, not to mention some fine Art Nouveau buildings by Hector Guimard – there's a concentration on rue de la Fontaine, the best known at no. 14, Castel Béranger, with exuberant decoration and shapes in the windows, the roofline and the chimney.

Villa La Roche

square du Dr Blanche. Ⓜ Jasmin. Mon 1.30pm–6pm, Tues–Fri 10am–12.30pm & 1.30pm–6pm, till 5pm on Fri, Sat 10am–5pm; closed Aug. €2.50. Le Corbusier's first private houses, dating to 1923, were the adjoining Villa Jeanneret and the Villa La Roche. The latter is in strictly Cubist style, very

plain, with windows in bands, the only extravagance being a curved frontage. It may look commonplace enough now from the outside, but at the time it was built it was in great contrast to anything that had gone before, and once you're inside, the spatial play still seems groundbreaking. The interior is appropriately decorated with Cubist paintings.

Place de Passy

Ⓜ Passy. The heart of the Passy *quartier* is pleasant little place de Passy, with its crowded but leisurely *Le Paris Passy* café. Leading off from here is the old high street, rue de Passy, with its eye-catching parade of boutiques, and the cobbled, pedestrianized rue de l'Annonciation, an agreeable blend of genteel affluence and the down-to-earth.

The Musée Marmottan

2 rue Louis-Boilly. Ⓜ Muette. Ⓦwww.

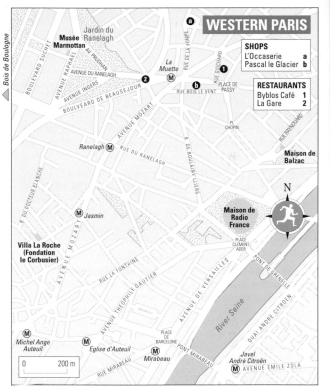

Within the map:

WESTERN PARIS

SHOPS
L'Occaserie a
Pascal le Glacier b

RESTAURANTS
Byblos Café 1
La Gare 2

Jardin du Ranelagh
Musée Marmottan
Bois de Boulogne
La Muette
PLACE DE PASSY
RUE BOIS LE VENT
Ranelagh (M) RUE DU RANELAGH
Maison de Balzac
Jasmin
Villa La Roche (Fondation le Corbusier)
Maison de Radio France
PLACE CLEMENT ADER
RUE LA FONTAINE
River Seine
Michel Ange Auteuil
Eglise d'Auteuil
Mirabeau
Javel André Citroën
AVENUE EMILE ZOLA
0 200 m
N

---

marmottan.com. Tues–Sun 10am–6pm. €7. The Musée Marmottan is best known for its excellent collection of Monet paintings. One of the highlights is *Impression, soleil levant*, a canvas from 1872 of a misty Le Havre morning, and whose title the critics usurped to give the Impressionist movement its name. There's also a dazzling selection of works from Monet's last years at Giverny, including several *Nymphéas* (Waterlilies), *Le Pont Japonais*, *L'Allée des Rosiers* and *Le Saule Pleureur*. The collection also features some of his contemporaries – Manet, Renoir and Berthe Morisot – and a room full of beautiful medieval illuminated manuscripts.

Maison de Balzac

47 rue Raynouard. (M) Passy. Tues–Sun 10am–6pm. Free. The Maison de Balzac is a summery little house with pale-green shutters, tucked away down some steps that lead through a shady, rose-filled garden – a delightful place to dally on wrought-iron seats, surrounded by busts of the writer. It was here that Balzac wrote some of his best-known works, including *La Cousine Bette* and *Le Cousin Pons*. The museum preserves his study, while other exhibits include a highly complex family tree of around a thousand of the four thousand-plus characters that feature in his *Comédie Humaine*.

▲ MAISON DE BALZAC

Bois de Boulogne

Ⓜ Porte Maillot/Porte Dauphine. The Bois de Boulogne was designed by Baron Haussmann and supposedly modelled on London's Hyde Park – though it's a very French interpretation. The "bois" of the name is somewhat deceptive, but the extensive parklands (just under 900 hectares) do contain some remnants of the once great Forêt de Rouvray. As its location would suggest, the Bois was once the playground of the wealthy. It also gained a reputation as the site of the sex trade and its associated crime; the same holds true today and you should avoid it at night. By day, however, the park is an extremely pleasant spot for a stroll. The best, and wildest, part for walking is towards the southwest corner. Bikes are available for rent at the entrance to the Jardin d'Acclimation adventure park and you can go boating on the Lac Inférieur.

Parc de Bagatelle

Bois de Boulogne. Ⓜ Porte Maillot. Daily 9am–7pm. €1.50. The Parc de Bagatelle, within the Bois de Boulogne, comprises a range of garden styles from French and English to Japanese. Its most famous feature is the stunning rose garden, at its best in June, while in other parts of the garden there are beautiful displays of

▲ BOIS DE BOULOGNE

tulips, hyacinths and daffodils in early April, irises in May, and waterlilies in early August. In June and July the park's orangery is the attractive setting for the prestigious Chopin Festival (Ⓦwww.frederic-chopin.com).

The Jardin d'Acclimatation

Bois de Boulogne. Ⓜ Porte Maillot. Ⓦwww.jardindacclimatation.fr. Daily: June–Sept 10am–7pm; Oct–May 10am–6pm. €2.70 or €5.20 including return train ride from métro; rides from €2.50. The children's Jardin d'Acclimatation is an action-packed funfair, zoo and amusement park all rolled into one. The fun starts at the Porte-Maillot métro stop: a little train runs from here to the Jardin (every 15min 11am–6pm). The park's many attractions include bumper cars, donkey rides, sea lions, bears and monkeys, a huge trampoline and a magical mini-canal ride (*la rivière enchantée*). There are also two museums: the high-tech Exploradôme (daily 10am–6pm; €5), designed to help children discover science and art, and the Musée en Herbe (Mon–Fri & Sun 10am–6pm, Sat 2–6pm), which brings art history alive through workshops and games.

La Défense

Ⓜ/RER Grande-Arche-de-la-Defense/Esplanade de la Défense. An impressive complex of gleaming skyscrapers, La Défense is Paris's prestige business district and an extraordinary monument to late-twentieth-century capitalism. Its most popular attraction is the huge Grande Arche. Between the arch and the river, apartment blocks and big businesses compete to dazzle and dizzy you, while avant-garde sculptures by artists such as Joan Miró and Torricini relieve the jungle of concrete and glass. For the most dramatic approach to the Grande Arche it's worth getting off the métro a stop early, at Ⓜ Esplanade-de-la-Défense, and walking along the Esplanade de Général de Gaulle.

Grande Arche de la Défense

Ⓜ/RER Grande-Arche-de-la-Defense. Lifts daily 10am–8pm. €7.50. The Grande Arche de la Défense, built in 1989 for the bicentenary of the Revolution, is a beautiful and astounding 112-metre-high structure, clad in white marble, standing 6km out and at a slight angle from the Arc de Triomphe, completing the western axis of this monumental east–west vista. Lifts take you up past a "cloud canopy" to the roof of the arch, from where on a clear day you can see as far as the Louvre and beyond, though the views from the bottom of the arch are almost just as good.

PLACES

Western Paris

▲ GRANDE ARCHE DE LA DEFENSE

▲ LA GARE

Shops

L'Occaserie

30 rue de la Pompe. Ⓜ Muette/
Passy. Ⓦwww.occaserie.com.
Tues–Sat 11am–7pm. Specialists in
secondhand haute couture and a
great hunting ground for Chanel
suits, Louis Vuitton handbags
and the like. While prices are
much cheaper than new, you're
still looking at around €700 for
a designer suit and about €300
for a handbag. There are several
smaller branches nearby at 16 &
21 rue de l'Annonciation, 14 rue
Jean-Bologne and 19 rue de la
Pompe.

Pascal le Glacier

17 rue Bois-le-Vent. Ⓜ Muette.
Tues–Sat 11am–6pm; closed Aug.
Exquisite home-made sorbets in
fruity flavours, such as sanguino
orange and mango.

Restaurants

Byblos Café

6 rue Guichard. Ⓜ Muette.
☎01.42.30.99.99. Daily 11am–3pm
& 7–11pm. An excellent Lebanese
restaurant, serving traditional
mezzes, moussaka and the
like in relaxed and convivial
surroundings. €15–20 a head.

La Gare

19 Chaussée de la Muette. Ⓜ
Muette. ☎01.42.15.15.31. Daily:
restaurant noon–3pm & 7–10.30pm,
bar noon–midnight. This renovated
train station is now an elegant
restaurant-bar serving, among
other things, a very popular set
lunch (€17). You can sit out on
the attractive terrace on sunny
days.

Excursions

Even if you're on a weekend break, a handful of major sights may tempt you beyond the city limits. There's the château de Versailles, the ultimate French royal palace, awesome in its size and magnificence. St-Denis, just beyond the city centre, is principally famous for its historic Gothic cathedral, the burial place of the kings of France. As for Disneyland Paris, 25km east of the capital, there are no two ways about it – children will love it. It offers a good variety of fear-and-thrill rides along with the Disney-themed spectacles, and it's easy to visit as a day-trip.

Château de Versailles

RER Line C to Versailles-Rive Gauche station (40min); signposted 10min walk from the station. ⓦwww. chateauversailles.fr. Tues–Sun except hols; May–Sept 9am–6pm; Oct–April 9am–5pm. €8, or €20 all-areas "passport" ticket. In the early 1660s, the "Sun King" Louis XIV recruited the elite design team of the day – architect Le Vau, painter Le Brun and gardener Le Nôtre – to create a palace that would be the apotheosis of French royal indulgence. Work lasted virtually until Louis XIV's death in 1715. Rather than a royal home, Versailles was

the headquarters and lodgings of every arm of the state, and the entire court of some 3500 nobles – plus administrative staff, soldiers, merchants and servants – lived in the palace, in a state of unhygienic squalor, according to contemporary accounts. For the nobility, every minute of the day revolved around the actions of the king, which were minutely regulated and rigidly encased in ceremony.

Following Louis' death, the château mostly remained the residence of the royal family until the Revolution of 1789, when the furniture was auctioned off

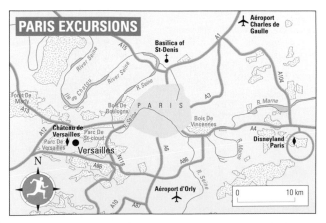

and the pictures dispatched to the Louvre – a process that took a year. Restoration only began in earnest between the two world wars, but today it proceeds apace, Versailles' curators scouring the world's auction houses in search of the original furnishings from the eve of the Revolution.

The palace's main **entrances** lie beyond the giant gates, past the equestrian statue of Louis XIV, in the glorious, half-enclosed cour de Marbre. The door marked "A", often signalled by long queues, gives access to the main showcase rooms of the palace, the **State Apartments**. The route leads past the royal chapel, a grand structure that ranks among France's finest Baroque creations, and through a procession of gilded drawing rooms to the king's throne room and the dazzling Galerie des Glaces, or Hall of Mirrors, which runs in one chandelier-strewn, mirrored sweep along the length of the garden front. It's best viewed at the end of the day, when the crowds have departed and the setting sun floods in

from the west. The queen's fabulous apartments line the northern wing, beginning with her bedchamber, restored exactly as it was in its last refit of 1787, with hardly a surface unadorned by gold leaf.

A separate entrance in the cour de Marbre, marked "D", is the place to book the excellent **guided tours** (€5–9.50 on top of entry ticket), which take you to wings of the palace that mostly can't otherwise be seen (though a few are covered by "self-guided" tours using audio-visual guides). Various itineraries depart throughout the day, including English-language tours; they must all be booked the same morning, so arrive early.

Versailles Jardin and park

Daily: April–Oct 9am–dusk; Nov–March 8am–dusk. Mid-April to Sept Sat & Sun €7, otherwise free. Le Nôtre's exquisite, statue-studded garden terraces lie between the château and the landscaped part of the park. On summer weekends the fountains here "dance" to the tune of classical music

▲ VERSAILLES

▲ GALÉRIE DES GLACES

(mid-April to Sept 11am & 5.30pm), a spectacle known as the Grandes Eaux Musicales. Beyond the gardens, the slope falls away to the Grand Canal and the "English" park, which is big enough to spend the whole day exploring, along with its lesser outcrops of royal building mania: the Italianate **Grand Trianon,** designed by Hardouin-Mansart in 1687 as a "country retreat" for Louis XIV; and the exquisite **Petit Trianon** (daily: April–Oct noon–6pm; Nov–March noon–5pm; ticket for both Trianons €5, or €3 after 3.30pm), built in the 1760s for Louis XV's mistress, Mme de Pompadour, as a refreshingly elegant change of scene from the over-indulgences of the palace.

Just beyond these is the bizarre **Hameau de la Reine**, a full-scale play village and thatch-roofed farm built in 1783 for Marie-Antoinette to indulge the fashionable, Rousseau-inspired fantasy of returning to the natural life. Around it, the park is being slowly returned to its original design from the time of Marie-Antoinette, which means some areas may be fenced off for re-landscaping.

Distances in the park are considerable but all the sights are well signposted. If you want to save time, take the **petit train**, which shuttles between the terrace in front of the château and the Trianons (about every 10min in summer; €5.80). There are **bikes** for hire at the Grille de la Reine, Porte St-Antoine and by the Grand Canal. Boats are for hire on the Grand Canal, next to a pair of **café-restaurants** – picnics are forbidden.

The basilica of St-Denis

Ⓜ St-Denis-Basilique, end of line 13. April–Sept Mon–Sat 10am–6.15pm, Sun noon–6.15pm; Oct–March Mon–Sat 10am–5.15pm, Sun noon–5pm. Free; tombs €6.50. The lofty basilica of St-Denis is the first great Gothic cathedral in Europe. It's also the melancholy burial place of almost all the kings of France. The church gets its name from its legendary founder, the early Parisian bishop St Denis – who was decapitated for his beliefs at Montmartre but promptly picked up his own head and walked all the way to St Denis but the present basilica was begun only in the first half of the twelfth century by Abbot Suger, friend and adviser to kings. Only the lowest storey of the choir remains from this era, as much of the rest of the church was rebuilt in the Rayonnant Gothic style in the mid-thirteenth century. The

▲ ST-DENIS MARKET

from the centre of Paris, but if you're here visiting the basilica it's well worth exploring the area around. Modern St-Denis is the most infamous of Paris's "hot" suburbs, previously for its radically Communist population, now for its supposedly volatile ethnic mix. In fact, it's a fascinating place to visit, characterized by the extraordinary, fortress-like architecture of its shopping and housing complexes. Try to time your visit to coincide with market day (Tues, Fri & Sun mornings), when the main place Victor-Hugo is crammed with shoppers.

abbey's royal connections date back to the coronation of Pepin the Short, in 754, but it wasn't until Hugh Capet, in 996, that it became the royal necropolis. Since then, all but three of France's kings have been interred here. Their very fine tombs, often graced by startlingly naturalistic effigies, are distributed about the transepts and ambulatory (closed during services). Among the most interesting are the enormous Renaissance memorial to François I on the right just beyond the entrance, and the tombs of Louis XII, Henri II and Catherine de Médicis on the left side of the church. On the level above – invariably graced by bouquets of flowers – are the undistinguished statues of Louis XVI and Marie-Antoinette.

St-Denis market

Ⓜ St-Denis-Basilique, end of line 13. You probably wouldn't make a special trip out to St-Denis

Disneyland Park

The introduction to Disneyland Park is Main Street USA, a mythical vision of a 1900s American town, that leads up to Central Plaza, the hub of the park. A steam train **railroad** runs round the park with stations at each "land" and at the main entrance. Sleeping Beauty's Castle, directly opposite Main Street across Central Plaza, belongs to **Fantasyland**, which is aimed at the youngest children. There are no height restrictions here, and rides are mostly gentle. Each of the other three themed areas offers a landmark roller coaster and a theme: **Adventureland** has the most outlandish, jungly sets, **Frontierland** is set in the Wild West, while **Discoveryland** emphasizes technology and the

Visiting Disneyland Paris

RER line A to Marne-la-Vallée/Chessy station (40min). ⓦ www.disneylandpar-is.com. Park hours variable, but roughly: Disneyland Park daily 10am–8pm; Walt Disney Studios Park daily 10am–6pm.

The Disneyland complex is divided into three areas: Disneyland Park; Walt Disney Studios Park; and Disney Village and the hotels. If you plan to stay here, booking an accommodation-and-entry package through Disney or a travel agent offers the best value for money.

The best time to go is on an off-season weekday (Mon & Thurs are best). At other times, longish waits for the popular rides are common in the middle of the day. The most popular attractions use the Fastpass scheme, where you book yourself a later time slot at the entrance to the ride and go on some less popular rides while you wait.

Tickets can be purchased in advance – in order to avoid queues at the park itself – online, at the Paris Tourist Office and at all Disney shops, or you can buy admission passes and train tickets in Paris at all RER line A and B stations and in major métro stations. The one-day one-park ticket (April–Sept €43, under-12s €35) allows you to visit either Disneyland Park or the Walt Disney Studios Park, but if you choose the Walt Disney Studios, you're entitled to move on to Disneyland Park after the Studios close. "Passe-Partout" or "Hopper" tickets (1-day €53, under-12s €45; 2-day €96/79; 3-day €115/95) allow you to move freely between both parks, and you don't have to use the ticket on consecutive days. Prices are usually discounted by around twenty percent in winter, except over Christmas. There are licensed cafés inside the park but expect the usual captive-audience prices and quality; the swankier restaurants in Disney Village aren't great value, but the various hamburger joints around the park aren't too pricey.

space age. As for rollercoasters, the runaway train on Frontierland's Big Thunder Mountain and the mine-carts of Adventureland's Indiana Jones and the Temple of Peril: Backwards! are fast and exciting, but the emphasis is on thrills rather than sheer terror. The two Space Mountain rides, in Discoveryland, are a different matter altogether: the upside-down loops, corkscrews and terrifying acceleration require you to have a strong constitution to enjoy it. Be warned that the experience can be so intense that the park's gentler rides may seem disappointing. Children, in particular, will want to return again and again.

Walt Disney Studios Park

Other than the Rock 'n' Roller Coaster Starring Aerosmith, a terrifyingly fast, corkscrew-looping, Metal-playing white-knuckler, the new Walt Disney Studios Park complex lacks the big rides offered by its older, larger neighbour. In some ways it's a more satisfying affair, focusing on what Disney was and is still renowned for – animation. You can try your hand at drawing, there are mock film and TV sets where you can be part of the audience, and the special-effects and stunt shows are impressive in their way. The Studio Tram Tour Featuring Catastrophe Canyon is more of a true ride, taking you past various fake film lots and pausing inside the accident-prone Catastrophe Canyon. The Armageddon Special Effects spaceship simulation is also pretty scary, while it lasts.

The Manchester United Soccer

School offers three two-and-a-half-hour football training sessions a day for budding Beckhams (aged 7–14 only; €25). It's best to book at the park entrance when you arrive, or with a Disney hotel concierge.

▲ DISNEYLAND PARIS

Accommodation

Hotels

Paris is extremely well supplied with hotels. The ones reviewed here are all classics, places that offer something special – whether it's a great location, unusually elegant decor or a particularly warm welcome. Some are sights in themselves. The grandest establishments are mostly found in the Champs-Elysées area, while the trendy Marais quarter is a good bet for something elegant but relatively relaxed. Over on the Left Bank – around the Quartier Latin, St-Germain and the Eiffel Tower quarter – you'll find more homely, old-fashioned hotels.

Most hotels offer two categories of rooms: at the bottom end of the scale this means choosing between an en-suite bathroom or shared facilities, while more expensive places may charge a premium rate for larger or more luxurious rooms. Overseas visitors may find that prices aren't exorbitant, by European standards, but then rooms can be surprisingly small for the money.

Continental **breakfast** is normally an extra €5 to €9 per person; you'll usually be asked if you want to have breakfast when you check in.

All hotels are marked on the maps in this chapter unless otherwise stated.

The Islands

Hôtel Henri IV 25 place Dauphine. Ⓜ Pont Neuf/Cité. ☎01.43.54.44.53. The best thing about this well-known cheapie is its location on handsome place Dauphine right in the heart of Paris. A handful of the twenty rooms have been spruced up and fitted with showers, but most are very run down and have just a *cabinet de toilette*. The five floors are accessed via a narrow, squeaky staircase; there's no lift. It's best to book well in advance and then to confirm nearer the time. No credit cards. €32–56.
Hôtel du Jeu de Paume 54 rue St-Louis-en-l'Île. Ⓜ Pont-Marie. ☎01.43.26.14.26, ⓦwww.jeudepaume

hotel.com. Located on the most desirable island in France, this quiet, charming hotel occupies the site of a tennis court built for Louis XIII in 1634 ("jeu de paume" is "real tennis"). The wood-beam court is now a breakfast room, from which a glass lift whisks you up to the 28 rooms, decorated in soothing colours. From €250.

The Champs-Elysées and Tuileries

Hôtel Brighton 218 rue de Rivoli. Ⓜ Tuileries. ☎01.47.03.61.61, ⓔhotel. brighton@wanadoo.fr. An elegant hotel dating back to the late nineteenth century

---

Booking accommodation

It's wise to **reserve** your accommodation as early as possible, as the nicest places are quickly booked out for all but the quietest winter months. All receptionists speak some English – but it's worth bearing in mind that more and more places offer **online** booking as well. If you book by phone you may be asked for just a credit card number, or sometimes for written or faxed confirmation. The tourist office can also make bookings for you for free – either in person at one of their offices (see p.215 for addresses) or online at ⓦwww.parisinfo.com; many hotels on the site offer discounted rates.

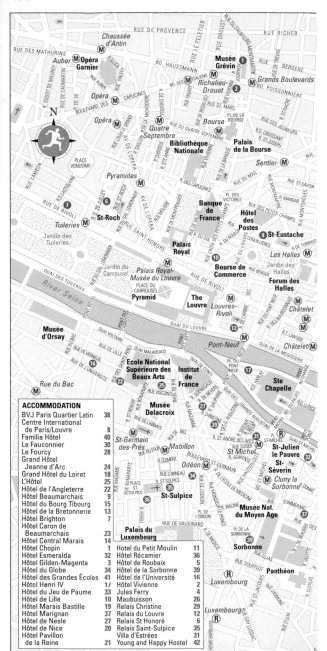

ACCOMMODATION

BVJ Paris Quartier Latin	38
Centre International de Paris/Louvre	8
Familia Hôtel	40
Le Fauconnier	30
Le Fourcy	28
Grand Hôtel Jeanne d'Arc	24
Grand Hôtel du Loiret	18
L'Hôtel	25
Hôtel de l'Angleterre	22
Hôtel Beaumarchais	9
Hôtel du Bourg Tibourg	15
Hôtel de la Bretonnerie	13
Hôtel Brighton	7
Hôtel Caron de Beaumarchais	23
Hôtel Central Marais	14
Hôtel Chopin	1
Hôtel Esmeralda	32
Hôtel Gilden-Magenta	3
Hôtel du Globe	34
Hôtel des Grandes Écoles	41
Hôtel Henri IV	17
Hôtel du Jeu de Paume	33
Hôtel de Lille	4
Hôtel Marais Bastille	19
Hôtel Marignan	37
Hôtel de Nesle	27
Hôtel de Nice	20
Hôtel Pavillon de la Reine	21

Hôtel du Petit Moulin	11
Hôtel Récamier	36
Hôtel de Roubaix	5
Hôtel de la Sorbonne	39
Hôtel de l'Université	16
Hôtel Vivienne	2
Jules Ferry	4
Maubuisson	26
Relais Christine	29
Relais du Louvre	12
Relais St Honoré	6
Relais Saint-Sulpice	35
Villa d'Estrées	31
Young and Happy Hostel	42

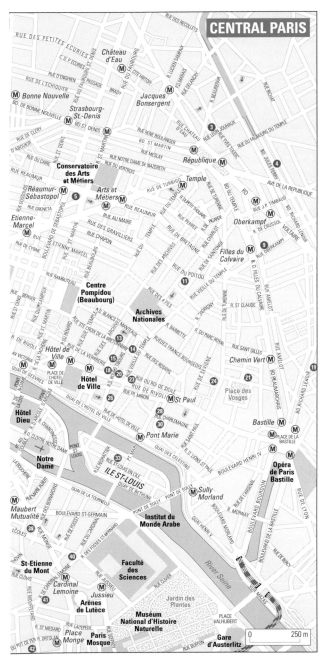

CENTRAL PARIS

RUE DES RECOLLETS
RUE DES PETITES ECURIES
Château d'Eau
C.D.P. ECURIES
RUE D'ENGHIEN
RUE DE L'ECHIQUIER
BRADY
Bonne Nouvelle
BD DE BONNE NOUVELLE
Strasbourg-St.-Denis
BD ST DENIS
Jacques Bonsergent
RUE DU FAUBOURG DU TEMPLE
RUE DE CLERY
D'ABOUKIR
RUE DU CAIRE
RUE REAUMUR
BD ST MARTIN
RUE RENE BOULANGER
BD ST MARTIN
RUE MESLAY
RUE NOTRE DAME DE NAZERETH
République
AVE DE LA REPUBLIQUE
Conservatoire des Arts et Métiers
RUE DE TURBIGO
Temple
BD DU TEMPLE
Réaumur-Sébastopol
Arts et Métiers
Etienne-Marcel
RUE DES GRAVILLIERS
RUE CHAPON
BOULEVARD DE SEBASTOPOL
RUE AU MAIRE
RUE REAUMUR
Oberkampf
RUE DE CYGNE
BOULEVARD ETIENNE MARCEL
RUE DU TEMPLE
RUE DE BRETAGNE
Filles du Calvaire
B.D. FILLES DU CALVAIRE
RUE RAMBUTEAU
RUE DES ARCHIVES
RUE DU POITOU
RUE VIEILLE DU TEMPLE
Centre Pompidou (Beaubourg)
RUE DES 4 FILS
RUE ST DENIS
RUE BERGER
RUE QUINCAMPOIX
RUE ST MARTIN
RUE ST CROIX DE LA BRETONNERIE
Archives Nationales
R. BARBETTE
R. DU PARC ROYAL
R. DE RIVOLI
Hôtel de Ville
RUE DE LA VERRERIE
RUE DES FRANCS BOURGEOIS
Chemin Vert
AV VICTORIA
PLACE DE L'HOTEL DE VILLE
Hôtel de Ville
RUE VIEILLE DU TEMPLE
RUE DES ROSIERS
RUE DE SEVIGNE
RUE DU ROI DE SICILE
RUE DE RIVOLI
St Paul
Place des Vosges
QUAI DE L'HOTEL DE VILLE
R. FIGUIER
RUE DE L'HOTEL DE VILLE
RUE CHARLEMAGNE
Bastille
Hôtel Dieu
QUAI DES CELESTINS
Pont Marie
BOULEVARD HENRI IV
PLACE DE LA BASTILLE
Notre Dame
ILE ST-LOUIS
QUAI DE BETHUNE
Sully Morland
Opéra de Paris Bastille
QUAI DE LA TOURNELLE
PONT DE SULLY
Institut du Monde Arabe
RUE DE LYON
Maubert Mutualité
BOULEVARD ST-GERMAIN
QUAI HENRI IV
St-Etienne du Mont
Faculté des Sciences
River Seine
Cardinal Lemoine
Jussieu
Jardin des Plantes
Arènes de Lutèce
Museum National d'Histoire Naturelle
PLACE VALHUBERT
Place Monge
Paris Mosque
Gare d'Austerlitz

0   250 m

and affording magnificent views of the Tuileries gardens from the front-facing rooms on the upper floors. More than half of the 65 rooms have recently been renovated; the standard of the others varies, though many retain period charm and ambience. Doubles €137–255.

Hôtel Le Bristol 112 rue du Faubourg St-Honoré. Ⓜ Miromesnil. ☎01.53.43.43.00, ⓦwww.lebristolparis.com. The city's most luxurious hotel manages to remain discreet and warm. Gobelins tapestries adorn the walls and some rooms have private roof gardens. There's also a large colonnaded interior garden, as well as a swimming pool, health club and gourmet restaurant. Doubles from €690.

Hôtel des Champs-Elysées 2 rue d'Artois Ⓜ St-Philippe-du-Roule. ☎01.43.59.11.42, ⓕ01.45.61.00.61. The rooms at this two-star hotel are small but nicely decorated in warm colours, and all come with shower or bath, plus satellite TV, minibar, hairdryer and safe. Breakfast is served in a cool, relaxing converted stone cellar. Doubles €98.

Hôtel Lancaster 7 rue de Berri. Ⓜ George V. ☎01.40.76.40.76, ⓦwww.hotel-lancaster.fr. Once the pied-à-terre for the likes of Garbo, Dietrich and Sir Alec Guinness, this elegantly restored nineteenth-century town house is still a favourite hideout for those fleeing the paparazzi. The rooms retain original features and are chock-full of Louis XVI and rococo antiques, but with a touch of contemporary chic. To top it all off, there's a superlative restaurant and zen-style interior garden. Doubles from €470.

Hotel de Lille 8 rue du Pélican. Ⓜ

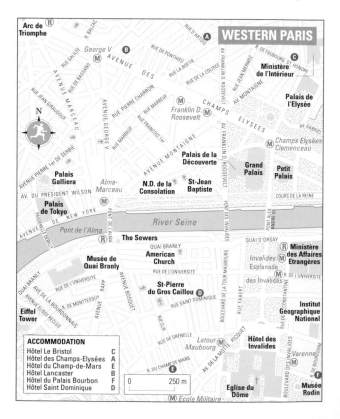

WESTERN PARIS

ACCOMMODATION

Hôtel Le Bristol	C
Hôtel des Champs-Elysées	A
Hôtel du Champ-de-Mars	E
Hôtel Lancaster	B
Hôtel du Palais Bourbon	F
Hôtel Saint Dominique	D

0   250 m

Palais-Royal-Musee-du-Louvre. ☎01.42.33.33.42. A thirteen-room budget hotel on a quiet street. The rooms, some en suite, are small and fairly basic, but not unattractive, with a nod to belle époque style. There's no lift to serve the five floors, and no breakfast. Singles €35; doubles €48–55; triples €60–65.

Relais St Honoré 308 rue St Honoré. Ⓜ Tuileries. ☎01.42.96.06.06, ℻01.42.96.17.50, ⓦhttp://sainthonore. free.fr. A snug little hotel run by friendly and obliging staff, and set in a stylishly renovated seventeenth-century town house. The pretty wood-beamed rooms are done out in warm colours and rich fabrics. Facilities include free broadband Internet access and flat-screen TVs. Doubles €196.

The Grands Boulevards and passages

Hôtel Chopin 46 passage Jouffroy, entrance on bd Montmartre, near rue du Faubourg-Montmartre. Ⓜ Grands-Boulevards. ☎01.47.70.58.10, ℻01.42.47.00.70, ⓦwww.hotelbreton nerie.com/chopin. A charming, quiet hotel set in an atmospheric period building hidden away at the end of a picturesque 1850s passage. Rooms are pleasantly furnished, though the cheaper ones are on the small side and a little dark. Doubles €77 and €88.

Hôtel Vivienne 40 rue Vivienne. Ⓜ Grandes-Boulevards/Bourse. ☎01.42.33.13.26, ℮paris@hotel-vivi enne.com. Ideally located for the Opéra Garnier and the Grands Boulevards, this is a friendly place, with good-sized, cheery rooms done up in rather nice woods and prints, a number of which have recently seen a full renovation. Doubles with shower only and shared toilet €69; doubles with full bathroom €81.

Beaubourg and Les Halles

Hôtel de Roubaix 6 rue Greneta. Ⓜ

Réaumur-Sébastopol/Arts et Métiers. ☎01.42.72.89.91, ⓦwww.hotel-de-rou baix.com. A stone's throw away from the Pompidou Centre and the Marais, this old-fashioned two-star hotel has 53 well-maintained and spotlessly clean en-suite rooms; the decor is nothing special, but this is great value for the location. Doubles €65.

Relais du Louvre 19 rue des Prêtres St-Germain l'Auxerrois. Ⓜ Palais-Royal/ Musée-du-Louvre. ☎01.40.41.96.42, ⓦwww.relaisdulouvre.com. A discreet hotel with eighteen rooms set on a quiet back street opposite the church of St-Germain l'Auxerrois. The decor is traditional but not stuffy, with rich, high-quality fabrics, old prints, Turkish rugs and solid furniture. The relaxed atmosphere and charming service attract a faithful clientele. Doubles €150–190.

The Marais

Grand Hôtel Jeanne d'Arc 3 rue de Jarente. Ⓜ St-Paul. ☎01.48.87.62.11, ⓦwww.hoteljeannedarc.com An attractive old Marais building, just off pretty place du Marché Ste-Catherine. The rooms are a decent size, with nice individual touches, plus cable TV. The triple at the top has good views over the rooftops (€115). Doubles from €82.

Grand Hôtel du Loiret 8 rue des Mauvais-Garçons. Ⓜ Hôtel-de-Ville. ☎01.48.87.77.00, ⓦwww.hotel-loiret.fr. A budget hotel, grand in name only, though it has recently renovated its foyer and installed a lift. The rooms are essentially unexceptional, but acceptable for the price; cheaper ones have washbasin only, all have a TV and telephone. The two triples (€80) on the top floor have views of Sacré-Coeur. Doubles €45–60.

Hôtel du Bourg Tibourg 19 rue du Bourg-Tibourg. Ⓜ Hôtel-de-Ville. ☎01.42.78.47.39, ℻01.40.29.07.00, ⓦwww.hotelbourgtibourg.com. Oriental meets medieval, with a dash of Second Empire, at this sumptuously designed boutique hotel. Rooms are tiny, but packed with rich velvets, silks and drapes. A perfect romantic hideaway. Doubles €220–250.

Hôtel de la Bretonnerie 22 rue Ste Croix de la Bretonnerie. Ⓜ Hôtel-de-Ville. ☎01.48.87.77.63, ℻01.42.77.26.78, 🖳www.bretonnerie.com. A charming place on one of the Marais' liveliest streets; the rooms, all different, are decorated with quality fabrics, oak furniture, and, in some cases, four-poster beds. The beamed attic rooms on the fourth floor are particularly appealing. The location's perfect for exploring the Marais, though front-facing rooms may suffer from street noise at night. Doubles from €116.

Hôtel Caron de Beaumarchais 12 rue Vieille-du-Temple. Ⓜ Hôtel-de-Ville. ☎01.42.72.34.12, 🖳www.carondebeau marchais.com. Named after the eight-eenth-century French playwright Beaumar-chais, who lived just up the road, this gem of a hotel has only nineteen rooms. Every-thing – down to the original engravings and Louis XVI-style furniture, not to mention the pianoforte in the foyer – evokes the refined tastes of high-society pre-Revolutionary Paris. Rooms overlooking the courtyard are small but cosy (€125–142), while those on the street are more spacious, some with a balcony (€162).

Hôtel Central Marais 33 rue Vieille-du-Temple, entrance on rue Ste-Croix-de-la-Bretonnerie. Ⓜ Hôtel-de-Ville. ☎01.48.87.56.08, 🖳www.hotelcentral marais.com. The only self-proclaimed gay hotel in Paris, with a relaxed bar downstairs. Seven small rooms with shared bathrooms €87.

Hôtel de Nice 42 bis rue de Rivoli. Ⓜ Hôtel-de-Ville. ☎01.42.78.55.29, ℻01.42.78.36.07, 🖳www.hoteldenice. com. A delightful old-world charm pervades this six-storey establishment, its pretty rooms hung with old prints and furnished with deep-coloured fabrics and Indian-cotton bedspreads. Double-glazing helps to block out the traffic on rue de Rivoli. Singles €75; doubles €105; triple €130; family room €140.

Hôtel Pavillon de la Reine 28 pl des Vosges. Ⓜ Bastille. ☎01.40.29.19.19, www.pavillon-de-la-reine.com. A perfect honeymoon or romantic-weekend getaway in a beautiful ivy-covered mansion secreted away off the place des Vosges,

it preserves an intimate ambience, with friendly, personable staff. The rooms mostly have a distinctively 1990s "hip hotel" feel, and could probably use another makeover. Doubles from €350.

Hotel du Petit Moulin 29–31 rue du Poitou. Ⓜ Saint Sébastien Froissart/ Filles du Calvaire. ☎01.42.74.10.10, 🖳www.paris-hotel-petitmoulin.com. A glamorous boutique hotel, set in an old bakery and designed top to bottom by Christian Lacroix. The designer's hallmark *joie de vivre* reigns in the seventeen rooms, each a fusion of different styles, from elegant Baroque to Sixties kitsch: shocking pinks and lime greens give way to *toile de jouy* prints, pod chairs sit alongside antique dressing tables and old-fashioned bathtubs. Doubles from €180.

The Quartier Latin

Familia Hôtel 11 rue des Ecoles. Ⓜ Cardinal-Lemoine. ☎01.43.54.55.27, 🖳www.hotel-paris-familia.com. Friendly, family-run hotel in the heart of the *quartier*. Rooms are small but characterful, with beams, elegant wallpaper and pretty murals. Some top-floor rooms have views of Notre-Dame, while a few more expensive ones have balconies. Doubles from €100; breakfast included.

Hôtel Esmeralda 4 rue St-Julien-le-Pauvre. Ⓜ St-Michel. ☎01.43.54.19.20, ℻01.40.51.00.68. Nestling in an ancient house on square Viviani, this ancient, old-fashioned hotel has cosily unmodernized rooms, some with superb views of nearby Notre-Dame. A trio of faintly decrepit singles (€40) come with washbasin only; doubles €90–125.

Hôtel des Grandes Ecoles 75 rue du Cardinal-Lemoine. Ⓜ Cardinal-Lemoine. ☎01.43.26.79.23, 🖳www.hotel-grandes -ecoles.com. This pretty, welcoming three-star in the heart of the Quartier Latin has an attractive setting around a peaceful court-yard garden. Rooms are attractively bright, if rather heavy on the floral wallpaper, and cost €105–130, depending on size.

Hôtel Marignan 13 rue du Sommerard. Ⓜ Maubert-Mutualité. ☎01.43.54.63.81, 🖳www.hotel-marignan.com. The Marignan is totally sympathetic to the needs of backpack-toting foreigners, with free laundry facilities, a dining room with fridge and microwave and bedrooms for up to five people. Even if you don't have a backpack, you'll find it central and welcoming – one of the best bargains in town. Doubles €60 with shared bathroom; €82 en suite.

Hôtel de la Sorbonne 6 rue Victor-Cousin. ⓜ Cluny-La Sorbonne. ☎01.43.54.58.08, ⓦwww.hotelsorbonne.com. Housed in an attractive old building almost on top of the Sorbonne, and close to the Luxembourg gardens, this is a quiet, comfortable hotel with a few modest designer touches. Doubles €110–130.

Villa d'Estrées 17 rue Gît-le-Coeur. ⓜ St-Michel. ☎01.55.42.71.11, ⓦwww.paris-hotel-latin-quarter.com. Luxurious and deeply discreet four-star with just six elegant rooms tucked away in a tiny street behind place St-Michel. Staff are friendly and not at all snooty. Great deals available, but standard rates for a double are €225 and up.

St-Germain

L'Hôtel 13 rue des Beaux-Arts. ⓜ Mabillon/St-Germain-des-Prés. ☎01.44.41.99.00, ⓦwww.l-hotel.com. This extravagant four-star place is a destination in itself, with a celebrity clientele and prices climbing above the €300 mark – notably for the room Oscar Wilde died in. The twenty sumptuously decorated, almost kitsch rooms are set round a light-well-like central atrium, and there's a tiny pool underground.

Hôtel de l'Angleterre 44 rue Jacob. ⓜ St-Germain-des-Prés. ☎01.42.60.34.72, ⓦwww.hotel-dangleterre.com. Top-class hotel in a building that once housed the British Embassy and, later, Ernest Hemingway. The luxury rooms (€260) are huge, and many have beautiful original roof beams. Standard rooms start at €185.

Hôtel du Globe 15 rue des Quatre-Vents. ⓜ Odéon. ☎01.43.26.35.50, ⓦwww.hotel-du-globe.fr. Welcoming hotel in a tall, narrow, seventeenth-century building decked out with a faintly medieval theme: there are four-posters, stone walls, roof beams and even a suit of armour in the lobby. Doubles from €95, going up to around €130 in high season.

Hôtel de Nesle 7 rue de Nesle. ⓜ St-Michel. ☎01.43.54.62.41, ⓦwww.hoteldenesleparis.com. Friendly, offbeat hotel with themed rooms decorated with wacky cartoon murals – of French history, mostly – that you'll either love or hate. There's even a *hammam*. Smaller rooms cost €75, some of which have shared bathrooms. En-suite rooms are €100.

Hôtel Récamier 3 bis place St-Sulpice. ⓜ St-Sulpice. ☎01.43.26.04.89, ⓕ01.46.33.27.73. Old-fashioned and rather plain hotel, but it's comfortable and attractively tucked away in a corner behind St-Sulpice. Doubles €110–130 – the more expensive have views onto the square. There's also a couple of rooms at €90 with shared bathroom, and views.

Hôtel de l'Université 22 rue de l'Université. ⓜ Rue du Bac. ☎01.42.61.09.39, ⓦwww.hoteluniversite.com. Gorgeously cosy three-star place with two dozen rooms filled with antique details. Beamed ceilings and fireplaces in the larger rooms. Doubles €165–175; €200 with a private terrace.

Relais Christine 3 rue Christine. ⓜ Odéon. ☎01.40.51.60.80, ⓦwww.relais-christine.com. Deeply elegant and luxurious four-star in a sixteenth-century building set around a deliciously hidden courtyard. Doubles from €350, but at this level, it's well worth paying the premium for one of the stunning *supérieure* rooms, at around €400.

Relais Saint-Sulpice 3 rue Garancière. ⓜ St-Sulpice. ☎01.46.33.99.00, ⓦhttp://monsite.wanadoo.fr/relaisstsulpice. Set in an aristocratic town house immediately behind St-Sulpice, this is a discreet and classy three-star. The well-furnished rooms are painted in cheerful Provençal colours and start at €170.

Eiffel Tower area

Hôtel du Champ-de-Mars 7 rue du Champs-de-Mars. ⓜ Ecole-Militaire. ☎01.45.51.52.30, ⓦwww.hotel-du-champ-de-mars.com. A friendly and well-run hotel just off the rue Cler market. The rooms are decidedly cosy, with swathes of colourful fabrics. Doubles €80–90.

Hôtel du Palais Bourbon 49 rue de Bourgogne. Ⓜ Varenne. ☎01.44.11.30.70, ⓦwww.hotel-palais -bourbon.com. This handsome old hotel on a quiet but sunny street by the Musée Rodin offers spacious and prettily furnished double rooms from €125, plus one tiny double at €68. Breakfast is included.

Hôtel Saint Dominique 62 rue Saint-Dominique. Ⓜ Invalides/La Tour Maubourg. ☎01.47.05.51.44, ⓦwww. hotelstdominique.com. The posh, village-like neighbourhood of the rue St-Dominique is the perfect setting for this welcoming two-star place. The prettily wallpapered rooms are arranged around a bright little courtyard. Rooms cost around €120, less in quieter seasons.

Montparnasse

These hotels are all marked on the map on p.149.

Hôtel Istria 29 rue Campagne-Première. Ⓜ Raspail. ☎01.43.20.91.82, ⓦwww. istria-paris-hotel.com. Beautifully decorated hotel near the cafés of Montparnasse, with legendary artistic associations: Duchamp, Man Ray, Aragon, Mayakovsky and Rilke all stayed here. Doubles €80–150, depending on the time of year.

Hôtel des Voyageurs 22 rue Boulard. Ⓜ Denfert Rochereau. ☎01.43.21.08.20, ⓦwww.hoteldesvoyageursparis.com. A truly original, great-value, Montparnasse establishment, with an original, warm and friendly spirit – the annexe is covered in frescoes by local artists. Rooms are simple, but comfortable, bright and modern, with air-conditioning and free Internet access, and guests can use the kitchen and living room. Doubles €50.

Southern Paris

These hotels are all marked on the map on p.154–155.

Hôtel de la Loire 39 rue du Moulin Vert. Ⓜ Pernety/Alésia ☎01.45.40.66.88, ⓦwww.hoteldelaloire-paris.com. Behind the pretty blue shutters lies a delightful family hotel with a genuinely homely feel. Doubles are a real bargain at €59, or €52 for the slightly darker rooms in the annexe, which runs the length of the peaceful garden.

Hôtel Printemps 31 rue du Commerce. Ⓜ Avenue Emil Zola. ☎01.45.79.83.36, ⓔhotel.printemps.15e@wanadoo.fr. A friendly welcome and sparsely furnished but clean rooms make this popular with backpackers. €40–43 for the room, whether used by one or two people, plus some inexpensive rooms with just sinks and toilets for €34.

Hôtel Port-Royal 8 bd Port-Royal. Ⓜ Gobelins. ☎01.43.31.70.06, ⓦwww. hotelportroyal.fr. The rooms at this excellent budget address wouldn't disgrace a three-star. It's immaculately clean, attractive and friendly, though right at the southern edge of the Quartier Latin. Fifteen inexpensive rooms (around €55) are available with shared bathroom facilities, though showers cost €2.50. En-suite doubles €80–90.

Hôtel Tolbiac 122 rue de Tolbiac. Ⓜ Tolbiac. ☎01.44.24.25.54, ⓦwww.hotel-tolbiac.com. Situated on a noisy junction, but all rooms are clean and decently furnished, and very inexpensive – doubles cost from €34. In July and August you can rent small studios by the week.

Résidence Les Gobelins 9 rue des Gobelins. Ⓜ Gobelins. ☎01.47.07.26.90, ⓦwww.hotelgobelins.com. A pleasant, quiet and old-fashioned establishment within walking distance of the Quartier Latin's rue Mouffetard. With its large, comfortable double rooms at €79, this is a well-known bargain, so book well in advance.

Montmartre and northern Paris

Hôtel Bonséjour Montmartre 11 rue Burq. Ⓜ Abbesses. ☎01.42.54.22.53, ⓦwww.hotel-bonsejour-montmartre. fr. Set in a marvellous location on a quiet, untouristy street, this hotel is run by friendly and conscientious owners, and the rooms, which are basic, but clean and spacious, are one of the city's best deals. Doubles with shared shower facilities €25–30,

otherwise €30–36, or €46 for the corner rooms (23, 33, 43 and 53) with balconies.
Hôtel Caulaincourt 2 sq Caulaincourt, by 63 rue Caulaincourt. Off map: from Ⓜ Lamarck-Caulaincourt head west along rue Lamarck, and take the first left. ☎01.46.06.46.06, ⓦwww.caulaincourt. com. One of the nicest and friendliest of Paris's budget hotels. The rooms are well kept, and decent value at €52–59, or €69–79 en suite. From the larger dormitory room of the hostel section (€24 a night), the lucky backpackers get a fine view.
Hôtel Ermitage 24 rue Lamarck. Ⓜ Anvers. ☎01.42.64.79.22, ⓦwww.crmit agesacrecoeur.fr. A discreet, welcoming, family-run hotel, hidden away behind Sacré-Cœur. Rooms are slightly chintzy in the classic French manner, and the ones at the back have views out across northern Paris. Approach via the funicular to avoid a steep climb. Doubles €90, breakfast included.
Hôtel Langlois 63 rue St-Lazare. Off map: 150m directly east of Ⓜ Trinité, down rue St-Lazare. ☎01.48.74.78.24,

ⓦwww.hotel-langlois.com. Superbly genteel hotel that's hardly changed in half a century, with antique furnishings and period details, and unusually large rooms. Doubles €104–120, depending on size.
Style Hôtel 8 rue Ganneron. Off map: from Ⓜ Place-de-Clichy head 250m north up Av de Clichy and turn right onto rue Ganneron; the hotel is just round the corner. ☎01.45.22.37.59, ⓕ01.45.22.81.03. Wooden floors, marble fireplaces, a secluded internal courtyard, and nice people. No lift. Great value, especially the rooms with shared bathrooms for €35. En-suite doubles €50.
Timhotel Montmartre place Émile-Goudeau, 11 rue Ravignan. Ⓜ Abbesses. ☎01.42.55.74.79, ⓦwww.timhotel.com. Rooms are modern, comfortable and freshly decorated, albeit in a nondescript way. The location is classic, with views across the city from the more expensive rooms (€105–150, depending on season). The less appealing standard rooms cost around €20 less.

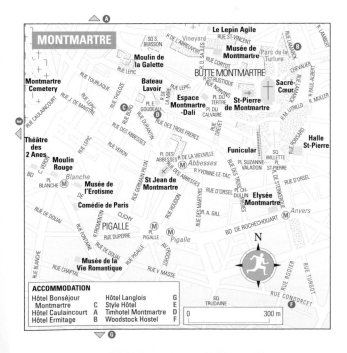

ACCOMMODATION			
Hôtel Bonséjour Montmartre	C	Hôtel Langlois	G
		Style Hôtel	E
Hôtel Caulaincourt	A	Timhotel Montmartre	D
Hôtel Ermitage	B	Woodstock Hostel	F

Bastille

**Hôtel Marais Bastille 36 bd Rich-
ard-Lenoir.** Ⓜ **Bréget Sabin.**
Ⓟ**01.48.05.75.00,** Ⓕ**01.43.57.42.85,**
Ⓦ**www.paris-hotel-marais-bastille.com.**
A decent three-star hotel on a fairly quiet
road, handily located for the Marais and
Bastille. Rooms are equipped with minibar,
TV and Internet point and are attractively
furnished in light oak and pastel colours.
Doubles €145, but check website for
regular special offers.

Eastern Paris

Hôtel Beaumarchais 3 rue Oberkampf.
Ⓜ **Filles-du-Calvaire.** Ⓣ**01.53.36.86.86,**
Ⓣ**01.43.38.32.86,** Ⓦ**www.hotelbeau
marchais.com.** A fashionable, funky hotel
with personal service and colourful 1950s-
inspired decor; all 31 rooms are en suite
with air-conditioning, safes and cable TV
and cost from €110.
**Hôtel Gilden-Magenta 35 rue Yves-
Toudic.** Ⓜ **République.**
Ⓣ**01.42.40.17.72,** Ⓦ**www.multi-micro.
com/hotel.gilden.magenta.** A friendly
hotel, with fresh, colourful decor; rooms
61 and 62, up in the attic, are the best
and have views of the Canal St-Martin.
Breakfast is served in a pleasant patio area.
Doubles €75; €68 in July & Aug.

Hostels

Hostels are an obvious choice for a tight budget, but you won't necessarily save money on sharing a room in a budget hotel. Many now take advance bookings, including all three main hostel groups: FUAJ (Ⓦwww.fuaj.fr), which is part of Hostelling International; UCRIF (Ⓦwww.ucrif.asso.fr), which caters largely to groups; and MIJE (Ⓦwww.mije.com), which runs three excellent hostels in historic buildings in the Marais district, all of which need to be booked long in advance. You don't need to be a member to book – just join when you arrive. Independent hostels tend to be noisier, more youth-oriented places, often with bars attached. Hostels usually have a maximum stay of around a week, and there is often a curfew at around 2am, though some offer keys or door codes. Except where indicated below, there is no effective age limit.

All hostels are marked on the maps in this chapter.

**BVJ Paris Quartier Latin 44 rue des
Bernardins.** Ⓜ **Maubert-Mutualité.**
Ⓣ**01.43.29.34.80,** Ⓦ**www.bvjhotel.com.**
Typically institutional UCRIF hostel, but spick
and span and in a good location. Dorm beds
(€26), plus single or double rooms (€35
and €28 per person, respectively).
**Centre International de Paris/Lou-
vre 20 rue Jean-Jacques-Rousseau.**
Ⓜ **Louvre/Châtelet-Les-Halles.**
Ⓣ**01.53.00.90.90,** Ⓦ **www.bvjhotel.com.**
A clean, modern and efficiently run hostel
for 18- to 35-year-olds. Book up to ten
days in advance. Accommodation ranges
from singles to eight-bed dorms. From €25
per person.
Le Fauconnier 11 rue du Fauconnier. Ⓜ
St-Paul/Pont Marie. Ⓣ**01.42.74.23.45,**
Ⓟ**01.40.27.81.64.** MIJE hostel in a superbly renovated seventeenth-century building.
Dorms (€28 per person) sleep three to
eight, and there are some single (€45) and
double rooms too (€33 per person), with
en-suite showers.
Le Fourcy 6 rue de Fourcy. Ⓜ **St Paul.**
Ⓣ**01.42.74.23.45.** Another MIJE hostel

housed in a beautiful mansion, this one has a small garden and an inexpensive restaurant. Dorms cost €28 per person, and there are some doubles (€33 per person with shower) and triples (€29 per person).

Jules Ferry 8 bd Jules-Ferry. Ⓜ **République.** ☎01.43.57.55.60, ⓦ**www.fuaj.fr.** Fairly central HI hostel, in a lively area at the foot of the Belleville hill. Difficult to get a place, but they can help find a bed elsewhere. Only two to four people in each room; beds cost €19.50.

Maubuisson 12 rue des Barres. Ⓜ **Pont Marie/Hôtel de Ville.** ☎01.42.74.23.45. A MIJE hostel in a magnificent medieval building on a quiet street. Shared use of the restaurant at *Le Fourcy* (see above). Dorms only, sleeping four (€28 per person).

Woodstock Hostel 48 rue Rodier. Ⓜ **Anvers/St Georges.** ☎01.48.78.87.76, ⓦ**www.woodstock.fr.** A well-run, friendly hostel in the Three Ducks stable, with its own bar. Set in a great location on a pretty street not far from Montmartre. Dorm beds €18–21, or twin rooms available for €21–24 per person. Book ahead.

Young and Happy Hostel 80 rue Mouffetard. Ⓜ **Monge/Censar-Daubenton.** ☎01.45.35.09.53, ⓦ**www.youngandhappy.fr.** Noisy, basic and studenty independent hostel in a lively location. Dorms, with shower, sleep four (€21–23 per person), and there are a few doubles (€23–26 per person). Curfew at 2am.

Essentials

Arrival

It's easy to get from both of Paris's main airports to the city centre using the efficient public transport links. The budget airline airport, Beauvais, is served by buses. If you're arriving by train, of course, it's easier still: just get on the métro.

By air

The two main Paris **airports** that deal with international flights are Roissy-Charles de Gaulle and Orly, both well connected to the centre. Information on them can be found on ⓦwww.adp.fr. A third airport, Beauvais, is used by low-cost airlines. Bear in mind that you can buy a **Paris Visite** card at the airports which will cover multiple journeys to and within the city (see p.213).

Roissy-Charles de Gaulle Airport

Roissy-Charles de Gaulle Airport (24hr information in English ☎01.48.62.22.80), usually referred to as Charles de Gaulle and abbreviated to CDG or Paris CDG, is 23km northeast of the city. The airport has two main terminals, CDG 1 and CDG 2, linked by a shuttle bus.

There are various ways of getting to the centre of Paris, but the simplest is the **Roissyrail** train link which runs on RER line B and takes thirty minutes (every 15min 5am–midnight; €8 one way). You can pick it up direct at CDG 2, but from CDG 1 you have to get a shuttle bus (*navette*) to the RER station first. The train is fast to Gare du Nord, then stops at Châtelet-Les Halles, St-Michel and Denfert-Rochereau, all of which have métro stations for onward travel. Ordinary commuter trains also run on this line, but make more stops and have fewer facilities for luggage storage.

Various **bus companies** provide services from the airport direct to various city-centre locations, but they're slightly more expensive than

Roissyrail, and may take longer. A more useful alternative is the Blue Vans door-to-door **minibus** service (€14.50 per head if there are two or more people, €22 for a single person; no extra charge for luggage; 6am–7.30pm). Bookings must be made at least 48 hours in advance (☎01.30.11.13.00, ☏01.30.11.13.09, ⓦwww.paris-blue-airport-shuttle.fr).

Taxis into central Paris from CDG cost around €40 on the meter, plus a small luggage supplement (€0.90 per item), and should take between fifty minutes and one hour. Note that if your flight gets in after midnight your only means of transport is a taxi.

Orly Airport

Orly Airport (information in English daily 6am–11.30pm; ☎ 01.49.75.15.15), 14km south of Paris, has two terminals, Orly Sud (south; for international flights) and Orly Ouest (west; for domestic flights), linked by shuttle bus but easily walkable.

The easiest way into the centre is the **Orlyval**, a fast train shuttle link to RER station Antony, from where you can pick up RER line B trains to the central RER/métro stations Denfert-Rochereau, St-Michel and Châtelet-Les Halles; it runs every four to eight minutes from 6am to 11pm (€9.05 one way; 35min to Châtelet). Another service connecting with the RER is the Orlyrail bus–rail link: a shuttle bus takes you to RER line C station Pont de Rungis, from where the Orlyrail train leaves every twenty minutes from 5.30am to 11.30pm for the Gare d'Austerlitz and other métro connection stops (€5.65 one way; train 35min, total journey around 50min). Leaving Paris, the train runs from Gare d'Austerlitz from 5am to 12.20pm.

Taxis take about 35 minutes to reach the centre of Paris and cost around €35.

Beauvais Airport

Beauvais Airport (☎08.92.68.20.66, ⓦ www.aeroportbeauvais.com) is a fair distance from Paris – some 65km northwest – and is used by some budget airlines. Coaches (€13 one-way) shuttle between the airport and Porte Maillot, at the northwestern edge of Paris, where you can pick up métro line 1 to the centre. Coaches take about an hour, and leave between fifteen and thirty minutes after the flight has arrived and about three hours before the flight departs on the way back. Tickets can be bought online via the airport's website, at Arrivals or from the Beauvais shop at 1 boulevard Pershing, near the Porte Maillot terminal.

By rail

Eurostar (☎08.36.35.35.39, ✆www.eurostar.com) trains terminate at the **Gare du Nord**, rue Dunkerque, in the northeast of the city – a bustling convergence of international, long-distance and suburban trains, the métro and several bus routes. Coming off the train, turn left for the métro and the RER, immediately right and through the side door for taxis (roughly €10 to the centre). The Eurostar offices and check-in point for departures are both located on the mezzanine level, above the main station entrance.

Gare du Nord is also the arrival point for trains from Calais and northern European countries such as Belgium, Germany and the Netherlands. Paris has five other mainline train stations, part of the national SNCF network: the **Gare de l'Est** (place du 11-Novembre-1918) serves eastern France and central and eastern Europe;

the **Gare St-Lazare** (place du Havre), serves the Normandy coast and Dieppe; the **Gare de Lyon** (place Louis-Armand) serves Italy, Switzerland and TGV trains to southeast France. South of the river, the **Gare Montparnasse** (bd de Vaugirard) is the terminus for Chartres, Brittany, the Atlantic coast and TGV lines to southwest France and the Loire Valley; the **Gare d'Austerlitz** (bd de l'Hôpital) serves ordinary trains to the Loire Valley and the Dordogne. The motorail station, **Gare de Paris-Bercy**, is down the tracks from the Gare de Lyon on boulevard de Bercy.

For **information** on national train services and reservations phone ☎08.36.35.35.39 (if you dial extension 2 you should go through to an English-speaking operator) or consult the website ✆www.sncf.fr. For information on suburban lines call ☎01.53.90.20.20. You can buy **tickets** at any train station, at travel agents and online at the SNCF website.

By road

If you're arriving by bus – international or domestic – you'll almost certainly arrive at the main **Gare Routière** at 28 av du Général-de-Gaulle, Bagnolet, at the eastern edge of the city; métro Gallieni (line 3) links it to the centre. If you're driving in yourself, don't try to go straight across the city to your destination. Use the ring road – the **boulevard périphérique** – to get around to the nearest *porte*: it's much quicker (sometimes frighteningly so), except at rush hour, and far easier to navigate.

City transport

While walking is undoubtedly the best way to discover Paris, the city's integrated public transport system of bus, métro and trains – RATP – is quick, inexpensive and efficient. Even the Batobus along the river comes under part of the same network. Taxis are surprisingly thin on the ground.

RATP

For 24-hour recorded information in English on all RATP services call ☎08.92.68.41.14 (premium rate) or visit ✆www.ratp.fr.

Tickets and passes

The standard RATP **ticket** (€1.40) is valid for any one-way métro, bus or RER express rail ride anywhere within the city limits and immediate suburbs (zones 1 and 2). Only one ticket is ever needed on the métro system, but you can't switch between buses or between bus and métro/RER on the same ticket. For a short stay in the city, consider buying a reduced-price **carnet** of ten tickets (€10.70). All tickets are available from stations and *tabacs* (newsagent/tobacconist) – don't buy from the illegal touts. **Children** under 4 travel free, and kids aged 4 to 10 pay half price. Officially, you're supposed to keep your ticket until the end of the journey but you only actually need it to get through the entrance gates.

If you're travelling beyond the city limits (zones 3–5), to La Défense, for example, note that you'll need a separate RER ticket. **Mobilis day passes** (€5.40) give unlimited access to the métro, buses and RER trains within the city limits (zones 1 and 2).

Paris Visite cards can be good value if bought at the airport when you arrive, as they cover all travel within the city limits plus the airport rail links, Versailles and Disneyland Paris, as well as offering minor reductions on a few more touristy attractions. They cost €8.35, €13.70, €18.25 and €26.65 for one, two, three and five days respectively, and can begin on any day. A half-price child's version is also available. You can buy these passes from métro stations and tourist offices.

The Métro and RER

The **métro**, combined with the **RER** suburban express lines, is the simplest way of moving around the city. Both run from around 5.30am to roughly 12.30am. Lines are colour-coded and designated by numbers for the métro and letters for the RER. Platforms are signposted using the name of the terminus station; travelling north from Montparnasse to Châtelet, for example, you need to follow the signs for "Direction Porte-de-Clignancourt", at the northernmost end of the line. For RER

journeys beyond the city, make sure that the station you want is illuminated on the platform display board. Free **maps** are available at most stations.

Stations (abbreviated: Ⓜ Concorde, RER Luxembourg, and so on) are evenly spaced and usually very close together, though interchanges can involve a lot of legwork. Many lines simply shadow the boulevards above.

Buses

Buses are often neglected in favour of the métro but can be very useful where the métro journey doesn't quite work. Every bus stop displays the numbers of the buses that stop there and a map showing all the stops on the route. Free **route maps** are available from métro stations. Generally speaking, buses run from 6.30am to 8.30pm with a reduced service continuing to 12.30am; around half the lines don't operate on Sundays and holidays. **Night buses** (Noctilien; Ⓦwww.noctilien.fr) ply 35 routes at least every hour from 12.30am to 5.30am. Among the most useful are N01 and N02, which run a circular route linking the main nightlife areas (Champs-Elysées, Bastille, Pigalle etc) and a number of train stations; they run every ten minutes at weekends (Fri night to Sun morning) and every twenty minutes during the rest of the week.

Tickets (€1.40) are interchangeable with métro tickets, and can be bought from the driver; make sure you put your ticket in the little stamping machine at the entrance to validate it.

Some bus routes are particularly good for sightseeing, notably bus #20; bus #29, which has an open platform at the back; bus #24, along the Left Bank; and bus #73, down the Voie Triomphale. A number of bus routes are **wheelchair accessible**; for a full list visit Ⓦwww. infomobi.com.

Taxis

The best place to get a taxi is at one of the **taxi ranks** found at major junctions or railway stations (*arrêt taxi*) – usually more effective than trying to hail one from the street. Taxis can be any colour but carry distinctive roof lights – the large white light signals the taxi is free; the orange light means it's in use. You can also call a taxi out: phone numbers are shown at the taxi ranks, or try Taxis Bleus (☎08.91.70.10.10, Alpha Taxis (☎ 01.45.85.85.85) or Artaxi (☎01.42.03.50.50). That said, finding a taxi at lunchtime and any time after 7pm can be almost impossible.

Charges – always metered – are fairly reasonable: between €7 and €12 for a central daytime journey, though considerably more if you call one out. Different day/night and city/suburb rates apply per kilometre, and there's a minimum charge of €5.20, a time charge of around €25 an hour for when the car is stationary, an extra charge of €0.70 if you're picked up from a mainline train station, and a €0.90 charge for each piece of luggage carried. A discretionary ten percent tip is usual. Taxi drivers do not have to take more than three passengers (they don't like people sitting in the front); if a fourth passenger is accepted, an extra charge of €2.60 is added.

Batobus

A pleasant alternative to road and rail, the **Batobus** boat shuttle (ⓦwww.batobus.com) stops at eight points along the Seine in the following order: Port de la Bourdonnais, under the Musée du Quai Branly and near the Eiffel Tower (Ⓜ Bir-Hakeim/Trocadéro & RER Champ de Mars); Cours la Reine, beside the Petit Palais and near the Champs Elysées and Les Invalides (Ⓜ Champs Elysées–Clemenceau); quai de Solférino, below the Musée d'Orsay (Ⓜ Assemblée Nationale); quai du Louvre, for the Louvre (Ⓜ Musée du Louvre); quai Malaquais, beside the Pont des Arts (Ⓜ St-Germain-des-Prés); quai de Montebello, opposite Notre Dame (Ⓜ Notre-Dame); quai de l'Hôtel de Ville (Ⓜ Hôtel de Ville/Centre-Pompidou); and quai St Bernard, beside the Jardin des Plantes (Ⓜ Jussieu/Cardinal-Lemoine). Boats run roughly every twenty to thirty minutes from 10am to 9pm from May to September, from 10am

to 7pm in March, April and October, and 10.30am–4.30pm in November, December, January and February. The €11 Batobus day-ticket (€5 for under-16s) allows you to get on and off as many times as you like in one day; and there are two- and five-day options for €13 and €16.

Cycling

Cycling in Paris is as scary as you'd expect in a capital city, and there are lots of awkward one-way streets to find your way around. That said, you can almost always find a quiet back route, and the town hall has made great efforts to introduce cycle lanes. You can pick up a free leaflet, **Paris à Vélo**, outlining the routes, from town halls, the tourist office or bike rental outlets.

Between May and September, a number of the roads along the Seine (the *quais*) are closed off on Sundays and public holidays (10am–6pm). They're popular places for cyclists and in-line skaters to meet up. The right bank of the Seine is freed of traffic from the Tuileries to Trocadéro, in the west, and from the Pont d'Austerlitz to the edge of the city, in the east; over on the Left Bank the roads are shut off from the Musée d'Orsay to the western side of the city. The *quais* along the Canal St-Martin are also closed on Sundays (2–6pm).

Prices for **bike rental** usually range from about €15–20 a day.

Paris À Vélo C'est Sympa 37 bd Bourdon (Ⓜ Bastille) ☎01.48.87.60.01, ⓦwww.parisvelosympa.com. One of the least expensive (from €25 for the weekend). Also does excellent three-hour bike tours of Paris (€34). Daily 9.30am–5.30pm, closed 1–2pm.

Paris-Vélo 2 rue du Fer-à-Moulin (Ⓜ Censier-Daubenton) ☎01.43.37.59.22, ⓦwww.paris-velo-rent-a-bike.fr. 21-speed and mountain bikes. Mon–Sat 10am–6/7pm, Sun 10am–2pm & 5–7pm.

RATP/Maison Roue Libre 1 passage Mondétour (Ⓜ Etienne-Marcel/Les Halles) ☎01.44.76.86.43. RATP, the public bus- and métro-operating company, rents out bikes from this site, open daily 9am–7pm. On Sundays and public holidays between

April and October, RATP also rents out bikes from "cyclobuses" parked on the Esplanade St Louis at the Bois de Vincennes; and at the Butte Mortemart, near the Hippodrome d'Auteuil in the Bois de Boulogne.

Information

The main Paris **tourist office** is at 25 rue des Pyramides (Mon–Sat 10am–7pm, Sun 11am–7pm; ☎08.92.68.30.00, ⓦ www.parisinfo.com; Ⓜ Pyramides). There are useful branch offices at the Gare du Nord (daily 8am–6pm), 11 rue Scribe, near the Opéra Garnier (Mon–Sat 9am–6.30pm), and under the Louvre in the Carrousel (daily 10am–6pm). They give out information on Paris and the suburbs, can book hotel accommodation for you, and they also sell the Carte Musées et Monuments (see overleaf), travel passes and phonecards. The Louvre office also has information on the whole region around Paris. It's also worth picking up the free *Paris Map* – this might be behind the counter, so you'll need to ask.

For information on city affairs, including city museums, parks, sports facilities and other amenities, contact the Hôtel de Ville Bureau d'Accueil, at 29 rue de Rivoli (Mon–Sat 10am–7pm; ☎01.42.76.43.43, ⓦwww.paris.fr; Ⓜ Hôtel de Ville).

For detailed what's-on information it's worth buying one of Paris's inexpensive weekly **listings magazines** from a newsagent or kiosk. The best and glossiest is *Zurban* (ⓦwww.zurban.com), though *Pariscope* has a comprehensive section on films and an English-language end-page section put together by *Time Out*. For more detail, French speakers should check out the monthly *Nova* magazine, while the free English-language monthly magazines *Paris Voice* (ⓦwww.parisvoice.com) and *GoGo Paris* (ⓦhttp://gogoparis.com), available from Anglo bars and bookshops, have good listings and small ads.

The **maps** in this guide and the free *Paris Map* (see above) should be adequate for a short sightseeing stay, but for a more detailed map your best bet is one of the pocket-sized "L'indispensable" series booklets, sold everywhere in Paris. The Michelin 1:10,000 *Plan de Paris* is comprehensive but unwieldy; more convenient is the *Rough Guide Map: Paris*, produced on waterproof, crease-resistant paper.

Museums and monuments

Entrance tickets to **museums and monuments** can really add up, though the permanent collections at all municipal museums are **free** all year round, while all national museums (including the Louvre, Musée d'Orsay and Pompidou Centre) are free on the first Sunday of the month – see ⓦwww.rmn.fr for a full list.

Each institution has its own policy for **children and teenagers**. In many museums under-18s go free, while all monuments are free for under-12s. Under-4s almost always get free admission. Half-price or reduced admission is normally available for 5- to 18-year-olds and **students**, though some commercial attractions charge adult rates from 12. The ISIC Card (International Student Identity Card; ⓦwww.isiccard.com) is usually the only card accepted for reduced-price student admission – often around a third off. For those **over 60 or 65**, depending on the institution (regardless of whether you are still working or not), reductions are often available; you'll need to carry your passport around with you as proof of age.

If you are going to do a lot of museum duty, consider buying the **Carte Musées et Monuments** (€18 one day, €36 three day, €54 five day). Available from the tourist office, RER/métro stations and museums, it's valid for seventy museums and monuments in and around Paris, and allows you to bypass the ticket queues.

Festivals and events

Paris hosts an impressive roster of festivals and events. Arguably the city's biggest jamboree is Bastille Day on July 14 but there's invariably something on to add extra colour to your stay.

France celebrates thirteen **national holidays** – May is particularly festive: January 1; Easter Sunday; Easter Monday; Ascension Day; Whitsun; Whit Monday; May 1; May 8; July 14; August 15; November 1; November 11; December 25.

Foire du Trône

Funfairs make a regular appearance in the capital, one of the most popular being the Foire du Trône (ⓦwww.foiredutrone. com), held in April and May in the Parc de Reuilly in the Bois de Vincennes (Porte Dorée entrance).

Fête de la Musique

On June 21, the Fête de la Musique (ⓦ www.fetedelamusique.culture.fr), buskers take to the streets and free concerts are held across the whole city in a fun day of music making.

Pride March

The Marche des Fiertés LGBT (ⓦhttp:// marche.inter-lgbt.org), or gay pride march, is held on the last Saturday of June. A flamboyant parade of floats and costumes makes its way to the Bastille, followed by partying and club events.

Bastille Day

On Bastille Day, July 14, the city celebrates the 1789 storming of the Bastille. The party starts the evening before with dancing around place de la Bastille; in the morning is the military march-past down the Champs-Elysées followed by fireworks.

Tour de France

On the third or fourth Sunday of July, Paris stages the final romp home of the Tour de France (ⓦ www.letour.fr) and thousands line the route to cheer the cyclists to the finish line on the Champs-Elysées.

Paris Plage

Paris Plage ("Paris Beach") is the transformation of part of the Seine into a "beach" from mid-July to mid-August, complete with real sand, deckchairs and palm trees.

Journées du Patrimoine

On the third weekend in September, off-limits and private buildings throw open their doors to a curious public for the "heritage days" (ⓦwww.journeesdu patrimoine.culture.fr).

Festival d'Automne

Running from the last week of September until Christmas, the Festival d'Automne (ⓦ www.festival-automne.com), is an international festival of theatre and music, much of it avant-garde and exciting.

Nuit Blanche

Nuit Blanche (@www.paris.fr), held in early October, is a night-long festival of poetry readings, concerts and performance art held in galleries, bars, restaurants and public buildings across the city.

Directory

ADDRESSES Paris is divided into twenty districts, or arrondissements. The first arrondissement, or "1er" is centred on the Louvre, in the heart of the city. The rest wind outward in a clockwise direction like a snail's shell: the 2e, 3e and 4e are central; the 5e, 6e and 7e lie on the inner part of the left (south) bank; while the 8e–20e make up the outer districts. Parisian addresses always quote the arrondissement, along with the nearest métro station or stations, too.

BANKS AND EXCHANGE All **ATM**s – *distributeurs* or *points argent*, found everywhere – give instructions in French or English. You can also use credit cards for (interest-paying) cash advances at banks and in ATMs.

On the whole, the best **exchange rates** are offered by banks, though there's always a commission charge on top. Be very wary of bureaux de change, which cluster round arrival points and tourist spots, as they can really rip you off. Standard banking hours are Monday to Friday from 9am to 4 or 5pm. A few banks close for lunch; some are open on Saturday 9am to noon; all are closed on Sunday and public holidays. Money-exchange bureaux (poor value, on the whole) stay open until 6 or 7pm, tend not to close for lunch and may even open on Sundays in the more touristy areas.

BATEAUX MOUCHES Tourist boats operating on the Seine are known in general as "bateaux mouches". You won't need to book in advance, just turn up at one of the jetties – they're frequent enough to sit and wait. Bateaux-Mouches (@www.bateaux-mouches.fr) boats depart from the Embarcadère du Pont de l'Alma on the Right Bank; rides last an hour and cost €8, or €4 for under-12s and seniors. Bateaux Parisiens (@www.bateauxparisiens.com) boats run from the Port de la Bourdonnais, under the Musée du Quai Branly – and in summer, also from the Quai de Montebello, on the Left Bank opposite Notre Dame; trips cost €10, or €5 for children. More flexible, and a touch less touristy, is the Batobus, which has eight stops along the Seine between the Eiffel Tower and the Jardin des Plantes (see p.214).

CINEMAS Paris has a world-renowned concentration of cinemas, and moviegoers can choose from around three hundred films showing in any one week. Tickets rarely need to be purchased in advance and are good value at around €8–10. Among the more interesting cinemas in the city are: **Le Grand Rex**, 1 bd Poissonnière (Ⓜ Bonne Nouvelle), a famously kitsch Art-Deco cinema showing blockbusters (usually dubbed); **Max Linder Panorama**, 24 bd Poissonnière (Ⓜ Bonne Nouvelle), a 1930s cinema showing films in the original format, with state-of-the-art sound; **La Pagode**, 57 bis rue de Babylone (Ⓜ François-Xavier), a reproduction Japanese pagoda and the most beautiful of the city's cinemas; and the cluster of inventive cinemas at the junction of rue Champollion and rue des Ecoles, **Reflet Medicis Logos**, **Quartier Latin** and Le Champo (Ⓜ Cluny-La-Sorbonne), which offer up rare screenings and classics. **The Cinémathèque Française**, 51 rue de Bercy (@www.cinemathequefrancaise.com; Ⓜ Bercy) shows dozens of different films every week, including lots of art-house fare, and costs just €6.

CRIME Petty theft sometimes occurs on the métro, at train stations and at tourist hotspots such as Les Halles and around rue de la Huchette, in the Quartier Latin. Serious crime against tourists is rare. To report thefts, you have to make your way to the commissariat de police in the arrondissement where the theft took place. The Préfecture de Police de Paris is at 7 boulevard du Palais (☎01.53.73.53.73). For rape crisis (SOS Viol) call ☎08.00.05.95.95.

DISABLED TRAVELLERS Paris has no special reputation for providing easy access or facilities for disabled travellers. The narrow pavements make wheelchair travel stressful, and the métro system has endless flights of steps. Museums, however, are getting much better. Up-to-date information is best obtained from organizations at home before you leave.

EMBASSIES AND CONSULATES Australia, 4 rue Jean-Rey, 15e (Ⓜ Bir-Hakeim) ☎01.40.59.33.00, @www.france.embassy.

gov.au; **Canada**, 35 av Montaigne, 8e (Ⓜ Franklin-D-Roosevelt) ☎01.44.43.29.00, ⓦwww.amb-canada.fr; **Ireland**, 4 rue Rude, 16e (Ⓜ Charles-de-Gaulle-Etoile) ☎01.44.17.67.00; **New Zealand**, 7 rue Léonard-de-Vinci, 16e (Ⓜ Victor-Hugo) ☎01.45.00.24.11; **UK**, 35 rue du Faubourg St-Honoré, 8e (Ⓜ Concorde) ☎01.44.51.31.00, ⓦwww.britishembassy. gov.uk/france; **US**, 2 rue St-Florentin, 1er (Ⓜ Concorde) ☎01.43.12.22.22, ⓦwww. amb-usa.fr.

EMERGENCIES Ambulance ☎15; police ☎17; fire ☎18.

GAY AND LESBIAN TRAVELLERS Paris has a vibrant, upfront gay community, and full-on prejudice or hostility is rare. Legally, France is liberal as regards homosexuality, with legal consent starting at sixteen and laws protecting gay couples' rights. The Centre Gai Lesbien Bi et Trans, 3 rue Keller, 11e ☎01.43.57.21.47, ⓦwww.cglparis.org (Mon–Fri 4–8pm; Ⓜ Bastille/Ledru-Rollin/ Voltaire) is a useful port of call for information and advice. Useful contacts and listings can be found in the excellent glossy monthly magazine, *Têtu* (ⓦwww.tetu.com).

HEALTH Pharmacies can give good advice on minor complaints, offer appropriate medicines and recommend a doctor. British citizens with a European Health Insurance Card (from post offices) can take advantage of French health services. Non-EU citizens are strongly advised to take out travel insurance.

INTERNET Internet access is everywhere in Paris – if it's not in your hotel there'll be a café close by, and there are lots of *points internet* around the city centre. Most post offices, too, have a computer geared up for public Internet access.

POST French post offices (la Poste) – look for bright yellow-and-blue signs – are generally open Mon–Fri 8am–7pm, Sat 8am–noon. However, Paris's main office, at 52 rue du Louvre, 1er (Ⓜ Etienne-Marcel), is open 24 hours for all postal services (but not banking). The easiest place to buy ordinary stamps (*timbres*) is at a *tabac* (tobacconist). Postcards (*cartes postales*) and letters (*lettres*) up to 20g cost €0.55 for the UK and EU, and €90 for North America, Asia and

Oceania. For anything heavier, most post offices now have yellow-coloured *guichet automatiques* that weigh your letter or package and give you the correct stamps.

RACISM Paris has an unfortunate reputation for racism, but harassment of tourists is unlikely to be a problem. That said, there are reports of unpleasant incidents such as restaurants claiming to be fully booked, or shopkeepers with a suspicious eye, and travellers of north African or Arab appearance may be unlucky enough to encounter outright hostility or excessive police interest.

TELEPHONES Almost all public phones take phonecards (*télécartes*), sold at railway stations and *tabacs*. Many call boxes also accept credit cards, but coin-operated phones are rare. For calling within Paris, you'll always need to dial the regional code first – ☎01. Local calls are inexpensive, especially off-peak, though hotel phones usually carry a significant mark-up. Domestic and international off-peak rates run at weekends and weekdays from 7pm to 8am. At peak rates, €1 gets you about five minutes to the US or Britain. The number for French directory enquiries and operator assistance is ☎12.

France operates on the European GSM mobile phone standard, so travellers from Britain can bring theirs from home; US cellphones, however, won't work in Paris unless they're tri-band.

TIME DIFFERENCE Paris, and all of France, is in the Central European Time Zone (GMT+1): one hour ahead of the UK, six hours ahead of Eastern Standard Time and nine hours ahead of Pacific Standard Time. In France, and all of the EU, Daylight Saving Time (+1hr) lasts from the last Sunday of March through to the last Sunday of October, so for one week in late March and/or early April North American clocks lag an extra hour behind.

TIPPING Service is almost always included in restaurant bills, so you don't need to leave more than small change. Taxi drivers and hairdressers expect around ten percent. You should tip only at the most expensive hotels; in other cases you're probably tipping the proprietor or their family.

Fly Less – Stay Longer!

Rough Guides believes in the good that travel does, but we are deeply aware of the impact of fuel emissions on climate change. We recommend taking fewer trips and staying for longer. If you can avoid travelling by air, please use an alternative, especially for journeys of under 1000km/600miles. And always offset your travel at ⓦwww.roughguides.com/climatechange.

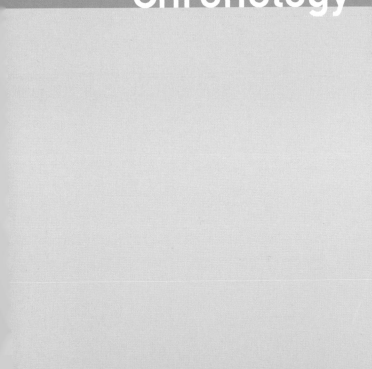

Chronology

Paris chronology

Third-century BC The Parisii Celtic tribe settles in the Paris area and builds an Iron-Age fort on the eastern part of what is now the Ile de la Cité.

52 AD When Julius Caesar's conquering armies arrive they find a thriving settlement of some 8000 people.

Around 275 St Denis brings Christianity to Paris. He is martyred for his beliefs at Montmartre (Mount of the Martyr), but then picks up his own head and walks as far as St-Denis – signalling that an abbey should be built on this spot.

486 Paris falls to Clovis the Frank. His dynasty, the Merovingians, govern Paris for the next two hundred bloodthirsty years.

768 Charlemagne is proclaimed king at St-Denis, ruling most of northern France, but spending very little time in Paris.

845–85 Paris suffers a further decline in fortunes when the city is repeatedly sacked by the Vikings.

987 Hugues Capet, one of the counts of Paris, is elected king of Francia and makes Paris his capital. Things start to look up for the city.

1200s Fuelled by river-borne trade and agriculture, Paris booms and its university becomes the centre of European learning. King Philippe-Auguste constructs the Louvre fortress and erects a vast wall around the city.

1330s to 1430s Parisians endure poverty and misery as the French and English nobility engage in the long and destructive Hundred Years' War.

1348 The Black Death kills some 800 Parisians a day, and over the next 140 years, one year in four is a plague year. The city's population falls by half.

1429 Joan of Arc attempts to drive the English out of Paris, but it is not until 1437 that Charles VII regains control of his capital.

1528 François I finally brings the royal court back to Paris from the pleasant security of châteaux in the Loire. He sets about building the Tuileries palace and reconstructing the Louvre.

August 25, 1572 One of the worst atrocities in the long-running conflict between Catholics and Protestants is committed in Paris on Bartholomew's Day: some 3000 Protestants are massacred at the instigation of the ultra-Catholic Guise family.

1607 The Pont Neuf is completed. The first bridge in Paris to be built without the usual medieval complement of houses, it's hugely symbolic of the city's renewal under Henri IV.

1661–1715 Louis XIV transfers the court to Versailles, but the city continues to grow in size, wealth and prestige. The first boulevards are created, but much of the city centre remains an unsanitary warren of crowded tenements.

1789 Longstanding tensions between the privileged classes and the lower orders explode into revolution. Ordinary Parisians, the "sans-culottes", storm the Bastille prison on July 14.

1793 The revolutionaries banish the monarchy and execute Louis XVI. A dictatorship is set up, headed by the ruthless Robespierre, and some 2600 victims are guillotined in a period known as The Terror.

1799 Army general Napoleon Bonaparte seizes control in a coup and in 1804 crowns himself emperor in Notre-Dame. He erects grandiose monuments such as the Arc de Triomphe and the Madeleine, and extends the Louvre to accommodate his looted treasures.

1820s Paris acquires gas lighting and its first omnibus.

1830 Conflict breaks out between absolutist monarch Charles X and liberal politicians. There is revolt on the streets of Paris and 1800 people die in three days of fighting, known as *les trois glorieuses*. Louis-Philippe is elected constitutional monarch.

1848 Revolution erupts once again against a background of mounting unemployment and intolerable living conditions. In June, thousands of workers and students are killed in street fighting with government troops.

1851 The elected president, Louis Napoleon Bonaparte – Napoleon's nephew – declares himself Emperor Napoleon III.

1850s and 1860s Baron Haussmann, Napoleon III's prefect, bulldozes the city into the modern age, demolishing hundreds of cramped medieval buildings to make way for long, straight boulevards and squares. The poor are driven out to the suburbs.

1863 At the Salon des Refusés, Manet's proto-Impressionist painting *Déjeuner sur l'Herbe* scandalizes all of Paris.

1870 Hundreds die of starvation as the city is besieged by the Prussians.

1871 Paris surrenders in March, but the Prussians withdraw after just three days. In the aftermath, socialist-inspired workers rise up and proclaim the Paris Commune, which lasts just 72 days before being bloodily suppressed by French troops.

1889 The all-new Eiffel Tower steals the show at the Exposition Universelle, or "great exhibition". Parisians are typically appalled.

28 December 1895 Parisians enjoy the first, jerky films, the documentaries of the Lumière brothers, which are given their first public screening at the *Grand Café*. Paris's enthusiasm for cinema will never wane.

1900 The Métropolitain underground railway, or "métro", is unveiled as the flagship engineering marvel of this year's great exhibition.

1914 War with Germany calls time on the belle époque. In September, the Kaiser's armies are just barely held off by French troops shuttled from Paris to the front line, just fifteen miles away. Physically, Paris escapes World War I lightly.

1920s In the aftermath of war, the decadent *années folles* (or "mad years") of the 1920s rescue Paris's international reputation for hedonistic, often erotic, abandon.

1934 Politicized thuggery grows rife in an increasingly depressed city. At a pitched battle outside the Chamber of Deputies in February, Socialist leader Léon Blum narrowly escapes being lynched by fascists.

1936 Newly elected left-wing Prime Minister Léon Blum pushes through a forty-hour week and paid annual leave for workers, but panicky market fluctuations cause his government to collapse.

1940 In June, German troops enter Paris. The government flees, and four years of largely collaborative fascist rule ensue.

1942 Parisian Jews are rounded up – by other Frenchmen – and shipped off to Auschwitz.

1944 As Allied forces draw near the city in June, the left-wing Resistance movement calls its forces onto the streets. Paris is liberated on August 25. General de Gaulle takes the credit, motoring up the Champs-Elysées to the roar of a vast crowd.

1961 As France's brutal repression of its Algerian colony reaches its peak, at least two hundred Algerians are murdered by police during a civil rights demonstration. This "secret massacre" is covered up for the next thirty years.

1968 In May, a radical, leftist movement gathers momentum in the Paris universities. Students occupying university buildings are supported by millions of workers, and opposed by brutal detachments of paramilitary police. France's conservative "silent majority" responds with a mass demonstration in favour of President de Gaulle.

1969 De Gaulle loses a referendum. His successor, Georges Pompidou, only survives long enough to begin the giant Les Halles development, and the construction of expressways along the *quais* of the Seine.

1973 Paris's first skyscraper, the Tour Montparnasse, tops out at 56 hideous storeys. The *périphérique* ring road is completed in April, sealing off an increasingly fossilized city from its impoverished and ever-growing suburbs.

1981 Socialist François Mitterrand becomes president but Paris remains firmly right wing, under Mayor Jacques Chirac.

1995 Jacques Chirac is elected president in May. Thanks to corruption scandals and economic austerity measures, public confidence in the government collapses by November and some five million people take to the streets.

1996 Mitterrand steps down at the end of a second term. His most visible legacies to the city are his presidential "grands projets", including the Louvre's glass pyramid, the Grande Arche de la Défense and the Bibliothèque Nationale.

July 1998 France wins the World Cup at the new Stade de France, in the ethnically mixed Paris suburb of St-Denis. For once, support for "les bleus" overrides all other colour distinctions.

March 2001 Unassuming Socialist candidate Bertrand Delanoë is elected Mayor of Paris: the Left controls the capital for the first time since the Paris Commune in 1871.

January 1, 2002 Parisians find themselves paying a little extra for their coffees and baguettes with the introduction of the euro.

April 21, 2002 Far-Right candidate Jean-Marie Le Pen knocks Socialist Lionel Jospin into third place in the first round of presidential elections. As France reels from the shock, Jacques Chirac duly sweeps the board in the run-off, winning 82 percent of the vote – 90 percent in Paris.

2002 Mayor Bertrand Delanoë turns three kilometres of riverbank expressway into a summer beach. "Paris Plage" is an immense success.

2003 In March, Chirac vows to veto any resolution committing the UN to war with Iraq. US tourists temporarily vanish from the capital's bars and restaurants. In the summer, millions of workers protest against economic "reforms", and temperatures soar above an unprecedented 40 degrees C (104 degrees F).

2005 In late October, disaffected youths begin to torch cars in the impoverished Paris suburbs. By mid-November, two hundred cars are burning every night, and riots have spread nationwide. Right-wing interior minister, Nicolas Sarkozy, declares a state of emergency.

2006 In March, violent protests erupt against a new law allowing young people to be more easily hired and fired. The Sorbonne is occupied, and for two weeks riot police confront wildcat demonstrators throughout Paris. On April 10, Prime Minister Dominique de Villepin withdraws the law.

2007 onwards Mayor Delanoë's deputy for transport policy, Green Party councillor Denis Baupin, plans to run river buses on the Seine and gradually force cars out of the city centre.

Language

Basics

Paris isn't the easiest place to learn French: many Parisians speak a hurried slang and will often reply to your carefully enunciated question in English. Despite this, it's worth making the effort, and knowing a few essentials can make all the difference. Even just saying "Bonjour monsieur/madame" and then gesticulating will usually secure you a smile and helpful service.

What follows is a rundown of essential words and phrases. For more detail, get *French: A Rough Guide Dictionary Phrase Book*, which has an extensive vocabulary, a detailed menu reader and useful dialogues.

Pronunciation

Vowels are the hardest sounds to get right. Roughly:

a	as in hat	i	as in machine
e	as in get	o	as in hot
é	between get and gate	o/au	as in over
è	between get and gut	ou	as in food
eu	like the u in hurt	u	as in a pursed-lip, clipped version of toot

More awkward are the combinations in/im, en/em, on/om, un/um at the end of words, or followed by consonants other than n or m. Again, roughly:

in/im	like the "an" in anxious	on/om	like "on" said by someone with a heavy cold
an/am, en/em	like "on" said with a nasal accent	un/um	like the "u" in understand

Consonants are much as in English, except that ch is always sh, h is silent, th is the same as t, ll is like the y in "yes" when preceded by the letter "i", w is v, and r is growled (or rolled).

Words and phrases

Basics

Yes	Oui
No	Non
Please	S'il vous plaît
Thank you	Merci
Excuse me	Pardon/excusez-moi
Sorry	Pardon, madame/Je m'excuse
Hello	Bonjour
Hello (phone)	Allô
Goodbye	Au revoir
Good morning/ afternoon	Bonjour
Good evening	Bonsoir
Good night	Bonne nuit
How are you?	Comment allez-vous?/Ça va?
Fine, thanks	Très bien, merci

I don't know	Je ne sais pas
Do you speak English?	Vous parlez anglais?
How do you say …in French?	Comment ça se dit…en français?
What's your name?	Comment vous appelez-vous?
My name is …	Je m'appelle …
I'm English/ Irish/ Scottish/ Welsh/ American/	Je suis anglais(e)/ irlandais(e)/ écossais(e)/ gallois(e)/ américain(e)/
OK/agreed	D'accord
I understand	Je comprends
I don't understand	Je ne comprends pas
Can you speak more slowly?	S'il vous plaît, parlez moins vite
Today	Aujourd'hui
Yesterday	Hier
Tomorrow	Demain
In the morning	Le matin
In the afternoon	L'après-midi
In the evening	Le soir
Now	Maintenant
Later	Plus tard
Here	Ici
There	Là
This one	Ceci
That one	Cela
Open	Ouvert
Closed	Fermé
Big	Grand
Small	Petit
More	Plus
Less	Moins
A little	Un peu
A lot	Beaucoup
Half	La moitié
Inexpensive	Bon marché/Pas cher
Expensive	Cher
Good	Bon
Bad	Mauvais
Hot	Chaud
Cold	Froid
With	Avec
Without	Sans

Questions

Where?	Où?
How?	Comment?
How many	Combien?
How much is it?	C'est combien?
When?	Quand?
Why?	Pourquoi?
At what time?	À quelle heure?
What is/Which is?	Quel est?

Getting around

Which way is it to the Eiffel Tower?	S'il vous plaît, pour aller à la Tour Eiffel?
Where is the nearest métro?	Où est le métro le plus proche?
Bus	Bus
Bus stop	Arrêt
Train	Train
Boat	Bâteau
Plane	Avion
Railway station	Gare
Platform	Quai
What time does it leave?	Il part à quelle heure?
What time does it arrive?	Il arrive à quelle heure?
A ticket to …	Un billet pour …
Single ticket	Aller simple
Return ticket	Aller retour
Where are you going?	Vous allez où?
I'm going to …	Je vais à …
I want to get off at …	Je voudrais descendre à …
Near	Près/pas loin
Far	Loin
Left	À gauche
Right	À droite

Accommodation

A room for one /two people	Une chambre pour une/deux personnes
With a double bed	Avec un grand lit
A room with a shower	Une chambre avec douche
A room with a bath	Une chambre avec salle de bains
For one/two/ three nights	Pour une/deux/trois nuit(s)
With a view	Avec vue
Key	Clef
To iron	Repasser
Do laundry	Faire la lessive
Sheets	Draps
Blankets	Couvertures
Quiet	Calme
Noisy	Bruyant
Hot water	Eau chaude
Cold water	Eau froide
Is breakfast included?	Est-ce que le petit déjeuner est compris?
I would like	Je voudrais prendre

breakfast	le petit déjeuner
I don't want breakfast	Je ne veux pas le petit déjeuner
Youth hostel	Auberge de jeunesse

Eating out

I'd like to reserve	Je voudrais réserver
…a table	…une table
…for two people	…pour deux personnes
at eight thirty	à vingt heures et demie
I'm having the €15 menu	Je prendrai le menu à quinze euros
Waiter!	Monsieur/madame! (never "garçon")
The bill, please	L'addition, s'il vous plaît

Days

Monday	Lundi
Tuesday	Mardi
Wednesday	Mercredi
Thursday	Jeudi
Friday	Vendredi
Saturday	Samedi
Sunday	Dimanche

Numbers

1	un
2	deux
3	trois
4	quatre
5	cinq
6	six
7	sept
8	huit
9	neuf
10	dix
11	onze
12	douze
13	treize
14	quatorze
15	quinze
16	seize
17	dix-sept
18	dix-huit
19	dix-neuf
20	vingt
21	vingt-et-un
22	vingt-deux
30	trente
40	quarante
50	cinquante
60	soixante
70	soixante-dix
75	soixante-quinze
80	quatre-vingts
90	quatre-vingt-dix
95	quatre-vingt-quinze
100	cent
101	cent un
200	deux cents
1000	mille
2000	deux mille
1,000,000	un million

LANGAUGE Words and phrases

Menu reader

Essentials

déjeuner	lunch
dîner	dinner
menu	set menu
à la carte	individually priced dishes
entrées	starters
les plats	main courses
pain	bread
beurre	butter
fromage	cheese
oeufs	eggs
lait	milk
poivre	pepper
sel	salt
sucre	sugar
fourchette	fork
couteau	knife
cuillère	spoon
bio	organic
à la vapeur	steamed
au four	baked
cru	raw
frit	fried
fumé	smoked
grillé	grilled
rôti	roast
salé	salted/savoury
sucré	sweet
à emporter	takeaway

Drinks

eau minérale	mineral water
eau gazeuse	fizzy water
eau plate	still water
carte des vins	wine list
une pression	a glass of beer
un café	coffee (espresso)

Words and phrases LANGUAGE

un crème	white coffee
bouteille	bottle
verre	glass
un quart/demi de rouge/blanc	a quarter/half-litre of red/white house wine
un (verre de) rouge/blanc	a glass of white/red wine

Snacks

crêpe	pancake (sweet)
un sandwich /une baguette	sandwich
croque -monsieur	grilled cheese & ham sandwich
panini	flat toasted Italian sandwich
omelette	omelette
nature	plain
aux fines herbes	with herbs
au fromage	with cheese
assiette anglaise	plate of cold meats
crudités	raw vegetables with dressings

Fish (poisson) and seafood (fruits de mer)

anchois	anchovies
brème	bream
brochet	pike
cabillaud	cod
carrelet	plaice
colin	hake
coquilles st-jacques	scallops
crabe	crab
crevettes	shrimps/prawns
daurade	sea bream
flétan	halibut
friture	whitebait
hareng	herring
homard	lobster
huîtres	oysters
langoustines	crayfish (scampi)
limande	lemon sole
lotte de mer	monkfish
loup de mer	sea bass
maquereau	mackerel
merlan	whiting
morue	dried, salted cod
moules (marinière)	mussels (with shallots in white wine sauce)
raie	skate
rouget	red mullet

saumon	salmon
sole	sole
thon	tuna
truite	trout
turbot	turbot

Meat (viande) and poultry (volaille)

agneau	lamb
andouillette	tripe sausage
bavette	beef flank steak
bœuf	beef
bifteck	steak
boudin noir	black pudding
caille	quail
canard	duck
contrefilet	sirloin roast
dinde	turkey
entrecôte	ribsteak
faux filet	sirloin steak
foie	liver
foie gras	fattened (duck/goose) liver
gigot (d'agneau)	leg (of lamb)
grillade	grilled meat
hachis	chopped meat or mince hamburger
jambon	ham
lapin, lapereau	rabbit, young rabbit
lard, lardons	bacon, diced bacon
merguez	spicy, red sausage
oie	goose
onglet	cut of beef
porc	pork
poulet	chicken
poussin	baby chicken
rognons	kidneys
tête de veau	calf's head (in jelly)
veau	veal
venaison	venison

Steaks

bleu	almost raw
saignant	rare
à point	medium
bien cuit	well done

Garnishes and sauces

beurre blanc	sauce of white wine & shallots, with butter
chasseur	white wine, mushrooms & shallots
forestière	with bacon & mushroom
fricassée	rich, creamy sauce

mornay	cheese sauce
pays d'auge	cream & cider
piquante	gherkins or capers, vinegar & shallots
provençale	tomatoes, garlic, olive oil & herbs

Vegetables (légumes), herbs (herbes) and spices (épices)

ail	garlic
artichaut	artichoke
asperges	asparagus
basilic	basil
betterave	beetroot
carotte	carrot
céleri	celery
champignons	mushrooms
chou (rouge)	(red) cabbage
chou-fleur	cauliflower
concombre	cucumber
cornichon	gherkin
échalotes	shallots
endive	chicory
épinards	spinach
estragon	tarragon
fenouil	fennel
flageolets	white beans
gingembre	ginger
haricots	beans
verts	string (french)
rouges	kidney
beurres	butter
lentilles	lentils
maïs	corn (maize)
moutarde	mustard
oignon	onion
pâtes	pasta
persil	parsley
petits pois	peas
pois chiche	chickpeas
poireau	leek
poivron	sweet pepper
(vert, rouge)	(green, red)
pommes	potatoes
(de terre)	
primeurs	spring vegetables
riz	rice
safran	saffron
salade verte	green salad
tomate	tomato
truffes	truffles

Fruits (fruits) and nuts (noix)

abricot	apricot
amandes	almonds
ananas	pineapple
banane	banana
brugnon, nectarine	nectarine
cacahouète	peanut
cassis	blackcurrants
cerises	cherries
citron	lemon
citron vert	lime
figues	figs
fraises	strawberries
framboises	raspberries
groseilles	redcurrants & gooseberries
mangue	mango
marrons	chestnuts
melon	melon
noisette	hazelnut
noix	nuts
orange	orange
pamplemousse	grapefruit
pêche	peach
pistache	pistachio
poire	pear
pomme	apple
prune	plum
pruneau	prune
raisins	grapes

Desserts (desserts or entremets) and pastries (pâtisserie)

bavarois	refers to the mould, could be mousse or custard
brioche	sweet, high yeast breakfast roll
coupe	a serving of ice cream
crème chantilly	vanilla-flavoured & sweetened whipped cream
crème fraîche	sour cream
crème pâtissière	thick eggy pastry-filling
fromage blanc	cream cheese
glace	ice cream
parfait	frozen mousse, sometimes ice cream
petits fours	bite-sized cakes/pastries
tarte	tart
yaourt, yogourt	yoghurt

Visit us online
www.roughguides.com

Information on over 25,000 destinations around the world

BROADEN YOUR HORIZONS

ROUGH GUIDES

WHEREVER YOU ARE,

WHEREVER YOU'RE GOING,

WE'VE GOT YOU COVERED!

Rough Guides Travel Insurance

Visit our website at www.roughguides.com/insurance or call:

- UK: 0800 083 9507
- Spain: 900 997 149
- Australia: 1300 669 999
- New Zealand: 0800 55 99 11
- Worldwide: +44 870 890 2843
- USA, call toll free on: 1 800 749 4922

Please quote our ref: *Rough Guides books*

Cover for over 46 different nationalities and available in 4 different languages.

small print & Index

A Rough Guide to Rough Guides

In 1981, Mark Ellingham, a recent graduate in English from Bristol University, was travelling in Greece on a tiny budget and couldn't find the right guidebook. With a group of friends he wrote his own guide, combining a contemporary, journalistic style with a practical approach to travellers' needs. That first Rough Guide was a student scheme that became a publishing phenomenon. Today, Rough Guides include recommendations from shoestring to luxury and cover hundreds of destinations around the globe, including almost every country in the Americas and Europe, more than half of Africa and most of Asia and Australasia. Millions of readers relish Rough Guides' wit and inquisitiveness as much as their enthusiastic, critical approach and value-for-money ethos. The guides' ever-growing team of authors and photographers is spread all over the world.

In the early 1990s, Rough Guides branched out of travel, with the publication of Rough Guides to World Music, Classical Music and the Internet. All three have become benchmark titles in their fields, spearheading the publication of a range of more than 350 titles under the Rough Guide name, including phrasebooks, waterproof maps, music guides from Opera to Heavy Metal, reference works as diverse as Conspiracy Theories and Shakespeare, and popular culture books from iPods to Poker. Rough Guides also produce a series of more than 120 World Music CDs in partnership with World Music Network.

Visit www.roughguides.com to see our latest publications.

Rough Guide travel images are available for commercial licensing at www.roughguidespictures.com

Publishing information

This second edition published March 2007 by Rough Guides Ltd, 80 Strand, London WC2R 0RL. 345 Hudson St, 4th Floor, New York, NY 10014, USA.

Distributed by the Penguin Group
Penguin Books Ltd, 80 Strand, London WC2R 0RL
Penguin Group (USA), 375 Hudson St, NY 10014, USA
14 Local Shopping Centre, Panchsheel Park, New Delhi 110017, India
Penguin Group (Australia), 250 Camberwell Rd, Camberwell, Victoria 3124, Australia
Penguin Group (Canada), 10 Alcorn Ave, Toronto, ON M4V 1E4, Canada
Penguin Group (NZ), 67 Apollo Drive, Mairangi Bay, Auckland 1310, New Zealand
Typeset in Bembo and Helvetica to an original design by Henry Iles.
Cover concept by Peter Dyer.

Printed and bound in China
© Rough Guides 2007

224pp includes index

A catalogue record for this book is available from the British Library

ISBN 13 9781843-53744-1

The publishers and authors have done their best to ensure the accuracy and currency of all the information in Paris DIRECTIONS, however, they can accept no responsibility for any loss, injury, or inconvenience sustained by any traveller as a result of information or advice contained in the guide.

5 7 9 8 6 4

Help us update

We've gone to a lot of effort to ensure that the second edition of Paris DIRECTIONS is accurate and up-to-date. However, things change – places get "discovered", opening hours are notoriously fickle, restaurants and rooms raise prices or lower standards. If you feel we've got it wrong or left something out, we'd like to know, and if you can remember the address, the price, the phone number, so much the better.

We'll credit all contributions, and send a copy of the next edition (or any other DIRECTIONS guide or Rough Guide if you prefer) for the best letters. Everyone who writes to us and isn't already a subscriber will receive a copy of our full-colour thrice-yearly newsletter. Please mark letters: "Paris DIRECTIONS Update" and send to: Rough Guides, 80 Strand, London WC2R 0RL, or Rough Guides, 4th Floor, 345 Hudson St, New York, NY 10014. Or send an email to mail@roughguides.com
Have your questions answered and tell others about your trip at www.roughguides.atinfopop.com

Rough Guide credits

Text editor: Alice Park
Layout: Diana Jarvis
Photography: James McConnachie
Cartography: Rajesh Mishra

Picture editor: Harriet Mills
Proofreader: David Price
Production: Aimee Hampson, Katherine Owers
Cover design: Chloë Roberts

SMALL PRINT

The authors

James McConnachie is also author of the *Rough Guide to The Loire Valley*, and he has travelled all over Europe and beyond for Rough Guides. His non-travel books include *Conspiracy Theories* (Rough Guides) and *The Book of Love: A Biography of the Kamasutra* (Atlantic Books).

Ruth Blackmore is a Senior Editor at Rough Guides in London. She is the co-author of the *Rough Guide to Paris* and a contributor to the *Rough Guide to France* and the *Rough Guide to Classical Music*.

Readers' letters

Sharmila Bagwe, Tim Ward

Photo credits

All images © Rough Guides except the following:

Front cover image: Eiffel Tower © 4cornersimages
Back cover image: Pont Alexandre-III © Chloe Roberts
p.12 Bastille Day © Peter Turnley/Corbis
p.13 Lance Armstrong on the Prologue of the Tour de France © Tim De Waele/Corbis
p.13 Forum des Halles, Nuit Blanch © Elisa Haberer/Corbis
p.17 Musée du quai Branly © Musée du quai Branly
p.18 Musée d'Art moderne de la Ville de Paris © Christophe Fouin, courtesy Musée d'Art moderne de la Ville de Paris
p.19 Portrait of Dora Maar, 1937 (oil on canvas) by Picasso, Pablo (1881-1973) © Musée Picasso, Paris, France/Bridgeman Art Library/DACS
p.23 St Sulpice © DK Images
p.25 Jardin de Bagatelle © DK Images
p.28 Taillevent © DK Images
p.31 Aux Lyonnais © Aux Lyonnais
p.37 Le Triptyque © letriptyque.com
p.38 Sally Nyolo at the Café de la Danse © Sebastien Cailleux/Corbis
p.44 Hôtel du Petit Moulin © Hôtel du Petit Moulin
p.44 Hôtel Bonséjour Montmartre © Hôtel Bonséjour Montmartre

p.48 Kong © Patricia Bellere, courtesy Kong
p.48 Costes lobby © Directphoto.org/Alamy
p.49 Bar Hemingway © Ritz Paris
p.49 Le Train Bleu © letrainbleu.com
p.51 Men carrying banner at Gay Pride © Owen Franken/Corbis
p.58 Les Amants du Pont Neuf (1991) Juliette Binoche © Ronald Grant Archive
p.58 View from the top of Notre Dame 1955 © Henri Cartier-Bresson/Magnum Photos
p.59 A Bout de Souffle (1960) Jean-Paul Belmondo and Jean Seberg © Ronald Grant Archive
p.59 Le Fabuleux Destin D'Amélie Poulain (2001) Audrey Tatou © Moviestore Collection Ltd
p.59 Ball at the Moulin de la Galette, 1876 (oil on canvas) by Renoir, Pierre Auguste (1841-1919) © Musée d'Orsay, Paris, France/Giraudon/Bridgeman Art Library
p.61 View from the Arc de Triomphe © Gordon R. Gainer/Corbis
p.62 Ice skating at the Hôtel de Ville © Magali Delporte/Axiom
p.63 Art Deco cinema Grand Rex © Directphoto.org/Alamy
p.72 L'Epicerie © DK Images

Index

Maps are marked in colour

INDEX